Kalamu ya Salaam is a renowned
fiction realities facing Black citize
Crow to the present. He's also an
oral tradition in New Orleans' legendary 9th Ward of his upbringing…and
outward into the rural "Deep South."

Kalamu's first published novel, *Walkin' Blues,* takes us into the mind, soul, and short life of the legendary blues songmaker, singer, and guitarist Robert Johnson with a magical realism of voice not previously imagined. Johnson's many acolytes from outside the culture have listened to and described the sources and influences of his nearly 3 dozen compelling "platters" (recordings) made in Texas between 1936-37. Today the historians and fans still speculate on three possible burial sites, the circumstances of Johnson's death by poison from a jealous lover, and the significance of the crossroads of Mississippi Highways 61 and 49…not to mention his virtuosity, complexity, and stylistic innovation, as well as continuing influence on several generations of jazz, blues, rock, and pop musicians globally.

Yet the mysteries of Robert Johnson's spirit, life, and music remain. None of his many followers have mustered the vernacular cultural voice or social and emotional knowledge that Salaam brings in creating the blues hero's intimate thoughts and actions in his life's journey. The reader won't hear the songs or think of Robert Johnson the same way again.

—Nick Spitzer, host of public radio's *American Routes* & professor of anthropology, Tulane University

In this Robert Johnson-inspired novel, Kalamu ya Salaam brilliantly lures the reader into common folk living with literary wit and spirited imagery. From laughter to heartache to juke joint loving to plain folk politics to Southern everydayness, we are confronted with our own vulnerability and contradictions. Salaam uses vibrant characters to show us we are the Blues in all its hues and human complexities. Perhaps the novel's title, *Walkin' Blues*, is a metaphor for the current state of this country. We are walking the blues while making improvisations as we climb each unpredictable day. The Blues is our journey and our healing. We have this book to help us laugh, learn, and love along the way.

—Kelly Harris-DeBerry, author of *Freedom Knows My Name*

In *Walkin' Blues*, the life of legendary "Blues Hero" Robert Johnson who "sold his soul" is brought down to earth and earthiness in psyche and sounds in authentic rhythms and nuance of dialect in the stories of believable characters in conceivable circumstances at critical moments of the blues man's short documented life.

–Jerry Brock, co-founder of WWOZ and Louisiana Music Factory

Kalamu ya Salaam is the ultimate griot—poet, fiction writer, playwright, literary theorist, editor, educator, and revolutionary. Yet, at the core of all of this, he's a blues mane. After a lifetime of writing that spans almost sixty years, he has not only made plain the blues aesthetic, he has produced creative work that affirms and builds upon the living blues. As such, there is no one more fit to galvanize what the blues is than he has done in *Walkin' Blues*.

Through a blend of rhythmic lyrical diction, the most vivid imagery, and sharp wit combining to disseminate communal wisdom, Salaam lays bare the blues artist as shaman—a swirling concoction of poet, storyteller, shapeshifter, scoundrel, rolling stone, preacher, agitator, trickster, heel, and healer. It's fitting that the man who gave us one of the clearest definition of the blues aesthetic in *What Is Life?: Reclaiming the Black Blues Self*, gives us a novel that shows how blues music is a manifestation of blues culture, which is produced and driven by the reaction to and navigation of reneged Reconstruction, Black Codes, Jim Crow, segregation, and the continued attempt of white supremacy to bind the humanity of African peoples. At the core, Salaam uses Johnson to remind us that the blues is the manifestation of African-American genius from a people who, despite being forced to live in the bowels of hell, never forgot that they were human and divine, and used their music and culture to maintain their sanity and their spirituality, because they understood that, one day, what's wrong will be righted, what's crooked will be made straight, and that the Sun will shine on my porch.

—C. Liegh McInnis, poet, short story writer, Prince scholar, and Clarksdale, Mississippi literary bluesmane

WALKIN' BLUES

*a speculation and meditation on the life
and legend of Robert Johnson*

Kalamu ya Salaam

MBW
NEW ORLEANS

WALKIN' BLUES

By Kalamu ya Salaam

Printed in the U.S.A.

ISBN 979-8-9899197-1-0

Walkin' Blues

-1-

HE HAD HIS SHOES IN THE CROCUS SACK. AND HIS GUITAR. THREE JARS OF preserves (one jar of figs, the other two was watermelon rinds). Plus, two huge biscuits, larger than his fist, wrapped in the edge of her apron, which Sweetwater had torn without hesitation, and lovingly sacrificed as an offering she hoped would also be an enticement for Robert to return to her after he found whatever it was he was looking for in Louisiana, whatever it was that could not be found here in the warmth of a Mississippi woman's kitchen, the resting place and wrestling place of a Mississippi woman's bed. She had not been able to resist caressing his chest after she set the bundled biscuits on the table, next to the mug of steaming coffee—Sweetwater had not cared that all the fine food she had fed Robert would cost her two week's worth of work, his company had been worth much more than twelve or so dollars, especially that morning she awoke, looking at his naked back, as he sat on the edge of their bed (really it was *her* bed that she wished was *their* bed), his guitar in his lap, softly singing a blues that did not sound at all blue, but rather tender and gay, although she knew neither of those words through her own experience, so little in her life had exhibited either character, yet here was this slender man, an angel singing the devil's music, perched not even an arm's length away, and she had reached out to press her palm to his spine, tracing straight down to just above the cleavage of his butt, which is what all she was remembering when she placed that offering before him, she had cooked cornbread on the stove in a black skillet for a few mens before, but this was her first oven-baked delight lovingly given to a man, especially on the day when he was saying goodbye, well, at least it had been a wonderful eight day week.

They had met at the leaving-college dinner the judge had thrown for his son, who had requested the best blues singer around, which everybody who knowed anything said was that feller last heard from up round

Tutweiler, went by the name of Robert, and Robert had been summoned, the judge had even let Robert sleep in the shed out back and had instructed Sweetwater to tend to him, and Sweetwater had been surprised by how quiet-like Robert spoke, how mannerly he was.

"Where you playing next?" she had idly asked.

"What you want to hear?" he innocently inquired.

"Mister, I don't know nothing 'bout no blues."

Robert stopped chawing on the chicken leg, smiled, "And I don't know nothing 'bout cooking, but I know good food when I eat it. This here is good!" They both laughed.

Something deep inside of her enjoyed this laughing, enjoyed his laughter, enjoyed her laughing with him, and suddenly a great desire swept over her to laugh like that again. And again. And some more. Sweetwater, blushed. And looked away.

Robert did not misread her sudden shyness. "Well, just like I ain't got to be a cook, to know good food when I taste it, I reckon, you ain't got to be a musicianeer to know good music when you hear it."

Suddenly she became serious, "I do like your playing."

And they just looked at each other.

"I do. I mean…" What was she supposed to say next? Mens was always talking to her, she never talked to no man out of need before, no, this wasn't need. This was something else. Something stronger. "I need to get back to work. I got to clean up and…"

"When you finish cleaning, I'll play whatever you want me to play."

Her hand flew up to cover the surprised smile that was slow spreading across her flushed face. She backed away without saying a word. Robert smiled and waved the half-eaten chicken leg in her direction. She turned and briskly stumbled off.

Most of the women Robert frequented were the ones who danced in the jukes, and no matter how soft they felt, there was a hardness to them, but this woman was different, probably never been up in a juke, never had liquor all up on her breath. She was big, bigger than average, and getting on, wasn't no springer. He reached down and took a long swallow of lemonade from the tin cup she had provided with the chicken plate. Green beans. Rice with field peas mixed in. Cuts of cucumber and tomatoes. Robert sucked his teeth, used the tip of his tongue to dig out a sliver of chicken lodged between his left molars. Guess old folks was right, his stomach was most full and now he was wondering was she as good at other things as she was at cooking, cause, damn, she was mighty, mighty good at cooking.

He had gone home with her that same Sunday evening, just to play a few reels, and now it was an early-fall, shade-your-eyes-sun bright Monday morning, a full week later. There was not much to say. He knew she wanted him to stay and he knew she knew he was not going to stay. You don't find no rolling stones sleeping inside a kitchen, he needed road. "Thank you, mam, you been right kindly to me. I'll never forget you."

Although she would do so, many times in the weeks and months to come, Sweetwater did not then question how often and to how many others Robert had said: I'll never forget you.

The sun was in her eyes as he walked away without looking back.

Two years, and many, many, lonely nights later, she saw him from a distance, him and all the pretty, young gals vying for his attention. He did not see her. She heard the way his guitar responded to the sway of hussy hips. The toe-tapping that seemed loud, and louder, as they gathered up the edges of their skirts, one jezzy was even showing her knees, when Robert let out a little whoop, and struck a chord so hard, the unhitched mens on the porch outside found another reason to hate this women-stealing bastard. Sweetwater couldn't look and so, reluctantly, she turned and trudged the long road back home.

Even once she was inside, she could still hear Robert singing. And for a second, like a child, she covered her ears to stop hearing what she didn't want to hear. Except the sound was inside of her, so with her hands on the east side and west side of her head, it only made Robert's sound echo louder because her palms blocked the outside out and locked the inside in.

The moon shone so brightly, she had not needed to light her lamp. She was a hard working woman. Seven days a week cooking in the judge's mansion, up before dawn, well after sundown when she got home, sometimes even later when the judge had dinner guests. And she saved her money, did not allow her loneliness to empty her purse into the hands of worthless menfolk who somehow believed soft sucking on a woman's breast would exempt them from being required to plow or pick cotton. Why didn't she believe? Although she liked to sing, church just was not for her, and how had that come to be? She knew. The minister's daughter always knows, especially when the minister's daughter's mother is not the minister's wife. Mama, always said: Never hate a man for who he love, or who he sleep with—baby, mens can't help theyself, theys just born with a strong, strong urge to mate.

Turning from her bitter nostalgia, Sweetwater acknowledged her own humanness. One side of her mind tolt her she should have never fed Robert. Never enjoyed the joy of his shout as he flowed into her. But her heart, or some other insistent part of her anatomy, sighed, there was nothing wrong with living at least once before you died.

Just like he hadn't planned to come and see her, she had not planned to go see him. It wasn't even curiosity—his new reputation was miles ahead of him, everywhere peoples was talking about the nimble-fingered man who could play a guitar better than any two ordinary mens put together. Even without hearing a name, Sweetwater had known, it must be Robert back from Louisiana, done found the music he was dying to get hold to. She had gained twenty-seven pounds in the two years since he last saw her, heck, he probably wouldn't even have recognized her if she had served him a catfish plate. No. What had sent her down there had been that little piece of hope harbored in her heart that whispered to her inner ear suggesting how Robert most likely hankered, maybe, for another helping of chicken and biscuits, and she would never know, if she didn't ask him. Naw, her mind told her. He wouldn't care. Wouldn't remember. But, urged on by a mustard seed of hope, she had gone down there and looked in the window, and now here she stood in her kitchen, leaning over her number ten wash tub, looking out her window, wondering whatever in the world was she continuing to live for?

Even though she lived alone, Sweetwater was not without her admirers. Why, the judge even had reached out once. Once. Not hard like most white mens reached for colored womens, but with a sort of half-heartedness like he knew he was doing wrong. Whether he was serious or not, Sweetwater had set him straight: I cooks, I cleans, suh, but I ain't nobody's kept woman. If you wants a good meal and a clean house, I'se the one. If there's something more you wants from me, well, suh, I guess I best be moving on.

"Janie, that's fair enough. I didn't mean nothing by it. You know I'm a man full of feelings, but I'm also a gentleman who understands when a woman doesn't desire steady company. Janie, you got a job here long as I got life."

The judge wasn't the only one, wasn't even the last one to tug at the back of her dress. Look like every colored man in the county took up a bet on who could get to Sweetwater. That fool roustabout Brooks who worked the levee gangs and thought that silver dollars could buy any woman's attention, and Forester with his puffed-up chest just cause he had his own fourteen acres of crop land. And six-foot-seven Johnny Charles, a lumberjack with the sweetest tenor voice but was always cursing up a blue streak. And on and on. Sweetwater was standing there reciting the list like Mr. Highsmith auctioning off cattle.

Sweetwater called everybody's name except Tanner. She was hearing Robert's guitar and avoiding Tanner's soft stammer, standing there with a hoe in his hands, asking "Mis, Miss Janie, how-ow-ow you today? You, you needs anything let me know. I be right proud to, to, to helps you out, any, any, any which ways I can."

Tanner was always hanging round trying to talk to her, maybe she should give him a little conversation. Tanner was a good man. Never missed a day's work. Never took nothing. Never slacked off. Never even so much as looked at Sweetwater in an unwelcomed way. Not even after he loss his wife and children in that fire eight months back. But Tanner couldn't sing worth rooster eggs, was tone deaf as a hog. Always telling her how pretty she sing. But suppose Tanner was her last chance and here she is blowing on the cold charcoal of Robert Johnson, trying to light a fire when there wasn't nothing there but ash, and here was Tanner just a burning bright. Why was life so cruel as to make us not want a good thing we can easily have and instead be craving after a bad thing what wouldn't do nothing but bring us misery even if we was to get it?

Robert gone, been gone, two years gone, come back to town and didn't even pass by…why was she remembering this? Was this the curse of sex: no matter how wrong the whole of it goes, you never, never forget, no matter how brief, you never forget the good moments? This remembering was embarrassing, for it showed her a weakness, a weakness she previously had not known was there, a weakness never before manifest, and surely, never again to be allowed to flower. This moment let her know, no one was exempt from being human, being in need, being weak for a minute of relief during days and nights and months and years of…why? Why had she ever—was it really that good?—why, why had she ever been fool enough (or was it woman enough—do all women at some point hitch themselves to some lover's plow, vainly trying to furrow a rocky field in a driving rain)? Maybe she should talk to Tanner.

It wasn't six months after that dismaying looking-in-the-juke-window incident, that Sweetwater hooked up with Tanner, and all the rest of their days together, Tanner treated her better than any man except, well, he was an average man, nothing like Robert, and, Sweetwater would sigh often to herself as she kneaded bread dough in the judge's kitchen, what was there to think about: a steady good man is better than somebody you don't know when you going to see them next.

Sweetwater waved her hand in front her face, like tearing through a spider web blocking the entrance to a closed-off room where emergency provisions was kept. Her face was dry. Her vision steady. Even her voice was calm when she said to herself: ain't no man worth all this, especially not no worthless man. But, even as she said it, she knew he had been a valuable lesson: love comes costly when you ain't got nothing much to spend. What? What was there to think about? Why was she even thinking about thinking about it? She was not the first woman to be late for work cause of some man—not some man, some Robert, Robert Johnson man—nipping on her upturned bottom. Her left hand involuntarily reached down and brushed the backside of her lower hip, right where his teeth had dimpled the dark fullness of her. "Sweetwater, you got the best ass I ever tasted!"

Robert never expected to see Sweetwater again, even though he had stayed with her four or five days longer than he usually rested. If he had been any other man, he might have homesteaded, shoved his shoes deep under her bed, placed his hat on her pillow, his guitar in her cupboard. But I ain't no field hand, he renewed his daily vows. He would never stay in one place and end up quickly becoming a monument to how toil can tear a man down. It's ok for womens to stay put, they children needs food and shelter, and a mama, but mens, well, from what all his life taught him, Robert reckoned a man just needs a passing through moment.

Robert was whistling. He had shined his playing shoes and they was deep in his sack. His unshined brogans, should say, *never-shined* brogans, his walking shoes, the feets the white folks would look at and see a shod mule walking, thems the shoes was kicking up dust heading south to Louisiana to get his guitar hand fixed. Robert had heard tell there was two-headed people down there what could make your fingers grow long enough to wrap twice around the strings, teach you tunes nobody else could sing. As he walked, rich folk passing him in cars and carriages, poor folk bending barefoot in the fields, a white man on a wagon loaded down with cotton and a sad-faced negro on the back, as he walked, keeping a slow but steady, three-and-a-half-mile-an-hour gait, a whole month's worth of walking in front of him, Robert found himself wishing Sweetwater well, wishing the best for her, not cause he missed her but because she was, well, she was the kind of good woman ordinary mens really, really missed, even though she was not extraordinary enough for him to go back to or to think about when he was with whomever the next woman would be. Robert slowed a bit as he recalled how Sweetwater had been so willing, eager even, but then his pace picked back up, being willing ain't quite the same as being expert, what a person *can* do is right here, right now, what they *wants* to be able to do is down the road a spell, maybe, 'cause not all you want for is what you reach.

Sweetwater wasn't no virgin or nothing, she just wasn't experienced. Her hands might as well been elbows, she used them so little in bed. She was so talented with how she handled food, why, if she only knew how to handle a man like that, with the same, what was that word he heard some book-learned man comment on a card shark's dealing: you mighty dexteritous with them cards, my good fella, well, anyway if she had a handled up dexteritous on him like she did some pie crust... who was he kidding, wasn't no food good enough to make him stay anywhere forever. They had food everywhere. Love was everywhere. If you knew what you was looking for, you could find it. Everywhere.

Everybody got a need for love, most folk just don't know how to get that need satisfied. They ties the need to all kinds of things that ain't got nothing to do with the need. Going to work for Mr. Gilmore ain't got nothing to do... Robert tipped his broke down hat to the woman walking with the washing on her head. That could a been his mother.

Come to think of it, Robert had his good hat in the sack too, right along with his playing clothes, his shined shoes, his guitar, two biscuits wrapped in a strip of apron torn off, a jar of figs—damn, they was tasty—and two jars of watermelon rind. Watermelon preserves and biscuits, now that's some mighty good eating. And don't forget that goat-hide waterbag, Robert kept it full. Eight miles a day, huh, month and a half he'd be damn near to New Orleans. Shit, there wasn't a cloud in the sky. Robert looked up and felt like shouting, he had to restrain himself. He felt like whistling and doing a little jig, but this was Monday morning and he was on the road, wasn't no time for making merry.

Traveling was serious business. You had to camouflage your comings and goings though. White folks hated, absolutely hated, to see a negro walking free. That's why, whenever he was on the road, Robert always took to looking like a field hand toting some heavy load, even though, truth be told, right now, Robert felt like a king. Some distant train was baying off 'cross yonder field. Robert ain't paid it no mind. Riding the rails in this part of Mississippi was the fastest way to end up in some small town jail or on some sheriff's chain gang. Naw, he wasn't in no hurry, slow ain't fast, but it'll get you there just the same. 'Sides, since he was heading south, and most escaping negroes was running north, nobody ever suspected that he had freedom on his mind—at least not none of the white folks.

"You that guitar man, ain't cha?"

Robert looked up when he heard himself hailed by an approaching teenager headed in the opposite direction. The lanky manchild was carrying a rooster bound at the feet, it's unblinking eye cocked open and examining Robert with a disinterested stare, and it's dusty tailfeathers bouncing and bobbing, while its elongated, two-and-a-half-pound body, now and again, bumped against the rough denim covering the boy's lower thigh. The bird was quiet, neither flapping its clipped wings nor trying to use its dull yellow beak to peck at its captor's shin. Was this a gamecock or a breeder? Called to mind Sweetwater's quick, double spin wringing a fat hen's neck, the flapping body spun off in one direction, the decapitated head flung in the weeds by the fence post for the ants to eat, that's if-in some stray dog didn't get to chew on it first.

Watching Sweetwater work was fascinating. After a couple of minutes, Sweetwater had picked up the plump carcass and started in to stripping feathers and preparing dinner—she had worked so methodically, with the surety of a blind man playing a piano. Damn. Death made Robert uncomfortable but it didn't seem to bother Sweetwater none. And look at her, blood was all on the ground but nary a drop on her, her apron was spotless. Damn. That woman knew what she was doing.

"What, Robert? Why you looking at me like that?"

"Sweets, you good at what you do. I admires that."

"You good too, Robert. We just good at different things."

It's funny how a black boy holding a brown rooster set a man to thinking of how good a sweet woman is.

"Where you playing at tonight?" There was youthful admiration in the adolescent's voice.

Robert smiled a response, "Hard to say, son. When you rambles like I does, you can't hardly speculate from the morning, where at sundown gon find you, or what the evening gon find you doing."

-2-

Not quite a week later the biscuits was finished, but a good weekend at a juke had brought him both crumbling cornbread and a special treat flinched from some white man's kitchen, a half loaf of fresh-baked wheat. Plus he had done alright near the McComb train station playing for pennies and an occasional dime. Beer on the weekends and water during the week, he was doing alright.

One woman's husband, well, leastwise he acted like he had jumped the broom with her or something, the way he yanked her back from admiring her reflection in the shine on the shoe that Robert was tapping to the beat of the music he was making. Robert paid more mind to the man than to the woman. A too jealous man might cut you, even if you ain't said nothing to his woman. Robert knew the way to squash that foolishness was to demonstrate that he had another woman on his mind, so no sooner she tried to push back a little from the man's insistent pull, Robert turned his attention to the big redbone girl, and shouted out, "Mama, mama, if I could shake it like that, I wouldn't never no more need to work, neither worry nor want for nothing." Everybody laughed. Even the formerly outraged fool, even he was delighted about the way the short woman danced, her hips oscillating like she was churning butter, and the dimples on her freckled cheek, a clear enough flag signaling that she wasn't doing nothing but having some fun. For the moment that fool forgot, forgot it was Robert's guitar that was making the women dance. Rough stuff was back to feeling good. The sight of this other woman dancing was entertaining, but really it was the warmth of his own woman, secure now in his lap, her body pushed up close to his chest and pulsing in time to the music was exciting his manhood now. Robert's guitar, the dimpled woman's hips, his baby's lips brushing against his ear, her ass bouncing on his lap. All the male anger was forgotten. Robert knew, the way to get out alive was not to look at no man's woman like you wanted to stay behind. Besides, just like you don't soap up your hands, just to wipe your brow, Robert wasn't playing for a moment's pleasure, he was working. This was his profession, the way he made his living, wasn't nothing on his mind but making a few dollars, he'd settle for a buck and six bits, but two and a quarter sure would make for an easy week of traveling. That's what Robert was thinking about, that, and did that dimpled woman have a man lurking somewhere.

"Where you learn to play like that?"

Robert was taken aback. She was big-boned and built low to the ground, earth-toned hair with a hint of red, not unlike many a person in the delta, most likely her daddy had jumped the fence into some colored chicken coop. Them white mens all the times decrying how ugly blacks be, but, come nightfall, be steady shaking our women's trees. There was something about the way she held one hand on her hip and used the other to talk with that kind of told Robert this girl was used to getting attention. Add to it, she was a forward woman and, of course, in 1930s Mississippi a forward woman was trouble, the kind of trouble Robert most times tried to avoid, but sometimes allowed himself to be tempted by, depending on the whether—whether or not he felt like grabbing the short end of a fast burning stick just to light his cigarette.

"Mam?" and he caressed the strings on his guitar's neck.

"I was just asking, where you learned to play so good."

"I'm still learning."

"Sounds to me like you done learned more than most mens."

Robert looked her in the eye. She did not look away nor down. He continued the verbal foreplay, wanting to see whether the cow was just lowing for lack of anything better to do or was her mooing a sign she was ready to give milk, "You never know who the next lesson will come from, hump, no telling, you probably could teach me a thing or two."

"I ain't said nothing about teaching nobody nothing. I was just inquiring about all them songs you know, about how you gets people all excited."

Out the corner of his eye, Robert caught the jealous couple leaving, the woman playfully draped over the man's back, hanging on like a cape. For some reason that made Robert remember, wherever you sees women, eventually you sees children. Few of the women who grew up in Mississippi went childless, at least few of the poor women, cause children was labor and was security once you got old. One time Robert had gone home with a slender woman, girl couldn't of even weighed much as half a sack of wet cotton, anyways, when they got up in her place there was four children sleeping on the floor. Robert mentally slapped himself upside the head: how you gon really get down with eight eyes watching you screw they mama? What was that girl's name. Matilda. Yeah, that was it, Matilda and her four kids. Good thing he didn't stay that night cause later he found out, Matilda have five brothers what stayed in the next shack over, wasn't none of them older than twenty, but all of them liked to fish and hunt…

"You ain't gon charge me nothing for asking about how you make your music, is you?"

Something told Robert: Robert, Louisiana calling. No detours. Bottle up and go.

"Mam, I plays music cause I got to. If peoples likes the sounds I make, well, that's good. If they wants to give me something cause they really appreciates my reels. That's good too. But I makes music cause I likes making music."

Through now with tallying up the woman, Robert half turned his back and reached over to the table to grab his hat. Having already spied the room's far corner that might serve as a right nice sleep spot to accommodate him til the morning come, Robert was about to enquire about the whereabouts of the joint's owner when there was a gentle tug on his jacket sleeve. Dimples wasn't finished asking questions: "I likes to sing, too. Reckon you could show me a song or…?"

Damn. Robert could go for days, weeks even, without no nookie. And then, bam, when he wasn't even trying to get none.

The road was a hard life, not nothing to be messed with by a soft man. If you wanted regular that's what they made the fields for. You could walk for days and never come cross not even a pecan tree, and then bam, one day, the flowers is in bloom and some sugar-sweet pear is hanging just waiting for you to pluck it, but, you know, there was something wrong with this, dimples was too attractive to be unattached, or at least…

"Flora Mae, they still got cleaning up to do."

Robert looked up at Mr. Johnny. "Much obliged for the payday, Mr. Johnny. I'm going to be stepping in the morning. A-hem, would you mind if I was to use a corner of your establishment to grab forty winks? I'd be out your way directly, plans to shove off 'fore day in the morning."

"Flora Mae, go get Robert one of them empty sacks. Thanks to him, we had a good night."

Dimples said nothing. Moved off quickly, following her uncle's directions. "Thas my sister's child. My sister dead, I takes care of the girl. We be through cleaning up directly. You can rest long as you wants, let yourself out in the morning. Now, don't you forget us none, next time your travelings bring you out this here way."

Robert slept on hardwood that night, his back against the wall. Regardless of what jealous men or foolish women thought, making music was hard, lonely-ass work, full of making do. Robert was grateful for a roof as he curled up at the back of the juke, the floorboards didn't seem so hard what with a pallet of two cotton sacks beneath him, and certainly this was way better than cold ground under some roadside tree, which was, not infrequently, the onliest hospitality offered to a blues musician walking from town to town.

–3–

FOLKS SAY EVERYTHING COME LATE TO MISSISSIPPI, BUT, AIN'T SO, FACT IS, SEEMS like trouble and hardships be early to the table down here. They sits they rumps down on the gallery over to the general store and rests a spell before shoving off to visit other states. Like you take when 1928 rung in, while the rest of the country was still dancing and making merry, down in the delta the depression had already blowed the storm shutters off even the richest white folks' house. Shucks, when the official depression come, there wasn't hardly nothing left to depress on account of the 1927 mighty flood what had already knocked 'Sippi to its knees.

Walking on towards Greenwood or Ita Bena, even seven or eight months after the levees broke down, Robert had witnessed whole towns washed away, the general store a twisted skeleton, empty holes where windows and doors used to be, the town crossroads deserted, devoid of busy folks' comings and goings, acres and acres of fields lying fallow, even saw a cotton gin perched up in a cypress tree like some mechanical vulture, heaps of dead animal bones all over the place, somebody's boot sticking up heel first in the middle of the road, a leather tombstone marking what had once been a busy path, and a smelly muck coating everything what the waters didn't carry off.

Wasn't no odor worse smelling than the repulsive stench of flood funk, a combination of rot and outhouse excreta mixed with the foulness of dead fish, which there had been plenty of, all up and down the river roads. Robert would never forget that putridness, who could? 'Specially seeing as, for at least six or so months, the smell was able to fight off the bleaching powers of the sun. The bible had said no more water—well, somebody must done misunderstood God's word, cause the sun was hot alright, fire hot, but it had been the water that shouted and the funk the water left behind that whispered to folks: get out, go, go, go head on out of here.

The mighty flood had done run off heaps of people, run 'em clean out the state, well leastwise had run off them what had somehow survived the high waters. Plenty people didn't make it through the storm. Lots of folk went under, drowned or just plum disappeared. One day they was working, and cooking, and hauling stuff up and down the highway, and then like a candle snuffed out when a door blow open sudden like, just like that, peoples was gone. Gone. Just gone. Ain't nobody heard nothing no more from them. Gone, with nothing left behind to mark they had ever been there. Gone. Whole families, relatives and all they kin and friends, gone. It was horrible. It was so horrible you couldn't even stand to remember it. That's how horrible it was.

Though Robert was too young to have experienced the first one, and would die too early to know about number two, Robert guessed the devastation of the flood was like a world war or something. How could you beat the rain? How do somebody whip the river? Not even white folks with steel bridges and big levees, all kinds of boats with engines on them and fancy ways to tell when a storm was coming, naw, not even white folks could stop the flood from tearing up everything it touched. Robert would never forget what all he saw, and especially, he would not forget, what all he didn't see: the people, no animals, buildings and things that used to be here and there, now there was nothing there. Nothing. Just a big old emptiness. In fact, the loss hurt Robert so bad, he never could bring himself to write a song about it, and especially no song as deep powerful as Charley Patton's "High Water Everywhere."

One time when Robert was hoboing down to Yazoo, the guy he was trodding down with told Robert how his daddy and his five brothers got swept away. Said, from what all peoples told him, when the sun come out, all six of them just up and headed up to Memphis. Robert, nodded cause he knew Memphis from back when he was brung up in that big house his step-father had with Robert's mother and his daddy's other children's mama, and all them children, packed all up under one roof, and getting alone fine, well, fine for a while. Eventually Robert's mother left, and then when he was seven, it was time for him to go. But, still, Robert knew Memphis, especially Handwerker Hill where they stayed, knew it as well as a child can know any city.

"So, Bobo, how come you stay on?"

"I didn't. I was gone down river, the flood catched me."

"Yeah?"

"Yes, suh."

"What you was in a boat or something?"

"No, I was on our house."

"What?"

"Yeah, you see, when the water come up, it come up so fast, most us ain't had no time to run no wheres. My daddy was loading the family on a barn door with logs strapped on to it, what he was rigging up to serve like our ark. Mama Mary, wanted to stay on top the house, but daddy said it wasn't going to hold and if it started breaking to pieces, we all would drown. So between him and my brothers John, Mark, Matthew, Timothy and Luke, they lashed logs side to side and front and back on the barn door what was floating in the water that was rising. And everybody had to jump on. Except, my mama, she was clinging to the chimney, see, and my daddy was shouting for her to step onto the ark and she was saying no. And by then the waters was really flowing something fierce, I mean, Mr. Robert, you ain't never seen nothing like it. Cows was floating by, horses, mules, pigs. I don't know what happen to the chickens. And it was dark and the water was this muddy, ugly color and making this tearing sound, like you know when you cut a tree and it start to fall and the pieces of it what wasn't already cut, start to bend and snap and the tree be making that sick breaking up kind of sound, well, it was everything sounding like that, like the water was breaking everything it caught, breaking it all up in two, or three, or howsoever many pieces, and the rain was driving so you couldn't hardly seen nothing much."

Bobo stopped talking. Robert found himself trying to guess whether Bobo daddy named Bobo, Peter or Paul. Finally Robert broke the silence, "So you was in the ark?"

"No. I was on the rooftop with my mama. She was scared to let go. She was always 'fraid of water, ever since her sister drown long time ago. So, I was up next to her, cause I was the youngest and daddy said for me to stay with mama, while him and my brothers lashed up the ark, that's what he called the barn door. Called it our ark. And the water was coming up the whole time. Coming up real fast. By the time they finished lashing, they was floating. My daddy, he had done lassoed the chimney to keep the ark up close to the house, mama and me had climbed up on the rain barrow and from there up to the roof. My daddy had built our house. Built it strong, but it was a quivering, and we could hear things bumping into it beneath the water line. Daddy said stay with mama. I did what daddy told me. Mama Mary was brave. She wasn't crying, or shouting or nothing. But I could feel her shaking and I could tell she was scared, and she just kept calling out: Dear Jesus, dear Jesus, save us lord. And then she commence in to reciting that thing about 'the lord, is my shepherd'. You know what I'm talking about?"

Robert said, "Yeah."

Bobo said, "And then like a hog crumbling when you hit him upside the head with the flat part of an axe, the house give way and float off one direction with me and mama, and the ark kind of turned in a circle and went off somewheres else. I don't know where."

Robert let out a low whistle.

Bobo continued reciting.

"So we went to floating off. Look like we was outrunning a race horse. And all the while, pieces of the house was breaking off. I knew we wasn't going to last too long up on that roof, but it was either the roof or the water, so we clung to the roof. By and by, we started slowing down some and pretty soon I thought I saw a light or something flashing in the dark a little ways off. It was night time all the way now. When we started it was just 'fore sundown, if I 'member right. I know it was daylight when we broke up cause I never forget my daddy face when me and mama floated off. I saw my brothers grabbing hold to my daddy, I guess to keep him from jumping in the water to try and swim over to where we was, but everything was happening so fast, it wouldn't done no good for daddy to jump off the ark, cause by the time he would of cut one stroke, we was already racing off."

Robert agreed, quietly. "Yeah, I reckon you right about that."

"Never seen my daddy, no more. Neither none of my brothers."

For about a minute the only sound was Robert and Bobo's feet, crunching along the roadside.

"So it was just you and your mama what survived?"

"No. My mama died. I don't know what happened to daddy and them. When I went back home after everything dried up, somebody tolt me the last they heard, my daddy and my brothers took off for Memphis."

Robert kicked a rock. He wanted to ask Bobo when was it his mother died. Was it in the flood, or was it afterwards? But Robert figured that Bobo was telling his story and it was best if he, Robert, would be patient while Bobo gathered up the pieces of his story. Robert kicked another rock. This second rock bounded way up ahead of them and skidded off into the brush, where it startled a thrush which cooed in alarm and flew off. Robert looked to his left and saw a stubble of a shadow, another hour or so it would be time to stop. Walking in the sun after one o'clock was the fastest way to get heat stroke since the sun was at its hottest between two and four, the hours the field hands called the devil's time. Robert figured they had three hours or so to go before they got to Yazoo. It was doubtful that they w…

"See what had happened was: that light I thought I saw was sure enough real. It was a lamp on the front of two boats tied together. Man was in one boat and his wife was in the other, but they was right next to each other. Each one had a paddle and was using it to push stuff away, to hit at snakes and wild dogs that was trying to find a dry something to get up on. When we was close enough to see them and for them to see us, mama hollered, hallelujah, we saved. But we wasn't. Cause we hit something in the water and the house broke all up. Mama fell on one side and I fell on the other. The side I fell in kind of pushed me right on up by them people's boat. The man pulled me out the water, turns out he had two babies up in the boat, twins, look like they was maybe a year old. Had them tied down and covered up. He pushed me off his boat into the other boat where his wife was. I was spitting up water and what all and was hollering: Mary, Mary. That was my mama. Mary. I don't know why I was saying Mary instead mama or Mama Mary. I guess..." Bobo paused abruptly.

They walked on in silence. Robert offered Bobo a swig of water from the water sack. Bobo drank a short swallow, handed the bag back, and wiped his mouth with the back of his hand, before continuing.

"I was gon say I called her Mary on account of my daddy, who would all the time be calling her Mama Mary. Mama Mary this, Mama Mary that. Us kids ended up mostly calling her Mama Mary after the way daddy did, except laying on my back, choking up that filthy flood water, I just kept shouting, 'Mary, Mary, Mary,' and reaching out for her. My daddy had said, 'Paul, you stay with Mama Mary. Don't let nothing happen to her.

Me and your brothers gon build us an ark. We gon make our way out this flood, just like Noah'." Bobo paused.

It got so quiet, Robert could hear their regular breathing in addition to the crunch of their footfalls, and the irritating buzz of horse flies circling around a cow on the other side of the road off a little ways, what was just standing their flipping its tail and not even looking in their direction.

"The last thing I heard from Mama Mary was hallelujah. When I come to my senses and cleared my head a little, I tried to stand up. The woman say, 'no son.' the man he reached over and hit me on the shoulder with his paddle, not hard or nothing, but kind of to get my attention. 'Boy, you got to be still,' he hollered at me. Good thing he had hooked them two boats together, cause I would done have turnt over one boat, but with two of them side by side, you could of jumped back and forth and they wasn't going to flip over or nothing. That's when I hollered, 'Mary, Mama Mary.' he shouted over to me, 'Son, your mama gone. We is your family now. Here, take this here rowing stick,' and he handed me another paddle he had in the bottom, 'and help us stay to floating'."

After Bobo stopped talking that time, he didn't say nothing more for a good quarter mile. Robert respected Bobo's quietude.

"Yessir, I had me a new family. Daddy-Mann. Mann was his family name, double-n on the end. I guess in honor of Mama Mary, I took to calling him Daddy-Mann, and calling my new mother Mama Bell. Well, actually her name is Mabelline, but when she was growing up everybody started calling her Maybell, and Daddy-Mann when he was courting her took to calling her Bell cause he say she made him feel so good, good as a bell ringing for quitting time. We used to sit around after vittles was done and we all had ate our full, and we used to talk to each other. Tell each other stories. Daddy-Mann said it was right to remember where we come from and who we come from and what all we went through, and if it happened, it happened, and we should never try to hide the truth. You know, tell the truth, shame the devil and all that kind of stuff, except Daddy-Mann he wasn't no church going man. Mama Bell, she would go from time to time, but not him. My first daddy, well he was a regular church man through and through, but I guess I takes after my second daddy, Daddy-Mann, more than after my borning daddy 'cause I don't carry too much bible words with me. I kind of believe if God was God and we was his children than he ain't no kind of father to let all the things happen to his children what done happen to us. I know some people don't see it that way and I don't mean to offend you, Mr. Robert, if you see it that way, but I'm just saying what's real in my heart, just like Daddy-Mann taught me to do, say what's real, say what's in your heart. It took me a little bit to get used to just talking and telling what all is inside me, but once I got the hang of it, you know, sitting around following supper, six, seven days a week, and telling stuff. Daddy-Mann would tell us what to talk about and we would take turns talking. Everybody had to listen while one of us was talking, no breaking in on top somebody else's words. You just had to wait whilst someone was talking. And you know what? Surprising as it may sound, you learnt how to listen real good by telling stories, cause see you spent more time listening than you did talking, cause you had to be quiet and listen when you wasn't talking and there was always the three of us in a circle. So you spent two times more listening than talking. And once you got the hang of it, you could talk about anything that had done happened to you, or anything you seen, or anything you done, or even anything you thought about doing and didn't do. It's fun, ya know. Just like we talking now, walking down this road. Daddy-Mann got me to the place where I really appreciate both talking and listening. When I talk I learn a lot about myself and when I listen I learn a lot about somebody else. I remember the time Daddy-Mann talked about the first time he mated up with Mama Bell. That's the way he said it: mated up with. It was funny, cause he said, I can't talk like him cause I got a light voice and he have this deep, deep voice with rocks in it, you know, how when you knock a axe into a tree stump and it make that heavy kind of thunk sound, well, Daddy-Mann voice would always thunk like that, and to hear him you wouldn't think he was afraid of nothing. In fact that was a time we storying about being afraid. We was to tell about a time we was afraid to do something but we did it anyway. Daddy-Mann said the time he was most afraid was when he first mated up with Mama Bell. Daddy-Mann say, he was afraid on account he was a big man and he didn't want to hurt her or nothing, and he was afraid on account of he wanted to make sure he please her cause wasn't nothing worse than not pleasing somebody you love. So what he say he did was to tell her, Maybell, we's hitched now but that don't mean nothing if you don't love me like I love you. And he said, Mama-Bell said,

Manny—she called Daddy-Mann, Manny—so, she say, Manny I tell you if you hurting me. He said once they got to mating, all Mama-Bell kept saying is: don't stop hurting me, don't stop hurting me!"

Robert smiled to himself. What would he have said about fearing something? He didn't remember being scared of nothing except, well, except nothing, Ginny dying ain't scared him, just made him mad and sad and committed to the blues.

"Ain't that funny, Mr. Robert?"

"What?"

"Daddy-Mann thinking he hurting Mama-Bell by mating with her and she telling him to keep on hurting her?'

"Well sometimes the act don't hurt but the results do."

Bobo could see that Robert's body was walking down the road but his mind was way off somewheres else. Bobo knowed he had a habit of talking a lot and some people took displeasure out of being annoyed such a ways. Lots of folks like to do what they did without talking. Walking without talking. Working without talking. Even mating without talking. Bobo didn't mean no offense or nothing. Bobo just liked to talk. Bobo hoped Mr. Robert wasn't going to split off at the next crossroads on account of Bobo speechifying.

"Bobo, when bad, bad things happen, a lot of times people can't stand to remain where the badness is, so they haul up on out of there." Bobo though Robert was thinking of how back after the mighty flood lots of people just turned they back to the wasteland and walked on not stopping til they was someplace well north of the river, and cotton, and crackers, well, leastwise away from Mississippi crackers, who just went and got more ugly than the ugly they already was. The flood made them double ugly.

But, at first Robert wasn't thinking no such a thing. At first, when Bobo had said hurting, Robert couldn't help from thinking about Ginny. But then, to get his mind off the dead girl-child and the dead baby, Robert had gone into thinking about them places that a lot of Mississippi had run off to. Robert remembered how him and Shines had hoboed northward. Got far as Detroit, well really, they even stepped over into Canada for a brief spell, just to see what the promised land felt like. The ground ain't felt no different, except they had more different kinds of people, speaking all different kinds of tongues. Hell, you could walk down a street and not know nothing what people was saying to each other. On top of that, they had plantations up there, except the fields was inside big buildings.

For sure, you could make more money working them rows they called assembly lines, or covering your mouth with a rag and getting all bloody in them slaughter houses, or getting dirty down in their sewers, or even staying clean holding doors open and sweeping, but even if you made money, and even if the sun wasn't as shiny up there as it was in Mississippi, and even if the fields was called factories, it still seemed all the same to Robert. From what Robert saw, mens was just as broke-down by the time they reached forty-nine hard years, struggling to put in six more so they could retire with a watch and a couple of dollars, most all of which went for medicine to try to keep death from snatching you directly after the last day on the job.

Bobo saw Robert spit on the ground and thought Robert was saying shut up, so Bobo pulled a harp out his pocket and commenced to making sounds, couldn't hardly call it music. On account of Bobo would pull his lips back a little when he needed to breath in, he ended up interrupting hisself.

"Naw, Bobo. You got to make the music go in and out, not just out. In and out." Robert reached over, tapped Bobo on the shoulder, took the harmonica from Bobo, raised the wood and metal instrument to his own lips and expertly blew an easy song, for him, something that gave Bobo the right idea and at the same time would be easy for Bobo to pick up on. Afterwards Robert gave the harp back to Bobo, and Bobo proceeds to blow in and out, surprised at how good it sounds. Robert nods and smiles at Bobo. Bobo feels a whole lot better.

Robert wanted to make Yazoo 'fore nightfall, so he slowed down to a two-mile-an-hour pace instead of taking a siesta under a tree like he normally would do at the hottest part of the day. Bobo didn't seem to mind whether they walked fast or slow, or even whether they kept walking or was to stop and rest under a tree. Plenty negroes was like that, so used to working ten, twelve hours a day, til walking down a road under a blazing sun wasn't nothing. Robert wondered if there would ever come a time when colored people didn't have to work all day in the sun.

Ever since the mighty flood, Robert didn't cotton to being on the road after dark, seems like white folks had done got meaner than a stepped on rattlesnake. Robert knew that it was white folks' empty pockets riling them up. Ain't nothing meaner than a poor white man, especially one that used to have a little something but now done lost everything and ain't even got much as some negroes, he trudging along on shoes with paper in the bottoms and holes in the soles, and you got some darkie sporting around in a Model-T Ford, ain't right, ain't right at all.

When night fall, it was best to be wherever white folks wasn't. If they kept up this steady pace, they could make Yazoo right 'fore cut off time. Robert thought about his brother-in-law's car up round Robinsonville, Mississippi—it was old but it was running. He wondered what kind of blues man he would be if he had a car to ramble round in. Hell, he could be in Hazelhurst in the morning and up in Memphis by nightfall, he could even go over to Helena, catch up with Robert Jr. And shoot on across through Tennessee, where he had all kinds of followers. But then again, what he really needed was one of them aeroplanes, so he could rise up and touch down wheresoever and whensoever he felt an urge to be with somebody or be gone from somebody. Robert Johnson in an aeroplane, now that would really be something.

So they kept walking and made Yazoo a good half hour before the sun was setting for its nightly rest.

"Bobo, here's a dollar. Meet me here in the morning, just after day shine."

Bobo looked at the dollar 'most like it was turning his hand white. "Mr. Robert what the dollar for?"

"For to make it easy for you to sleep and easy to find your way back."

"Where you gon be, Mr. Robert, I mean, I don't know no peoples here bouts and…"

"Son, I make it a habit of not asking folks where they come from and where they going to."

Bobo looked at the ground.

"Bobo, I ain't ditching you, I just got somebody I got to see, and gots to run up on them alone, see it's a three way deal that the third partner thinks is a two way. So as I got to have negotiating room, and I ain't exactly sure what the situation gon be."

"So, you want me to wait here…"

"No, son. That's why I give you that dollar. Go have some fun. Find yourself something good to eat and somewheres soft to sleep, just don't forget to be here in the morning, and if I ain't here when you arrive, don't fret, I be long directly."

Bobo had been looking round and round. He didn't hardly see nothing he knew. Everything here was up and down, all he knew was flat land.

"Bobo, here," Robert pressed three nickels in his hand. "Give me that dollar back." confusion rushed cross Bobo's face, like chickens running from a fox. "I'm going to give you a bunch of coins, instead of that dollar piece. This way it look like you got more money than you got. Plus, this way, you ain't got to show all you got at one time. Put some in your shoe, some in your pocket and keep two bits in your hand. Most colored treat you kindly, but they always gon be some joker what want what you got and going to be doing his best to get it howsoever he can."

Bobo tried to follow what all Mr. Robert was saying, but things was coming faster than a jackrabbit lighting out with a hound dog on his tail.

"Times a wasting, son. Follow these here directions, follows them to a tee and you be ok. Go down this road til you see a shack with a sign what say fish for sale. Knock on the door, tell the lady who answer, you want to buy some perch. If a man come to the door, say you looking for work. Ask for perch if the woman come, ask for work if the man come. The man gon turn you way and the lady she take you in. You on your own from there. Be back here when the morning come. If you have to turn from there, further on up the road they got another jook what will offer you a resting spot for two bits, but I believes the perch is better than jook floor."

Robert squeezed Bobo's shoulder to let Bobo know he had confidence in the young man. Bobo was a-feared, but he was trying not to show it. He was a-feared that he wasn't going to find the place cause he didn't know how to read.

"Mr. Robert, I can't make out no sign."

"Yeah, you can, son. Maybe you can't make out no words, but you see a figure like this," and Robert use his right foot sweeping swiftly 'cross the sand to draw two arcs intersecting each other, looked something like a fish. "You see that?"

Bobo looked down, but ain't said nothing.

"Bobo, don't worry none 'bout no words, just look for the fish sign, sides don't recall no other place having no sign on it. So all you looking for is the sign, not the words. The fish sign. You follow what I'm saying?"

"Yes suh, Mr. Robert. I'm following you. I means, I gon look for a sign."

"Look. And if you don't see no sign, ask somebody where a man might find a resting spot for the night. But, if you goes the way I told you, you gon see a sign."

"Yes suh."

"And son, whatever you do, don't pay no more than four bits for that perch." Robert laughed and laughed some more as he turned, picked up his dusty crocus sack, and headed on to where-so-ever he was heading.

-4-

"I KNOWED HE WOULD BE HERE," BOBO SMILED LIKE THE TIME HE PEEPED IN THE shed upon overhearing the merriment of two voices seeping forth and catched his mama Mary just a gigglin' and daddy all over her, tickling her with his big hands, and she bending over laughing and trying (but not too hard) to make him stop, "Jeremiah, stop," and she would laugh some more and half-heartedly lunge forward, twisting like she was a filly slow running from a stallion, "Stop, Jeremiah, stop," but he was faster than a weasel in a hen house, grabbing her round the waist and picking her up and swinging her around, and she was laughing so hard she was 'most out of breath, and when he set her down, she kind of tripped a little bit, but he caught her up, his arms encircling her breast, and he look like he squeezed her like he was milking, and she playful kind of slap at him, and he grinned like he always do when he beat Chester and them at checkers, and that's when the two of them both look up and saw Bobo standing there, and mama Mary try to straighten her dress out a little, but daddy, he wouldn't turn her loose, and just bellowed out, 'Boy! What you looking at?" and Bobo ain't said nothing at first, just grinned at the rambunctious couple, and, without skipping a beat, his daddy had sternly questioned, "Ain't you got chores to do?"

"Yes suh," was all Bobo had said, but he had not moved, not even flinched, instead just stood there looking some more, drinking the happy commotion all in like it was honey-sweet lemonade, you know, something you rarely get, so rare 'til you remember every lil taste and texture of it. Bobo would always remember the way mama Mary's hair was moving in such beautiful disarray from rubbing up against daddy's chin and swinging side to side trying to escape his grasp, mama Mary's two thick dark braids flapping around her head like black angel wings, and there were a couple of buttons on her dress front unbuttoned up where her breasts is, and daddy still had his hand there, without no shame, like he was reaching into a satchel grabbing hold to a handful of planting seed, except her bosom was jiggling and jumping like a hooked big mouth bass straining to slip the hook. For some reason their playful tussling both fascinated and felicitated Bobo, made him happy like warm mud oozing up 'twixt his toes when him and his friends would be skinny dipping down at Robinson's Creek. And Bobo wasn't embarrassed or nothing, in fact he was bubbling with joy that his parents likeded each other so much they would be sneaking off in the shed like two adolescents looking for someplace to play fight with each other away from the reproachful eyes of grown folks. "Bobo, what you grinning at?"

And Bobo had responded with all the innocent honesty of a choir boy, "Something pretty, I mean, umm," forced by his own tongue-tiedness to look away, Bobo mumbled some sounds that never collected into words. How does one say to one's parents, yall look pretty horsing around, mama flushed and glowing, and looking like something any man would want to hug, and daddy standing gap-legged with two arms full of happy woman?

"Yeah, ain't she? Yo mama is so pretty I could just bite her like she was a ripe watermelon. Just bite her and…"

"Jeremiah! That's not no way to talk in front a young 'un."

"He know how good a watermelon is."

"That ain't what I'm talking about."

"Mama Mary, you pretty. If I was daddy, I would be trying to kiss you too."

"That's all you menfolk think about!" and Mama Mary had leapt from daddy's grasp, pushed past Bobo, her pigtails flapping, the laughter of father and son haloed around her head.

For some reason, a real young woman hanging astraddle Robert's left knee, bucking up and down, his guitar crisscrossed in front her midsection, his head buried into her back as he pounded out a stomp without missing a lick, maybe it was the way this not quite pretty girl (certainly far less pretty than Mama Mary) was smiling that called up to Bobo the memory of his parents making merry, except he had not hardly expected to see his parents in that shed, or maybe it was the happiness in the music that Robert was making that reminded Bobo of his Mama Mary giggling and his daddy's baritone voice tenderly teasing Mama Mary, which all was how Robert's music sounded, like grown folks laughing and enjoying each other.

"I knew it. I knew it," Bobo stood in the doorway shouting to no one in particular, besides wasn't no one paying no attention to the gawking youth, one foot cross the sill, standing there bug-eyed like he never before seed a Saturday night function. People was enjoying Robert Johnson's music, and Robert Johnson was enjoying the softness of this girl's butt cheeks pressing against him while he rakishly strummed a racy song, each downstroke of his hand ending up touching her firm thighs, each upstroke fleetingly touching an arching breast, and, up in between each time he sang "Shake 'em on down," Robert was just a nipping at the taunt flesh of her lean back, like a chicken pecking corn.

Old man Papa-Pea was hip popping by himself in the middle of the floor, his shoulders hunched up a little, doing something like a miniature bunny hop, except his feet was held together, when he would jump left, his hips swung right in an exaggerated sway, "Shake 'em on down," and Robert would playfully bite at a shoulder blade, and while chording on the upstroke would brush that swift hand of his up against an erect nipple straining against a thin cotton covering, and on the other way would thump insistently against a thigh whose intersection was beginning to dampen like as if Robert was priming a pump, "Shake 'em on down," and now everybody was shouting out the dance directive in response to Robert, "Shake 'em on down," even Bobo was moved to holler and ended up getting so excited he pulled out his harp playing the two in and out notes Robert had taught him, "Whoo – whoo" "Shake 'em on down,"

There was nothing more jubilee than a shake down, even though there wasn't but twenty-seven negroes crowded into what was originally designed as the main room of a two-room house that at most had held twelve when it was the Mayfield's home. Although folk respectfully created a little clearing for Papa-Pea, every other inch was inhabited by shaking humanity, most of whom were un-nattily attired in unwashed field clothes. Eula Jean, which was the young girl's name, was really most impressed with Robert's suit. She had never before seen any colored man wear a suit like that, not even the preacher whose suit was a faded blue and all shiny from constant use. Robert didn't smell nothing like field, or cotton, nor horse or mule, nor railroad tar, nor train smoke, nor sawmill dust, nor riverfront musk. All the young men she knew was rough, none of them ever bit at her shoulder blades or brushed up against her breast with a flutter like dragonfly wings, nor rested so briefly light-heavy on the soft inside of her thigh. All the mens she knew was grabbers and hard huggers, none of them had Robert's slow way of making haste. "Shake 'em on down." By now the crowd was singing so loud, you could hardly hear Robert's guitar. Robert mischievously reached out for Eula Jean's right hand and pushed her thumb up like he was shooting a marble and used her extended thumb to strum his guitar. Eula Jean liked to cried. She had never made music like this before. She was playing "Shake 'em on down." well, at least Robert was using her thumb to play "Shake 'em on down." and suddenly, without interrupting the music, Robert stood up, Eula Jean didn't know what was happening, but he was still using her thumb and he was pressing the guitar tightly against her stomach, and his legs was bumping up against the back of her thighs, and he was almost picking her up the way he was bucking her like, like a stud mounting a mare, and now putting his tongue up in her ear whispering, "Shake 'em, shake 'em, shake 'em on down." and, my God, what was she supposed to do? And then he leaned forward, the guitar was pointed slightly downward, and Eula Jean could feel him rubbing into her from behind, and he was still using her hand to strum the chords, and her knees was getting weak, "Shake 'em on down," and Eula Jean was feeling the music all up in her mid-section, feeling the way the guitar wood vibrated against her skin, and Robert was caressing her hand as he strummed, his long fingers playing in and around her short ones, squeezing and loosening, and rubbing into the cleavages of her fingers, and it was so arousing, even though he was only touching her hand, it was arousing, well, he was touching her butt too, but the way he was touching her hand was more arousing than the way he was humping her butt, she had felt men bucking up against her from behind before, but never before had no man make love to her hand, and all at the same time be playing a guitar and shouting and singing "Shake 'em on down."

And then sudden like a thunderclap that made you jump out your skin, Robert just up and stopped. Stopped playing, stopped singing. Stopped bucking up back of Eula Jean. Let her hand drop. Moved his guitar aside. And. And just plain stopped, like a country road they wasn't finished running. Dead stopped. And a great whooping "whoa" went up from the crowd. It was only then that Eula Jean opened her eyes.

She had been enjoying Robert's touch so much, with him gone so quick, she felt naked. Like as if they had been in bed one minute and was standing up in front the church the next. She spun around looking for Robert—what had she done wrong? And at that minute a childhood habit took hold, she unconsciously stuck her thumb in her mouth, the same thumb that had been hitting the guitar strings, as she sucked her thumb she realized that it was hurting a little, not really all that much but enough to notice and sucking on it made it feel better. Actually her thumb was somewhere between numb and all a tingle, just like some other parts of her body was, but where was Robert?

She looked from face to face, fast like when chasing a mouse darting through the house. When she saw Robert hugging some man-boy, Eula Jean was washed over with a rancid combination of shame jumbled up with intense feelings of inadequacy, and she sucked harder on her thumb. She knew that mens sometimes hugged each other, but why would Robert be hugging on a man up in here when she was here, he was just hugging her from behind, he could have hugged her all he wanted, why he didn't want to hug her, why he want to hug that old bug-eyed boy? And she sucked even harder on her thumb.

Papa-Pea broke her sight line to where Robert and Bobo was grinning in each other's face. Papa-Pea laughed his near toothless laugh, fanned at her with his weather beaten, broke-down field hat, hitched up his pants, pulled on his suspenders, hip-wiggled like a bull digging in, bent over slightly, his butt sticking out toward where Robert was, shook his rump like a dog flicking off water, and commenced to holler at Eula Jean, "Sha-shake 'em, sha-shake 'em, shake 'em on down."

Where was Robert going? Eula Jean sucked harder still as Robert threw an arm up around Bobo's shoulders and stepped toward the porch.

"I knew you'd be here, Mr. Robert."

"Glad to see you, son. Let's get us some air for a minute."

"Hey you!"

Robert immediately sensed the menace in the unseen man's voice. Robert knew it was better to step forward before turning around, in case the voice was aiming to cut at him.

"Eula Jean my girl."

Robert was figuring faster than a preacher eating chicken: he could walk away but he had money inside. He could try to talk but the man's voice sounded like declarations of war rather than a negotiating table. He could fight but he ain't had nothing but his guitar in his hands—and for sure he wasn't going to get his guitar hurted up. Then two things happened near simultaneously, neither one of which helped simmer down the situation. Bobo in all his sixteen and a half years of naiveté inquired of Robert, "Who Eula Jean?" which would have been ok, sort of, had not, like she was a seasoned actor making a grand entrance, right on cue Eula Jean come bounding through the door, rushing past the voice, whose back was to the doorway, so as the voice didn't see her come shooting out, and, for her part, Eula Jean did not pay no attention to the shape half blocking the path toward where Robert stood looking back her way.

"Mr. Robert, wait up."

"What the fuck!" was all the voice said.

Robert ain't said nothing.

Eula Jean acted like she ain't heard the voice, and jerked away from the voice's hand, which had shot sideways to keep her from approaching Robert, but in both her rush toward Robert as well as her resistance to the voice, her body moved faster than her feet, well, really it was the voice's left leg that he throwed out there to keep Eula Jean back, but being as her thighs was still feeling Robert, Eula Jean wasn't even much studying no voice and so she never saw the voice's leg blocking her path, which, of course, thoroughly enraged the voice.

So here was Eula Jean literally falling forward toward Robert with the voice rushing up behind her, and Robert swinging aside his guitar from the fast approaching flesh collision, and Bobo was still standing there waiting for an answer to who Eula Jean is, except that it was beginning to dawn on Bobo that the girl falling forward, who was the same girl Robert had been jacked-up on inside, well, surely, this was Eula Jean, so who was the voice, oh yeah, he had said Eula Jean was his girl, so the voice must be Eula Jean's man, which meant that silver thing gleaming in the moonlight was probably some sort of instrument of harm, most likely a knife, hopefully not no gun.

"Aw, fuck no."

Now that the girl was falling, Robert had but two choices: catch her or let her fall, and Robert knew, either way, the voice was not going to be happy about it, which is when Bobo stepped in to try to catch the girl, or was he trying to stop the voice?

Robert caught the girl. Bobo caught the knife.

"Aug, Mr. Robert, he gon cut you."

"Motherfucker."

Robert laid the girl down, fast like, but not hard, and then laid his guitar down gently, and then tenderly grasping Bobo's shoulder, Robert propped up Bobo. The knife was still sticking in Bobo's chest. It was awful.

By then Eula Jean was screaming incoherently. Bobo was spitting up blood. The voice was long gone in the shadows, crashing off in the cornfield out back.

"Bobo."

There wasn't nothing much Robert could do. Bobo was dying, fading fast, his eyes glazing over, a death rattle (a gurgle really) weak in his throat. Eula Jean had by now pushed herself halfway up and was screaming, "Cordell done it. Cordell jooged that man. Cordell jooged him."

A quiet crowd had rushed outside when they heard Eula Jean screaming and were now standing around silently observing the tragic tableau, none of the men offering any help nor even so much as a mumbled word of advice.

The knife was still in Bobo's chest. Eula Jean was still screaming. Cordell was still escaping (even though he had slowed to a dog trot). And Robert was once again left holding a dying person in his arms.

-5-

"ROBERT, I KNOWS YOU BEEN USED OF HAVING YOUR VERY WAY WITH EVERYBODY here 'bouts, and I knows people say you handsome and all, and gon be a great and famous musicianeer like David in the bible, but I see something else in you. I sees you when you be done slip off in the woods and go to writing in that lil book you keeps or else you be just looking real close up like at a leaf you turning over and over in your hands or you be scratching all sorts of squiggles and lines and such in the dirt with a stick. I knows you be figuring up on life and I admires that in you. That's the Robert Leroy I likes, the R.L. what be studying up on all kinds of stuff and…

"So you been following me?"

"I been studying you."

"When? I ain't never seed you…"

"Well, I do be seeing you. Yesterday, over to the twin oaks. Later on, I heard your pappy, Mr. Willis, asking after you, but I ain't said nothing."

Robert sat down on a log. He wasn't used to nobody looking at his mind. He had been over to the oaks yesterday, sure had. She had him right on that count. She wasn't but fifteen, but no other female had ever allowed that they liked him cause he was a thinker, everybody else said he looked good, or he could sing good, or… Ginny was confusing to Robert.

"Why you ain't never said nothing to me before?"

"It ain't right to disturb somebody when they thinking up on things."

Robert glanced at her. He wished she would sit down next to him.

"Ginny, you ever figure over on things?"

"Everybody study up on things, it just be that some of us only studies on the edges of things, and somebody like you, you considers all over a thing, inside and out."

"I believe I want to kiss you."

Robert tried to fascinate her, put the stare on her as he softly offered up his request.

Ginny smiled but stepped back a little.

"I got to go. I came over to fetch some feed corn," she held up a bandana in which she had wrapped the kernels.

She was running out of reasons to visit and was thankful he couldn't see inside her, or he would know the real reason she had to go was to keep from throwing herself on him. She had stepped back in case he had tried to reach out and grab her hand or something. She was wanting him so hard, but she knew he was quicksand and her feelings heavy-footed as a plow horse.

"Wait."

"Naw. I got to go."

"What I got to do to make you stay?" Ginny backed away even more quickly. Robert jumped up. "Ginny, I likes you."

Quick as a wasp, Ginny stung him, "You likes lots of girls. I wouldn't be nothing but another bit of cotton you pluck and shove off into your loving sack."

"Well, marry me then."

Ginny was so stunned she started to turn around to see who Robert was talking to, to see who had done snuck up behind her, or what. He couldn't be talking to her. She quick kind of peeked over her shoulder, when she turned back full to face Robert after making sure weren't no one else but her and Robert standing there, she suddenly got angry. He was playing with her deepest feelings for him. She hated when people treated her like a child, when people didn't take her for serious.

"I ain't no girl child, Robert Leroy. Please, don't play with my feelings like they was a pebble you skip cross some lil creek you making frisky in. Please. I got to go."

"I ain't playing."

"You is."

"I ain't."

"Is so."

"T'ain't so."

"Is."

"Marry me!"

"No!"

Ginny abruptly spun around and scampered away as quickly as her stiff legs would take her, which didn't hardly seem fast enough. Robert hollered after her.

"I'm gon keep after you 'til you say yeah."

Ginny increased her pace, biting the knuckles on her free hand to keep from shouting out a reply to Robert. Not seven steps later, something landed on her shoulder.

"Wait up. I wants to walk my future wife back home."

Ginny said nothing, she just kept swallowing whatever words or sounds tried to shake loose.

As they walked on in a strained silence, the both of them was thinking the same identical thought: how long would it be 'fore they got married.

Robert took to telling most everybody he was going to marry Virginia Travis, even asked her momma permission. Ginny mama said nothing too much, except to keep shelling her peas when she off-handedly mumbled, "Well, I reckon that's up to Ginny, ain't it? She the one gonna have to live with you." Ginny mama never did cotton to Robert, he was too much crazy up behind that sinful juke music.

Dusty, which was how most people called Willie Willis, who was Robert's step-daddy, allowed maybe, just maybe, being married might turn his lazy ass into a working man.

Seems wasn't nobody teetotally happy about it, not even Ginny, who was half-worried that Robert was doing it on impulse and not cause he really, really liked her enough to serious sort of want to be man and wife. Even Robert was having second thoughts about jumping that fence on account he was struggling with a growing desire to be a musicianeer and he was having a devil of a time seeing clear as to how he was going to keep up with improving on his music while at the same time meeting the settling down demands that he believed being married was mostly likely to require.

Grown folks all the time likes to advise young folks on the ups and downs of marriages, counsel them on what you supposed to do to keep it right and what twists to make to turn it back round whenever it be going wrong, but it wasn't nobody's words in particular that Robert heeded, instead, he took to peeping people's lives and nearest he could judge, there wasn't no experts on marriage in Robinsonville, Mississippi, neither in any of the nearby environs. Robert couldn't say for sure about

Memphis, 'cause he had been too young to know what to look for in the behavior of grown-ups when he lived in Memphis, but from what little he knew about the ways of grown folks, there probably wasn't much deep difference between folks in Memphis and folks in Mississippi, 'sides, half of Memphis was Mississippi born anyways.

And during that inbetween time of their relationship when it wasn't quite yet planting time even though they had acquired most of the permissions they needed, Ginny took inventory of herself. One October, Indian-summer Saturday morning when she had done gone over to her brother's place, while washing in a tub out back with a little fire to heat the water, Ginny decided to slip down to her favorite lollygagging spot: a little sliver of creek water what ran cross the property connecting up to a stream that emptied into the river what ran half a mile away on the north side. The ankle-deep waterway was a little diversion sort of that had birthed itself one spring when there was a blockage in the stream on account of a fallen tree and debris built up around it, and, of course, overflow naturally found itself another path to the river.

Even though the day wasn't summer hot, it was very warm and the water although cool was right pleasant once you was in it for a little bit. Everything was so nice, it even sounded like the birds took to singing just for her. Weren't nobody around neither, except her brother, who was way off yonder working in the fields, and his wife, who was a whole quarter mile back at the house, so when Ginny felt the urge to frolic in the water, there was no hesitation even though she was normally a cautious somebody who would blow on a candle twice just to make sure it was out.

As some young people do, when they just out of puberty and their juices is flowing close to the surface, Ginny started thinking about Robert, how it would feel for him to be feeling on her. Before she knowed it, her hands were groping at her breasts as she imagined Robert would. Ginny was proud of her breasts, which were heavier than most her friends and made her look more grown-up than she really was.

Right hand to left breast, Ginny caressed herself, thumb brushing nipple. A twitch run through her. The birds did not stop singing, so she knowed nobody was coming or nothing, plus, she figured that God wasn't disapproving, cause if he did, he would send her a sign.

Ginny moved a little ways upstream and to the water's far side, which was hardly three feet away, but on that side was a bluff with a tree overhang and roots exposed running into the creek bed. Ginny squatted on the biggest vein of the roots and looked down at herself. How would Robert touch her?

Ginny was resolved: Robert Leroy loved her as much as he knew how to love anyone, maybe more than he knew, but she knew, ever since the day when Robert had told her about how his mama had him by another man about a year after the white folks ran off Mr. Spencer, who was her husband. From that moment Ginny knew that Robert was offering her everything he was, just flat out exposing all his innermost stuff, the kinds of stuff most folk don't usually share with nobody but God.

Robert say, when he was small he ain't never knowed about his real daddy, only knew about Mr. Spencer and was under the general belief that Mr. Spencer and his daddy was one and the same, which all was why Robert thought his name was Robert Leroy Spencer even though the man he was named after had the real name of Charles Dodds, Jr. and not Charles Spencer.

Robert say when Spencer ended up in Memphis is when he had done left the name Charles Dodds, Jr., buried behind, 'cause he had shook the Mississippi mud off his shoes. Seems like leaving Mississippi is when things got all tangled up 'cause Spencer brung some woman name Serena up to Memphis and left his wife behind, which is when Julia took up with another man. And then over a year after Robert was born, Mrs. Julia Dodds hired on with some white man in the delta what was contracting out labor, and then she eventually made her way up to Memphis where she hook back up with the former Mr. Dodds who was now Mr. Spencer. So there was Mr. Spencer and Miss Serena and Miss Julia, actually Mrs. Julia Dodds (which, by inference, made her Mrs. Spencer, but wasn't nobody inferring nothing back then), and both them women's children, all living up under one roof and seemingly like they getting along as best you might expect from such a jumbling up. But after a little bit, Miss Julia ain't likeded living in a Memphis house with two womens running one kitchen.

When Robert had said the two kitchens part, Ginny thought about her mama telling Ginny wouldn't be but no one woman up in any kitchen of her's, 'cause too many cooks spoil the pot, and two women under one roof spoil the house, just like there wasn't but one man of the house, had to be but one woman of the house. Ginny kind of agreed with that even though Robert say from what he remember, "It worked out ok."

On account of the way he was talking about it in a kind of far off voice, so quiet-like, Ginny had to almost push up in Robert's lap to hear him clearly, well that led Ginny to believe the water was deeper than Robert was saying it was.

"Didn't none of us starve and there was not no whole lot of fighting over nothing. But, you know, after my mama moved on and left me behind, me and Mr. Spencer kind of started disagreeing on different things. Ya know how I mean?"

Ginny had this way of looking Robert dead up in his eyes and answering him with her eyes, maybe a little nod, but didn't need no words to communicate with him and that seem to bring peace to Robert that she could talk to him without words. So when he ask did she know what he mean, Ginny gave him the I'm-here-for-you look rather than the head nod yes, and to punctuate her look she real soft-soft placed her hand on his knee and squeezed it a little bit, and when he felt it and look into her eyes directly, she smiled at him, and he knew she understand him. Robert really liked talking with Ginny, and, for her part, Ginny deeply enjoyed communicating with Robert Leroy.

"I wasn't nothing but seven years old, but I knew even back then things weren't all the way right, so me and Spencer we took to butting heads, which is eventually how I come down here and hook back up with my mama and the other rest of my people and my new daddy."

Robert Leroy, he breath in and then slow exhale, making a sound like he heard one time when some boy stuck a dead dog with a sharp stick. And then he cough two short little coughs like he was trying to clear his throat but his throat was dry, and then he wipe his eyes with the back of his hand. "Ya know, I done had three daddies. I got Dusty now. Up in Memphis I had Mr. Spencer. And there was the man who put my mama in a family way."

Which is when Ginny knew for sure that Robert Leroy loved her, here he was getting all shiny-eyed and telling her stuff that didn't nobody else know and sharing all kinds of secret feelings and such, except…, no not except, 'cause this was not nothing she wanted to set aside, especial, yes, that was the word, this was especial, especial the way Robert was opening up to her. She didn't have nothing especial to share with Robert. She had one mama and one daddy. Her mama had never left her nowhere with some other woman her daddy was liking, and her daddy ain't never brought no other woman up under their roof.

For some reason Ginny was not afeared she would not be able to handle all this twisting and turning of Robert's inside-family matters. Ginny knew she was strong and always was level headed and careful like, so she was sure this would work out, besides maybe it was all this twisting-up stuff that made Robert Leroy especial, maybe to be especial you had to be kind of twisted by life, and since everybody needed somebody, maybe the twisted-up kind of peoples needed somebody who was good at untwisting things, which Ginny knew she was good at doing.

She could always keep her siblings from fighting up each other, could figure out what to say to make her daddy laugh, which was not no easy task, shucks, most people couldn't even get him to speak to 'em, Ginny reckoned there wasn't but maybe five or six people who had even much seen her daddy smile not to mention laugh out loud like she could make him do on the regular, and Ginny was also good with her mama, knowed how to do chores so that her mama approved, and, well, maybe Ginny was born to be Robert Leroy's especial companion.

"My real daddy name Noah Johnson and I was born on Eight-A-May holiday, either 1910 or 1911 down to Hazlehurst. I don't rightly know which, my mama told me different at different times." At seventeen going on eighteen, he was not quite three full years older than Ginny, he wasn't no sapling but he still ain't had growed up to his full height, which made it all the more especial since he could have had any number of other womens to talk to. Here Ginny was, a very young woman, girlhood barely behind her, and she was the one Robert Leroy conversated with.

"One day I'm going back down there to see my daddy just like," and Robert had hesitated a little, looking down and playing with a doddle-bug. Ginny patiently waited for Robert to stop pushing the tiny creature, making the bug ball up on itself. Finally, as though there had been no interruption, without bothering to look up, Robert re-commenced to talking, "Just like, one day my son going to see me," which is when Robert acknowledged Ginny's presence by turning to her, full face to full face when he said that last little bit, and then after a short while of swimming in her dark eyes, Robert looked back down to the dust and flicked the bug away with a twig, and then pushed himself up as though he was about to go off wandering but didn't do nothing but stand there quiet-like with his hands in his pockets.

Ginny had sort of hugged herself, she really wanted to hug Robert but more than that especial desire, she wanted to (and knew she needed to) give his silence safe space to flower. Most folks thought of Robert as talkative, but she knew both the quiet Robert and the talking Robert, and she loved the both of them enough to be happy with whichever Robert showed up at any particular time. And Robert for his part loved that he could be alone with her, be thinking and she would not try to crawl up inside his thoughts with all kinds of prodding and questions or comments and such.

"My mama done the best she could by me, now, by my reckoning, it's time for me to do the best I can by somebody... I mean, by you, Ginny. Do my best by you."

Ginny always turned that scene over in her mind, and each time she did, for some reason chewing over Robert's words made warmness rush through her and made desire to flower so strongly she would have to shut her eyes and sit on her hands to keep from touching herself. Except. Except when she was alone somewhere and knew nobody was going to be running up on her, then she would, well, she would, you know, kind of help the feeling along.

As the water swirled around her ankles, and as she recalled the way he had repeated those two words: "By you," Ginny granted herself permission to approach her privates. At first she pressed her legs together tightly without moving her hand, but then she fully surrendered to the glow of adolescent arousal, whatever this feeling was. The bible said it was a sin for a man to spill his seed on the ground, but ain't said nothing about if a woman touch herself. And when she spread her legs and scooted down slightly to make it easier to press her button, that little extension at the top part of her what lurked under soft folds of flesh, when she tapped that, Ginny gasped—something this powerful, God, why hadn't nobody ever told her about this?

Her second touch caused an even deeper gasp, a deep, deep up-rush that made her shudder and dig her heels hard into the loamy creek bottom as her toes curled. I better stop, Ginny lied to herself.

Heck, she was almost fifteen, the age when her mama said Ginny could decide for herself how she was to live her life, not only did she not have to stop touching herself, but better than that, she could be with Robert much as she wanted, or, well, at least as much as he wanted, cause she was not sure he would feel as strong about her as she felt about him, what with all them girls buzzing around him, even much her friend Sarah, asking her about doing it with Robert, and Ginny telling Sarah when you really love somebody things should stay between the two lovers and not be spread all over the fields like fertilizer for gossip.

"But I told you about me and Junie, and you told me about the time you and Thomas did it."

"Yeah, but that wasn't cause I wanted it, that was cause Thomas kind of made me, on account of you and Junie, and the four of us was supposed to be at the picnic and went off together 'cause nobody would suspicion that the four of us would be doing nothing like that together. And I could hear yall on the other side of that big tree and Thomas pull on me and wouldn't stop until I let him climb up on me, but that wasn't no love or nothing."

"I knows you ain't liked no Thomas. But I likes Junie and I tells you about how Junie do it, remember I…"

"Don't matter none. You knows I loves Robert Leroy and that's all you needs to know about that."

"What about William Charles?"

"What about him?"

"Vergie, you tolt me 'bout him."

"Sarah Ann, you know good and well that was cause that was the first time I was with somebody and we had promised each other to tell each other about our first time."

"Well, what was it like the first time with Robert?"

"What you studying up on Robert Leroy for? I guess I got to watch you."

"Vergie, it ain't nothing like that. He don't even much like me."

"Your toe must a been in the water if you know the temperature so good."

When her friend didn't respond except to look away, Ginny realized that when it came to Robert Leroy, she didn't have no trustworthy girl friend.

"Sarah," Ginny paused so the full weight of what was to follow could rain down on Sarah's silly head, "We both knows how mens is. Right?"

Although she couldn't see where Ginny was headed, Sarah knew it was not in no direction that she particularly wanted to journey down. "Yeah," Sarah reluctantly responded, "You could say that, but..."

"Well, what I got to say about all this is this: Robert Leroy was menfolk before I knowed him, and I knows that a lot of bees be buzzing around his honey, but no matter who he been with, he done announced to the whole wide world he gon marry me, and marry is better than fornicating."

"I ain't said nothing about fornicating no Robert."

"I ain't accusing you of getting with my Robert. I'm just answering your question about me being with Robert. I'm going to be Mrs. Robert Leroy Johnson and that's a big difference than just being another fast something he done rolled around in the hay with."

There was a huge silence that followed Ginny's retort to Sarah even though, in truth, Ginny 's words was just defensive maneuvering. Actually Ginny was scared to ask Robert about womens. She knew he had been with plenty women who was way more accomplished than her seven months or so of experience with only four other boys, and that was counting that one time with Thomas and that first (and only) time with William Charles. Truth was when it came to pleasing a man, Ginny really didn't much know how to do it.

Sarah Ann was the only somebody Ginny would talk with about they bodies and stuff, and Sarah herself had not started up to messing with men 'til almost a whole week after Ginny had been with William Charles—a nagging little ragweed of a thought suggested to Ginny that her friend Sarah was actually a follower trying to sound like a leader, which all kind of made sense of how Sarah Ann had said that all Junie liked to do was stick it in, shoot it off, roll over and fall asleep, wouldn't no man fall asleep if it was good, at least that's the way young Ginny speculated on the subject. Hump, Sarah Ann didn't hardly know no more than Ginny did, and for sure, probably both Sarah and Ginny added up together and doubled twice over wasn't no match for Robert Leroy's understanding of what to do when you was doing it.

Some of them songs Robert be singing talked about doing it all night long, Ginny hoped those songs was true, and prayed that she would be able to keep up her part for as long as Robert Leroy wanted to stay up.

"Robertttttt…" Ginny screamed when she couldn't contain the pleasure no more, and at the same time she was spasming, she bumped her head back of the tree, slipped and almost fell off the root, which is when she lurched against the bluff, reached out and used her left hand to steady herself, but even while scooting backwards, for some reason that didn't make no sense but felt right to do, Ginny kept her right hand hovering over her button. When the flood of feelings finally subsided and she was able to catch her breath, the first thing Ginny wondered was: does Sarah know about the button?

–6–

ROBERT'S SECOND FAVORITE, EARLY, BLUES TEACHER, THE INFAMOUS CHARLEY Patton, known far and wide as a hard-playing rounder, had advised Robert that music and marriage was a hard mix, well leastwise, was a hard mix on the woman, and, just like he wouldn't throw no bucket of water on laying hens, Robert was loving on Ginny too much to put her through the sure 'nuff trials and tribulations what would result from him being all the time gone off somewheres making merry, so Robert Leroy Johnson decided to buckle down and do all the things a marrying man should do, which mainly meant a whole heap of manual labor in the fields and down to the saw mill, not that he liked it, in fact he down-right hated it, but still and all, Robert loved Ginny and was willing to prove his love doing all them hard-ass things a good man does, like going to work every morning the good lord send, and coming home every evening, and trying not to stay too late out to the jukes on the weekends.

Robert made the mistake of taking Ginny down to a function once. Once. Only once did he make that mistake, got down there and he saw another side of Ginny that wasn't so sweet. Robert knowed Ginny was physically strong and was strong willed, but he never knew what a lil' hellcat she could be until when she tried to tear out some silly child's hair. The girl wasn't doing nothing but what most women be doing in a juke when they having themselves a good time and such, you know, dancing and prancing, cutting the fool, flirting with everybody and what all, you know, the normal stuff young womens do when they firm and fine and full of life and be feeling theyself, which is all the girl was doing, really, leastwise that's the way Robert looked at, it wasn't like he was angling to reel her in or nothing, he was just going along with the entertainment of the evening, making people feel good and all, laughing and drinking, dancing and hugging on each other.

Robert was framing, playing second guitar, not even having to sing at all, on account of farmer Brown was leading with both his box and his voice, and Junior Brown was blowing up a storm on the harp, so they actually had a hellacious sounding little pick up group getting on down with it, and everybody was enjoying it, everybody was dancing, and, lord, it was some crowded up in there, peoples was all on top each other, except, it seems, for Ginny, who wasn't dancing and was standing off to the side, in the corner all by her lonesome, but weren't nobody paying her no mind, not out of spite or nothing, but on account of Robert, everybody knew Robert and Ginny was hitched, so what with Robert being right there, less than four or five feet away, weren't nobody even much even trying to talk to Ginny. Every so often, Robert would look over towards where Ginny was, raise up the neck of his guitar, hit a double strum on a crazy chord, and then wink at her and smile his wide, wide charm-sweet-out-of-lemon smile, and do it all without missing a stroke, so naturally Robert felt like every little thing was jam tight and jellied up.

But just like a cottonmouth will strike all sudden-like without much a warning, well Ginny was a full bladder about to bust. Robert was used to girls getting crossed with each other behind liking him, but full fledged fighting for no good reason, well, this was a new twist on an old problem.

Now, some mens likes to see women fighting over them, but it hurted Robert to have to bear up behind Ginny cat fighting, cause Robert he loved Ginny, was crazy about her, but he wasn't jealous like Ginny was and didn't hardly know to what extent Ginny was jealous 'til she started scratching that Sarah child. From the way Ginny jumped the girl seems like they must of knowed each other and was toting some suit satchels of bad feelings from some time before, but the girl was only funning, dancing around and such, she ain't meant nothing, still and all Ginny didn't take it that way, and quicker than a peckerwood would call you a nigger, Ginny was on that girl like a hawk swooping down on a rabbit. Made Robert have to spring up, stop playing, grab Ginny and drag her out there, which of course meant that he couldn't make no money. When they got outside Ginny was shaking like she had a high fever but weren't not even one drop of water in her eyes, her little fists was balled up tight like she was Jack Johnson or somebody. And she wouldn't say nothing to him. Nothing. Robert knew he couldn't leave her outside and he dared not bring her back up in there, so he decided to call it quits and commenced to stepping off to hike the six miles back home.

Robert he call hisself clearing up the air, figuring after the each of them had their say, they both could put it behind them, but you know mens and womens that is yoked up can be mighty stubborn with each other, especially when they tugging off in different directions and the both of them thinking they in the right and the other is the one going astray.

"Ginny, 't'ain't right you be fighting up in there whilst I'm trying to play for the peoples."

"What peoples you was trying to play for Robert Leroy? Look like to me you was playing just for one particular person, the more she switch, the harder you was playing, and then when you went to rubbing her butt with your guitar that was just too much, but I'm the one who a fool for fighting Sarah, I should a been said something to you, 'cause that was powerful disrespect on your part acting like we ain't man and wife."

"Ginny, I'm a musicianeer. I plays for all the peoples not for no one particular person, and you knows I knows we together, if I disrespect you then I'm sor..."

"Robert Leroy, my eyes don't lie to me. There was no if in the way you was acting with Sarah."

Robert decided to give it a rest.

"You ain't got nothing to say about that, is you?"

Ginny insisted on a continuance of a conversation to nowhere.

"I says I'm sorry."

"So, I was right. You was rubbing up on Sarah?"

"I'm saying I'm sorry you mad."

"You ain't sorry about messing with Sarah?"

"I weren't messing with Sarah."

"Was too!"

"Was not."

"Was so."

"No, Gin..."

"Well, what you call it when a man be feeling on a woman."

"I ain't even much touch nobody."

"You telling me your guitar weren't rubbing all up sides Sarah's behind."

"She bumped into me, Ginny."

"And you bumped back."

"Ain't such."

"You must think I'm dumb cause I'm a few years younger than you, but even a baby could see what I saw."

"You ain't seen nothing."

"You mean you ain't want me to see nothing."

"What you saw, then?"

"I saw my Robert using that box," and Ginny scornfully flicked her index finger towards Robert's instrument, "Bumping up back a Sarah like you was some kind of dog with a hard on."

"Ginny, this crazy."

"So I'm crazy now, huh? How would you feel if I was to go to grabbing on John Jay?"

"What John Jay got to do with this?"

"I'm just saying if the rooster eat, the hen ought to eat too."

"What you saying? You saying you want to go lay up with somebody else?"

"I'm saying I'm content with what I got but what I got ain't content with me." Ginny had a little catch in her voice, made Robert look over at her, plus, she was almost whispering, and not all loud like she had been a minute ago, it was almost like she had given up and all the fire light done gone out, like she was kind of resigned to being sad and unhappy. "If you feels my pastures ain't green enough, well, I can't stop you from jumping the fence, but, at least respect me enough not to do it all up in my face."

Ginny was all knotted up inside on account she felt like she was losing Robert to the fast life up in them jukes, losing him 'fore she even had hold to him good, and crazy mixed-up about it on account she ain't wanted to do nothing to even one little bit slow down Robert's music 'cause music was the only thing in the world that Robert did that demonstrate everything Robert had to offer. Besides, Ginny knew she would have to be slow as molasses in the winter to even think about challenging that guitar for Robert's affection. Just as sure as a snake going to crawl and a rooster going to crow for day, Ginny knowed there was no way in the world she could win that tug-a-war. Her on one end and that guitar on the other, well, he might put it away for a day, or a month, or even for a year, but sooner or later…

Ginny wanted to stop thinking about it, but she just couldn't. She wanted to be slow walking all hand-in-hand up under the moonlight, all hugged up on Robert and everything, or maybe his long fingers tickling her waist, his hip bumping hers as they strolled, but, shucks, he had to want it too, it don't do no good for only one partner to wants to dance, if the other don't be feeling it.

Ginny knew she was right about that, he had to want her for her and not be choosing some Sarah over her, right there where everybody was looking at him igging his wife in favor some fast girl. She had a right to be mad, hell, he would be mad if she was dancing all close up on some one or the other of them mens up there, twisting her waist up and rubbing her hips up against they thing.

It was almost like Ginny had grabbed a skillet that was too hot to hold and still and all so hot she couldn't let go, besides, she loved Robert, loved him all hard and everything, with everything she had, every little bit of her, from hair-tip to toe-nail, all inside out and everywhere else, she loved Robert and it hurts something terrible when you be loving somebody with everything you got and they just ignore that love, especially in front of Sarah, Sarah knowed how much Ginny love Robert, Ginny told Sarah how much she love Robert, and for Robert to turn his back on her, his very own wife, and play around with Sarah's behind, well that was plain, teetotal wrong.

In her mind, Ginny was screaming at Robert: Robert Leroy you wrong, you wrong, you know you wrong for that, that's double-d wrong, all the way wrong, just plain wrong, why you want to be wronging me like that, I can understand if you want to play around a little, I understand mens be like that and you was playing around long before you married me, but, Robert, we married and when you married, you married. I wouldn't even so much as look at another man now that I'm married to you. If you don't love me why you married me?

Every time Ginny got to a stopping point in her thinking, she'd eased up a little but then keep rolling right on down the road. She kept on thinking on how bad she felt and how wrong Robert done her.

For his part, Robert Leroy was feeling lonely and sad mainly because, no matter which all way he examined what had happened, he couldn't make out how to straighten things out. He could have made three whole dollars back there, now he ain't had nothing in hand but a mad woman and a long, lonely walk back home.

Robert knew he loved Ginny, no doubt about that, but he didn't love what Ginny was doing now, acting like some lil' silly school girl. They was married. Everybody knowed that. Everybody knowed when the night was through Robert was going to be leaving with his Ginny, not with nobody else. Them other womens could shake and such all they want, wasn't nobody walking home with Robert but Ginny. Hell, that went without saying.

Robert gave up thinking about it. You know how sometimes you be wanting to say something to make somebody feel better, but at the same time you don't want to set them off or nothing, so you be real, real kind of careful with every word you say, every breath you take, and so you kind of caught betwixt trying to find the words to make them feel better and, on the other side, grabbing hold to the reins and trying to pull them up short, but you can't figure out what to do so you don't do nothing one way or the other, you just hold on and hopes you can ride it out, well, that's sort of the way Robert was caught that night.

Robert thought about it, he ain't wanted to be with no woman he couldn't control and at the same time he ain't wanted to be with no woman he *had* to control. He wanted to be free, so he guessed what was good for one, was good for the other. His woman should be free to do whatever she wanted to do, just like he wanted to be free to do what all he wanted to do, but, hell, freedom don't include fighting nobody just on account you don't like something they be doing, especially not when they don't be doing no harm to you, which, of course, was the big question maliciously running around Robert's chicken yard: was Ginny wrong, or was he wrong for thinking she was wrong?

Right is easy to recognize but sometimes wrong be hard to figure. And on that cool night not even two weeks shy of Ginny's upcoming birthday, the both of them walked all the way home in the unsettleness of heavy hearts and a hurtful mutual solitude.

-7-

ROBERT LOVED BEING MARRIED TO GINNY. SURE THEY HAD SOME WEEDS AND rocks in their garden, but there weren't no troublelation that they had not been able to deal with, and Robert liked that, really, really liked how they would work together on each other's faults (and he sure had a hamper full for his part).

Robert smiled thinking of Ginny 's faults, mainly her willfulness. Don't let her get a notion stuck up in her hair, you could be combing all day and wouldn't get it out. And she was so serious, even when she was dead wrong, serious as a rich man counting his money. Like when they argued about who should empty the night bucket in the morning.

When Robert got up early to feed the chickens he would empty the bucket and by the time he got back, of course, Ginny would be up fixing breakfast and, of course, would have left some night water in the bucket, but would be bustling about so he could have a hot meal before heading out to work, which meant that he would have to empty the bucket again, and, of course, it wouldn't do for him to leave the first taking-out 'til after he finished with the chickens 'cause if he had not taken it out when he first got up, Ginny would be burning up and would mis-fix the breakfast to let him know he done something wrong, and, of course, he would know, cause Robert always knew whatever was wrong, he was wrong, cause Ginny wasn't never wrong about them little such things, and she wouldn't say nothing, but he would know.

Robert smiled some more, remembering how dumb he was to argue with Ginny about the night bucket. He hated the smell of it in the house, mainly because they ain't had nothing but that little bitty room in his half-sister Bessie and her husband Granville's house, and once Ginny was in a family way, her smell was in a family way too, real strong, yet, even though he hated the smell (it was strong like deer musk), he could ignore the odor just like you stepped over cow patties in the field without breaking stride and without having to hold your nose. Ginny, on the other hand, couldn't stand that smell even notwithstanding it being her very own smell, but even though she couldn't stand it, she wouldn't take the bucket out back and would wait for him to finish with the chickens, which was like figuring two and two was three, seems like if she ain't like the smell she would of at least set the bucket outside the back door, but no, she let it wait for him to empty.

"Robert, while you waiting for vittles, take the night bucket out back, please."

"I took it out when I got up this morning."

"I know you did, but I… nevermind." Ginny turned back to the stove and mumbled to herself, "I got to do everything."

"I feeds the chicken, so you ain't…

Although she didn't want to be acting forward or nothing, she still was upset about Robert not willing to help when all he was doing was sitting and watching her work. Ginny never took her eyes off the coffee pot when she quietly asked, "You want to fix breakfast and let me feed the chickens?"

"You know I can't cook."

"And you act like you can't carry neither," Ginny spun around, unable to contain herself any longer, she put them iron eyes on him, sparking like a hammer hitting a hot horseshoe.

"I carried some this morning."

"And that left you so weak, you can't carry no more." Once Ginny got started her mouth just took over. She knowed she oughtn't been talking to her husband like that but she never could stand people wronging her, especially when they was acting like she was too childlike to understand what was going on.

"Well, Ginny, I figure, you know, whoever use it after the first emptying, well they ought to empty, I mean like, it ain't like it's none of mine that I left behind."

"So you'll carry your water, but you ain't going to carry none of mine?"

"That ain't what I'm saying."

Ginny bit her tongue, turned back to the stove and tried to control the angry creeping up in her voice, "But I suppose it's ok for you to eat even though you ain't did none of the cooking?"

"I ain't saying all of that."

"Well, what you saying then?" Now she was patting her foot from the strain of trying to act at least ten degrees cooler than she was feeling at the moment. After counting to twelve, Ginny released her anger slowly and carefully, wanting to make sure Robert heard what she had to say rather than simply heard that she was angry. "Here I am carrying your baby, getting up fixing your breakfast, and you saying I'm asking too much for you to carry the night bucket out back."

"Ginny, you know if you was a man, you could a been a preacher, cause you sure know how to shame a body into doing what you want."

It was hopeless. Anytime Robert Leroy go to referencing church, she knew good and well he was lying. She pulled open the oven door and, padding her hand with a bunched-up handful of her dress, Ginny grabbed the handle of the black skillet, set it atop the stove, softly closed the oven door, and even softer than that, intoned downward toward the skillet, "The shame ain't mine."

"See, you twisting my words all up some more."

Ginny paid no attention to Robert's response, clanging the tin plates around as she grabbed the second one in the short stack—she never served the top one without washing it first on account of bugs and mouses and who knows what all be scurrying around the kitchen. She wasn't really angry anymore because she recognized that Robert recognized he was wrong.

Ginny didn't expect an apology, his left-handed acknowledgement calling her a preacher gave her satisfaction enough. Besides, he was right, at least he did get up and feed the chickens, a task that most men expected their wives to do. But still the night bucket needed emptying too.

"Here's your breakfast, Robert Leroy. While you eating, I'm going empty out the night bucket."

Robert ain't said a word, instead he grabbed Ginny as she was play-mad sashaying out the kitchen. She wasn't hardly showing much, so she wasn't heavy or nothing. Robert picked her up off the floor and deposited her on the log-bench they used for sitting to the rough-plank table.

"Robert Leroy leave me go."

"Ginny Esther sit yourself down whilst your husband takes care of some light work, then we can eats together: me, you and the baby," and he was rubbing her belly while saying that last part, rubbing and laughing out loud like it all was a joke.

When he got back in the house, Ginny had her head down on the table. He sat down and started in on his food but she did not raise up to talk with him like she usually did over their coffee and cornbread-with-cane syrup breakfast. Robert was on his second mouthful before he fully missed Ginny 's conversating. Robert hunched Ginny a little bit with his elbow.

"The bucket empty, reckon you could spare me a smile or two now, Miss Ginny?"

Ginny sat up but she weren't hardly smiling. In fact, her eyes were wet. Instantly, Robert felt some bad that he had made her cry.

Ginny shook her head and wiped her face with her dress sleeve, and then looked at Robert with the most pitiful look this side of a bloodhound too old to hunt. Guess, Willie Brown was right about womenfolk being extra sensitive when they was carrying, every since Ginny figured she was in a family way, she had started being real tender-headed about every little thing that come along.

"Ginny, I'm sorry."

"No, Robert Leroy, it ain't you. I'm the one all the time complaining about this, that, or the other."

While he was outside, she had thought about the argument, it was her pride doing all the talking, but her heart told her, a too proud mouth is poison in the marriage well.

Ginny had seen it often enough and she remembered her mother's words of advice: Ginny you a headstrong little something, ain't you, but you best remembers no man likes no woman beating up on him. You might can lick him with your words or your fists, but sure as you beat him you gon lose him.

When Ginny spoke after swallowing the lump of shame in her throat, her words came out all croaky like she had a bad cold or something, and she weren't even able to give full voice to her deepest sentiments. "I loves you like I ain't never love nobody or nothing before in all my life, and sometimes, sometimes…"

Robert placed his spoon on the tin plate and sat up straight on the bench, and at the same time he reached out and gentle-like covered her hand with his long fingers and squeezed a little. Ginny faced him full on. A shy smile started peeking through the tears. She was overjoyed she hadn't made him mad.

Before Ginny realized what he was doing, Robert had scooted over close to her and was slow kissing every little wet spot on her face. He was drinking up each and every tear. And when he finished, he smoothed back her hair, and smiled his most genuine smile.

"What yall two fools grinning about?"

Bessie come bustling through the door and caught Ginny and Robert grinning up in each other's face like two thieves what done got away stealing chickens out the rich folks' yard.

"Sis, I loves me some Ginny, and Ginny, she loves her some me, and we both is grinning cause we both be loving the one who is loving us back."

And with that, Ginny smiled double-wide.

Even though they bumped heads from time to time, the both of them loved each other so strong, they was both weak for each other, and always ended up doing whatever the other wanted, which is why Robert emptied the night bucket for the second time that morning, and also why Ginny never bothered Robert about him going down to the juke and leaving her behind.

From time to time while working, Robert would break out smiling as he remembered some little specific something about Ginny, could be anything, the way she was so strong-willed and could out stubborn a mule, or how she was kind of bow-legged (actually more than "kind of," you could run your hand 'tween her legs when she was standing up straight), or could be grinning behind how high-pitched her sweet laughter was, remind you of a baby, or the cooing sound she made when he was loving her, sort of like a hoot-owl drunk on moonshine.

Robert liked thinking about Ginny, and more than thinking about her, he liked touching her, liked how, small as she was notwithstanding, she was a double-handful when they was loving. When she took to really feeling it, she would buck beneath him something fierce-like, she could of been a Brahman bull you had to hold on tight to or she'd tear you to pieces, like the first time she bit him while they was coupling.

Robert paused his hoeing and reached up with his left hand and rubbed the spot where his shoulder and his neck met, were her face usually rested, where she nipped him like a mule do when he mad, but Ginny hadn't been mad, just real excited, all bucking up and such, and, whew, when she bit him he shot off and screamed and she bit down harder and he screamed louder, and she was all out of control, shaking the way a woman shake when the feeling hit her, screaming and shaking and biting him all at the same time. Damn.

Robert ain't knowed how she learned how to love like that, just made fifteen in March, and claim she ain't never much cared about being with a man, that is before Robert, and, of course, that kind of puffed-up Robert's chest some to think he was the one turned her on, but, still and all, just as sure as fatback's greasy, Robert had to admit, Ginny had him just as crazy about her, crazy about being in her, about holding on to her and feeling that energy when she was shaking in his arms (and he even wondered how did he feel to her when she had him shaking and hollering her name).

As Robert was thinking on how bold his innocent Ginny was in making love to him, he looked over toward the tree line where the pines growed and saw a hawk with some poor animal clasped tightly in the hawk's claws. Two things, you always saw in the country, for sure: sex and death, almost like they was yoked together in life. Every where you looked some animal or the other was humping one another, and something was always killing something, be it a man slaughtering a cow or a pig to feed his family or some predator capturing some prey, just like that hawk had caught whatever it was the hawk had caught, or like when you shoot a rabbit, or a coon, or some other game. So, Robert guessed, it was natural for Ginny to know how to love like that, for sure she'd seen a bull coupling with a cow, or horses nipping at each other, not to mention dogs and whatnot. Hell, every country-bred child had witnessed both sex and death lots of times before they was old enough to mate up with someone or go to hunting to kill something, sex and death was just a daily part of country life, so, yeah, Ginny probably come by it natural like.

In November Ginny was starting to show some, and by December was sticking out, and became moody as all get out. One minute smiling, the next second snapping like a turtle, but even though her disposition was uneven she never lost her taste for loving Robert. They would walk out by the creek in the evenings and sometimes she'd spread out her shawl over the pine needles, and would playfully push Robert flat on his back and mount him, her knees on either side of his hips, and brace herself with her hands on his shoulders, pushing against him, rising up a little and lowering herself quickly. He liked it when she sat up straight. She liked it when she leaned forward, her pregnant stomach pressing firmly against him and making it hard for him to breath deeply.

"Ginny, ain't you scared we going to hurt the baby?"

"Don't be silly, this ain't hurting no baby 'cause I'm on top. It ain't like you weighing down on me or nothing. Besides, you know what they say?"

Robert knew that they said: pregnant pussy was the best pussy, but he didn't believe that was what Ginny meant. He ain't never heard her use no words such like that before, but he couldn't figure out what she meant.

"I know, but, Ginny, you can't believe everything folks say. Sometimes *they* don't be knowing what they talking about."

"Ain't you never heard that it's good to feed the baby?"

"Feed the baby?"

"You know, when you skeet off in me, that be feeding the baby."

"Oh, you mean like what they call irrigating?"

"Yeah, I guess, irrigating, if irrigating mean skeeting off."

Robert would have laughed but Ginny had already swiftly unbuttoned his britches and had him firmly in hand, rousing him. She stretched out next to him without letting go of his member. He had not noticed when it was she had slid down the top of her dress, but he did notice she was now exposing her breasts to him, pushing a nipple against his lips as she leaned over him propping herself up with her left elbow. Of course, he couldn't resist her encouragement and licked at her nipple, but before he could fully take her into his mouth, she pulled back slightly.

"Robert Leroy, the baby hungry."

"The baby hungry, huh?"

"Yeah, and it's your turn to feed him."

And then she swiftly mounted him. Although he had long ago recognized how wet she could get in a manner of minutes, still it never failed to surprise him how easily he fitted into her, how she was both slick and tight at the same time. And she had some kind of trick way of flexing around his thing on the upstroke making him want to up-thrust into her but as he was arching his pelvis to stay in her as she reared upward, she would quickly reverse her motion and push back down, at the same time digging her nails into shoulder.

"Feed the baby, Robert." and she was immediately upraising again, squeezing him. And then she started rocking forward and backward while going up and down, sort of like back and down in one motion, and forward and up in the other. "Feed him, Robert. Feed the baby." and, of course, Robert would try to resist, try to hold back, and he usually was pretty good at controlling himself. More than pretty good. Damn good, at holding back. "Feed the baby, Robert."

When her voice went up like that, Robert knew she was getting close to exploding, which is when he would whisk his hand over her breasts, first cupping them and then sliding quickly towards the nipples but instead of grabbing, he would be feather light and barely scrap across the top of her erect nipples.

"Feeeeeeeeeeddddd him, Robert! Feeeeeeeeeeddddd him!" By then Ginny wouldn't be moving up and down so much, instead she would be more pushing back and forth as she leaned forward over him, as far forward as her stomach would let her. It almost looked like she was humping him, especially with her on top, the way she had dropped her head down and was grunting when she wasn't cooing, which taken all together was the signal she was close. And she started moving so much faster all Robert could do was hold on, there was no way he could keep up with her motions cause she was pressing down on top him even as she was sliding back and forth, and also was digging her nails into his shoulders, and her mouth was working as she grunted and cooed, and one minute she would be clenching her teeth and the next second she would be ooohhh-ing, her mouth wide open, gasping for air.

When her time arrived, it was an out pouring like from a deep well when you pumped and pumped and pumped and pumped some more, real fast pumping, and just when you thought the well might be dry, the water come spewing forth. And she would twitch like a bull did after its throat was cut and the last death throes manifested in mass muscle contractions, Ginny would twitch two or three times, depending on how deeply she felt it. After a few moments of remaining stock still like a corpse when rigor mortis done set in, Ginny would catch her second wind and then take pleasure in bringing Robert around the bend.

He had made the mistake a couple of months ago of telling her how good it felt when she reached back and caressed his balls while she was mounted on him, it was a mistake cause she took delight in teasing him, sometimes lightly squeezing, other times soft scratching with just her fingernails, and then occasionally patting them rapidly, and he never knew which one of the three she would do, in what order or for how long.

That was her mischief: mixing up how she handled him, and all the time be gyrating atop him. Except when she would do nothing. Literally nothing. Just sit there for a second except, after a short pause, she would run her fingertips across his lips until he would suck one of her fingers, which the minute he focused on her finger in his mouth, she would use her other hand on his balls and start back in to gyrating, and it would get to be too much what with the finger sucking, the ball rubbing and her gyrating on his thing. But still he would try to hold out some more. And, just like a woman, she would know he was doing everything in his power to keep from irrigating, but, again, just like a woman, she knowed how to make his waters flow.

She would roll off of him, and kneel on all fours (that is on her knees and elbows) with her butt facing him and look back over her shoulder at him, almost daring him to mount her, and he would kneel behind her, obedient as a neophyte deacon, and she would reach between her legs and guide him into her, and wait, unmoving, just wait for him to start thrusting, taunting him: "You don't want to feed your baby? How would you like it if I didn't feed you?"

And of course, within twenty seconds or so, he was pushing and grunting like a hog wallowing in slop, and she wouldn't try to match his thrust but instead would do a little side to side rocking motion, and whenever she felt his thrusts getting harder, she would urge him on by reaching up between her legs and messing with his balls: patting, scratching, squeezing, in no particular order, just matching him as he got harder and faster, and, oh, my God, it wasn't this good when Ginny wasn't pregnant and they did it normal ways, face to face.

As his grunting got louder, she would verbally urge him on: "Come on, Robert. Come on, baby. Come on. Come on!" and he would. Invariably, he would. After which is when she would reach over and dip her sweat rag into the water basin in the corner and clean herself. And after that she would rinse out the rag and then slowly and gently wash Robert. Her manipulation of the cool cloth on his privates always caused an after-tremor. On the warmer nights, she would tenderly damp-wash him from head to toe, both starting and ending with gentle wipes between his legs almost like she was tending a baby. Sometimes he would fall asleep before she finished, but regardless, she was thorough in cleaning herself and cleaning him.

Three weeks before the baby was due, they were still making love.

Look like every month or else every five or six weeks, Robert and Ginny would ride the twenty-five or so miles up to Memphis with Bessie and Granville in Granville's old jalopy. Those were fun times, Robert would be in the backseat playing his harmonica and Ginny would try in vain to sing like Robert, but she couldn't 'cause she had a thin and terribly squeaky voice, but still they had a good time, especially if Bessie and Granville were of a mind to join in to singing, as the both of them had right nice sounding voices, even though the neither one of them liked sinful music, so they would only join in on the frolics like they played on the radio.

One time while coming back, Granville took a bend too fast and was unable to avoid some ruts in the road, as they bounced in the back, Robert interrupted his harp playing to remind Granville to be careful on account of Ginny 's condition.

"Don't you see she's percolating, man?" Robert huffed as he reached over to pat Ginny's stomach. Everybody, Ginny included, started laughing at Robert.

"Robert, you percolate coffee. Womens don't percolate, we be pregnant."

"Well, Bessie, when a body use a word to mean something extra to what the word mean, well they calls that poeting. Didn't yall all catch my meaning when I said 'percolating'? And besides you remember things better when I fix up my words that a ways."

Ginny beamed like a torch light. Even though she knew that Robert liked using words, it still made her feel mighty special when he used words on her. Most of the girls she knew, ain't had no man that was good with his mouth like her Robert was. He could blow that harp. He could sing. And he could speechify.

Even though carrying the baby was hard on her, from early on with heavy bouts of morning sickness, to now having always to relieve herself seven, eight or more times a day, from always feeling sleepy lately, to this strange new craving for the lick-taste on her hands after working the pump handle, or the mouth-puckering sharpness of creek water, or even swallowing a secret tiny handful of reddish dirt, still and all, even with dealing with all of that, Ginny was so terribly proud of Robert's ability to handle up on words and how good he was at using the handle of words to set her to flowing when what he was saying pertained to how he felt about her, all that made her wish she was double-pregnant, so he would twice-over talk pretty about her.

Like babies often do, especially when you ain't had no doctor to estimate arrival dates and such, the birthing time come about two weeks earlier than was expected. Almost caught all of them short. Granville had to rush over to fetch Miss Nan for the birthing. Bessie done the best she could while they was waiting for Miss Nan.

Mid-April wasn't really that hot, but Ginny was dripping sweat. Robert fetched in buckets of cool water, and didn't understand why Bessie was making him heat up a tub of water in the backyard. Ginny was sweating, she needed cooling off, not no putting on of more hotness.

By the time Miss Nan got there, Ginny was screaming and moaning. The first thing they did was put Robert out the house.

Robert walked around the house fourteen times, Ginny's wails accompanying each rotation. Robert was listening for the sound of a baby crying, but all he heard was Ginny screaming. Granville was standing out back chopping wood, said he had to do something with himself 'cause he couldn't stand to just stand around and wait.

Bessie come out and ask for more hot water.

Ginny was still screaming but it seemed to Robert some her screams was growing weaker, tapering off like she ain't had much strength left.

On his twenty-seventh time circling around the house, Robert couldn't take it no more, so he bust up in there. First he saw Bessie sitting at the table not doing nothing. And then he noticed it. Couldn't miss it, it was so quiet. Too quiet. Quiet is not what is supposed to go with a birthing. The sinister sound of silence dominated the atmosphere.

Bessie ain't even much look up at him when he stood in the doorway and asked, "What we got? Ginny ok?"

Bessie just turn her head away. Robert couldn't move, at first. And then all he could hear was the sound of Granville chop-chopping in the back. And Robert didn't hear no baby. Neither did he hear any Ginny. And Bessie still ain't said nothing. And Granville was steady wood chopping.

Robert didn't hear Miss Nan when she step out the room, her dress front all bloody. Miss Nan stood stone-faced looking pass Robert. Not saying nothing either. Bessie was silent. Miss Nan was silent. The only sound was Granvile's ax thunking logs down to size. Which all is when the silence run up and grabbed Robert, pushed him forward, even though Robert was suddenly afflicted with a terrible fear.

Robert started stumbling. Bessie never so much as blinked. Miss Nan ain't even turned her head to full on face him, but she weren't ignoring him, just kind of look at him sideways. There was nothing coming from the room where Ginny was but the sound of a fly buzzing.

Robert wasn't all the way in the room good when the horror hit him in the gut like a mule kick when a mule make up its mind it ain't going to plow and it ain't going to take no whipping, neither no beating. But what really, really hurted Robert was not the smell, nor the fear of what might done gone wrong, but what really, really hurted was the sighting of the horror. Robert had never seen so much blood come out of one human being in all his life. Look like all the bedding was a pool of blood. It really weren't that much blood, but that's the way it looked to Robert.

Robert didn't notice the bloody bundle in the corner. Nor the knife in the basin Ginny always used. Robert didn't hear Miss Nan walking up behind him prepared to do whatever needed to be done in case Robert couldn't bear up under witnessing the double death that not infrequently accompanied childbirth.

All (soon-to-be nineteen-years-old) Robert saw was a bloody heap that had once been his (just-made-sixteen-years-old) Ginny.

Robert would never remember what he did next. He would never remember howling with a raw urgency that sent a shiver through Granville in the back yard, the ax momentarily halted at the top of its swing. Never remember literally slumping to his knees and crawling on all fours to reach Ginny's body. Never recall clasping her mangled body up to his bosom and rocking with her. Never remember kicking the basin, the water sloshing over the edge, the knife clanging against the insides of the basin, sounding like the ringing a piece of scrap metal make when you throw it into a barrel.

Robert would not remember that he had not looked around the room. Had not searched for the dead baby. Had not wondered why Ginny's stomach was all cut up on the left side, nor why Ginny was only covered by a cloth what was bloody in the middle and dry at the top and bottom. Nor had he wondered why her blood was so red. Why she felt so cold. What? Nothing. He would remember very little: the blood, the knife, Ginny, her teeth still clinched tight. Lifeless Ginny. Dead Ginny. Dead. And he had her lifeless head cradled in his lap, just like she had so often cradled him. And shortly he didn't even see Ginny because his copiously descending tears veiled his sight.

He held her for over an hour. Nobody could make him turn her loose. Not that anybody tried real hard.

Later on, Granville took the dead baby out back and buried it still wrapped in the bloody swaddling. Bessie and Miss Nan took to scrubbing down the room.

Robert had sat with Ginny for what seemed like forever. Tears streaming silently down his face. After almost eighty full minutes of tortured solitude, Robert gently loosed her, looked at his bloody hands, smeared the blood all over his face, got up and walked out the house.

Ain't nobody seen him for three days after that.

Nobody.

–8–

THE GREEKS HAD A SCHOOL OF FOLK KNOWN AS STOICS, WHO STROVE FOR balance in life, seeking to follow logic rather than emotions. Their goal was to be indifferent to both pleasure and pain, to bear up under the weight of life with a calm dignity. They started on a porch (scholars believe at the agora, or marketplace, in Athens), in fact, they say, the very word "stoic" comes from the Greek word for porch. Led by Zeno, their founding teacher, the stoics established a major branch of Greek philosophy. But they were small fry when it came to bearing up to trouble. It took the good folk of Mississippi to teach us not only how to bear the troubles of the world, but, more importantly, how to make an art out of suffering, hence the blues.

Suffering in silence, just standing and saying nothing, could of come from being forced to watch a captured runaway get beat and/or maimed. Could of come from routinely being raped and not being able to say nothing. Could of come from owing everything to the same assessment man who is cheating you out your future earnings, as meager as the future may be. Could of come from a lot of things. Burying a son/father/brother/uncle/friend who was lynched. Laboring at gunpoint in the fields day after day after day, sunrise to sunset… you know?

No, unless you was born up in that, you don't really know about Mississippi, Goddamn. About a dark that's darker than any dark you can run from, a dark that just swallow you up 'til you get tired of trying to light it and give up. The sun laughs at you. The moon drives you crazy.

Zeno would have been awfully proud of the good folk of Mississippi. And for certain he would have been proud of the music makers who took tons of pain and distilled it down to a mouthful of blues, an artform what had pulled many a hurting somebody back from the edge of oblivion. The blues was like what they call a prosthesis for people what had been cut half in two by hard times, people who lost legs and arms to the evilness of man to man being so unjust. Watching certain things can put your eyes out. Hearing... well, let's just say, only a true stoic could have survived Mississippi without committing suicide.

When Robert come back from his three days in the wilderness—he had stayed out there eating nothing, drinking only creek water, saying nothing, not even talking to himself or the birds or the rocks or the water or nothing. Anyway, when he come back amongst his people, he had made up his mind to follow the blues, to ramble the rest of his life, in fact what was life anyway: a haywagon of shit for ever little taste of sweet you might get, a spoonful of love compared to a heavy barrel full of hate and hard times that you was forced to tote through life.

Robert was not bitter, just awful, awful wearied. Bessie swear his voice changed, got deeper, yet hollow and tormented, course, she was probably exaggerating on account of she seen how he took Ginny's death, and she knowed Robert before he knowed Ginny and she seen how much joy Ginny had brought up in his life, it was most like Robert was a big fat candle just waiting for a match like Ginny to make his light shine. She even seen her brother go whistling off to work, when before Ginny, nobody could never make him even so much as, like the old folks say, hit a lick at a snake (tell the truth, shame the devil, that was true), she seen it, seen Robert hoeing up in the garden and a snake come along, and he stop hoeing so as the snake could pass, and when she inquired why, he say cause the snake wasn't doing him nothing, so why should he harm the snake, ain't a snake got a right to life, ain't the same God what made man, the same God what made snake?

Bessie knew it was that death thing. Robert hated death. Couldn't much stand to kill a rat and chuck it out the window. Ginny could though, she'd do it without batting an eye, do it, do it in a minute. But Robert he ain't never cottoned to dealing with death, so Bessie knew—she ain't had to look at Robert crying and crawling on all fours, ain't had to seen how he hugged that poor girl to him like as if he was a farmer tending a sick calf, and, for sure, ain't had to look upon Robert's blood-smeared face, the ghost look in his eyes. Bessie would never forget that day, so she knowed Robert would always remember it, but, you know, Bessie was judging Robert based on how she herself felt.

Robert on purpose dis-remembered all that stuff. Put it someplace where his mind seldom would get at it. It was 1930 and Robert ain't had but eight more years to live, or, depending on how honest you wanted to weight his life, eight more years to be tortured by his sack full of misfortune, Ginny and the baby dying just being the most recent addition to the ever growing rock pile weighing down Robert Johnson.

It weren't the devil, it was life in Mississippi that was chasing Robert. And Robert, for his part, came to an agreement—he wouldn't study death, wouldn't even think on it for one minute, if he could just find a hiway without rocks and potholes, somewhere where it was ok for Robert Lonnie Johnson, which is what he now called himself, hence forth and forever more, no more Leroy, the name his mother give him, henceforth and so on, it was Lonnie, after the great guitarist from New Orleans, Lonnie Johnson, who was no relation as far as Robert knew, but as Robert well knew, didn't nobody really know who all Robert was kin to, not even Robert himself. Robert ain't had no roots, he was what they call a tumbleweed, going whatever way the winds in his life blowed him.

So now, here Robert stood hugging Bobo and more convinced than at any time in his short life that death was following him everywhere, except rather than killing him, death was snatching up whomever was with Robert, and just like after Ginny died Robert decided to ramble, now after Bobo's death, Robert knew he had to ramble alone, not 'cause he necessarily wanted to, but because Robert didn't want to be the cause of nobody else dying.

After a minute or so, Robert let Bobo down to the ground, and for lack of knowing whatever else to do, Robert placed one hand on Bobo's chest and, with his other hand, pulled the knife out of Bobo. And soon as he got the knife out good, he dropped, no, he threw it to the ground. Felt like his hand grabbed a poker in a fireplace, a poker what been in the fire place all night and the fire had been a raging all night, and the poker it ain't look hot, but it was hot, a whole heap hotter than it look like, yeah, that's what the knife had felt like. Hot with blood. It was bloody, a bloody hot knife in a basin of ruddy water. Sometimes you can't help thinking on things. Suddenly when he looked down upon Bobo all Robert saw was Ginny and the tin basin, and the knife in the basin, and the bloody water.

"Anybody know who this boy people is?" one of the men asked out loud, hoping Robert would speak up, but Robert ain't heard the man, Robert was listening to Ginny explaining how dealing with troubles was nothing but a session of cleaning chitterlings.

If you took your time and was thorough about it, life would be good to eat when you finished, but you had to be patient and extra vigilant getting into all the crevices and all, and be thorough about cleaning out the shit, and take your time with the cooking and use vinegar, he didn't want to think about it, didn't want to think about how Ginny had been so sure she could untwist him, "You just twisted up some on account of how you was brung up, but we can untwist you, we take our time, we young, we…" but in Mississippi death weren't respecter of nothing, especially not some short lasting thing like "youth," don't care if you was young or old, when death come a knocking, you got to answer the door, and in Mississippi, death be always a knocking.

Of course there was all kinds of dying. Robert had died before. He felt like he had died back in Memphis when the man he thought was his daddy told him the woman he knew was his mama had left them, gone somewhere—the man swore he didn't know where. Robert was six, or seven, or eight, who knows, his mama never did tell him directly when his birthday was, on account of… account of what? Robert didn't hardly even much know. Robert just knew how lost you feel when your mama don't care enough to keep you with her and you still not yet strong enough to walk out into the world on your own. Do anyone ever get strong enough to go it alone? Robert knew the answer to that question. No. We never get strong enough. But we do. We do go on in our weakness or we die. Die or keep somehow going, limping along some, running some but just in general trying to slow walk on down life's road. But mama, mama, mama why you got to go?

When you young and your mama leave you after she the one brung you up to Memphis, she the one birthed you, drug you round with her from camp town to camp town. Hell, you don't know nothing about living in one place, one house.

Memphis. Daddy Spencer. Robert he was the youngest of the brood, and Robert had thought that was all why Daddy Spencer didn't seem to care too much for him, what with Robert having ten other brothers and sisters, not to mention Serena's flock, guess Daddy Spencer was tired of children.

Taking the strap to Robert didn't do no good, Robert was tougher than some old barbershop strap. Plus Robert hated the furniture making trade. Daddy Spencer could make a chair out of anything, oak, cane, what they called wicker, or pine, you name it, but Daddy Spencer couldn't make lil' Robert like making furniture.

For sure it was by the time he was seven (or was it eight?), whenever, Robert was through with wood and Daddy Spencer was through with Robert, and there wasn't nothing to do but go after his mama. Daddy Spencer said she might be down somewhere round Robinsonville and he took Robert down there, left him, "Thas the house, you better hope she there and take you in 'cause me and you is parting ways."

"Anybody know who this boy people is?" the lady at the door asked some folk who was sitting inside, which is when nobody said nothing, and then the lady took Robert by the hand and started in to asking all kinds of questions that Robert couldn't answer, except to say his name was Robert Leroy Spencer and he was looking for his mama "Julia Dodds, I mean Spencer, Julia Spencer," and somebody say something about Dusty and Julia Willis down the lane, "Ain't she not too long ago come here from Memphis or some such," and the lady brung Robert down there and sure enough, there was Robert's mama, and Robert and Mama Julia had looked at each other and it ain't seem to him that she was particularly glad to see him or leastwise she didn't act so much overjoyed or nothing, just told the lady, "Thank you for bringing him by," and ushered him to the table, sat him down, ask him if he was hungry, and told him in a little bit his new daddy would be home.

"Anybody know who this boy people is?" Robert quietly repeated the question to himself.

Robert looked upon Bobo's cold continence and just kind of felt a chill. Robert knew that the death of an anonymous man wouldn't cause no notice round these parts. Them what cared couldn't do nothing about it except accept it, which seemed, most often to be the way Mississippi life and death was: you couldn't do nothing about it, you just had to accept it.

In these rough river camps nobody even cared if you lived or died unless you was a prized worker for some camp captain, but if you was an ordinary negro, wouldn't nobody even much ask where you was gone at and wonder why you was missing, well, leastwise none of the white folks would care, and the colored, no matter if they did care, the colored couldn't do nothing. Robert had seen it so much, he was tired of seeing it.

Robert was trying to focus his mind but it kept bounding off like a jack rabbit twisting this way and that in an attempt to dodge them hell hounds what was dogging Robert's trail.

Daddy Spencer. Mama Julia. Bobo. Who this boy people is?

Suddenly Robert felt like he was over round Tunica, which is where he last saw death work its show in a combination day pool room, night juke. When the fight had broke out, Robert had kept playing. Son House taught him that. "Unless they shooting or coming after you, you keep playing," and in most cases, people wanted to party more than they wanted to fight so either they would break the fight up or push the fight outside, in either case, the musicianeer's job was to protect his instrument and stay away from the fray. Now, of course, sometimes the fight was on account of the musician, you know, usually some woman taking a temporary liking to a musician and thereby incurring the wrath of her more or less permanent man-friend or even husband, or whatever, and sometimes the fight was even with the musicianeer, in which case, you had to conduct yourself like every other member of God's creation, you had to either fight back or flee.

This particular time the fight had happened so fast the killing was over before much fussing had even much started. The short guy shot the big guy, arguing about cheating or some such. The big guy had hit the little guy with a pool stick. The little guy fell to his knees. The big guy had his foot raised to kick the little guy, but instead of struggling to get up, the little guy had rapidly, but calm-like, pulled a short gun out his pocket and plugged the big guy twice. The big guy fell against the pool table. The little guy went over, and calm as a farmer pulling up weeds, grabbed the big guy by the collar and threw his body down on the floor and then stepped atop his body and continued playing his game of pool, "Eight ball, side pocket." When he made the last shot, the little guy stepped down, kicked the big guy's body and said, "I'm gooder than you ever was, I ain't got to cheat."

Robert would have thought somebody was funning him if they had tried to tell him about the little man standing atop the dead man's body to make his eight ball shot, but Robert was right there, playing when the whole commotion went down, playing right through the argument about whether the little guy had touched the cue ball twice, right through when the big guy grabbed the cue ball and the money that was laying on the table's edge, right through when the little guy said, "Hold up, horse, don't be grabbing my cue ball and for sure don't be grabbing my money," and the big guy replying "You lucky I ain't grabbed your cheating ass!," right on through, "And I'd be the last thing in life you ever laid hands on," and when the little guy reached for the cue ball, the big guy swung on him with the pool stick, and through it all Robert had kept playing a variation of the Mississippi Sheiks' "Sitting On Top Of The World."

Death always left Robert somber. He couldn't hardly play but for two more songs after the little guy shot the big guy. And after Bobo took that knife, Robert didn't play no more that night. And after Ginny, Robert…

Robert stood up. Made himself stop thinking about death.

"I met him on the road. I don't know who his people is."

And with that benediction, most of the people quietly melted into the surrounding areas leaving the embattled trio of Robert standing silent over Bobo, and the man whose juke it was standing disgusted in the doorway, and Eula Jean sitting on the step, her face all twisted up.

Robert picked up his guitar, dusted it off, "Reckon we can find some place to lay him out proper. I'd pay two or three dollars for the burying."

The owner man, he turned to the crying woman, "Eula Jean you best go call pastor. Me and Mr. Robert here will tote this boy on down to the graveyard. Tell pastor we got to bury him tonight. I ain't going to keep no body here. Tomorrow Sunday, ain't no telling how long they be up in that church. I got work to do. Tell pastor we help him dig the hole."

Eula Jean ain't made no response except to get up and trudge off in the same direction Cordell had gone.

Ain't this a bitch, Robert thought to himself, you know you in a one horse town when the preacher and the grave digger is one and the same.

-9-

"BOY, DON'T BE BEATING ON THAT BOX LIKE THAT. YOU ANNOYS PEOPLES WHEN you does that. Stay to blowing that harp, you good at that. You ain't no good trying to play the guitar. You understand? Leave it alone."

Son House was not smiling. He had that stern, scare a white man look. Deep, dark eyes squinting mean like he was sighting a rifle. His jaw clinched, his lips set into a tight, stiff unmoving line, look like the next word he was going to say weren't going to be no word at all, was going to be a harking up of some spit and letting you have it, full in the face. Robert felt like a kicked dog, cowering under the whip of the severe words lashing out of Mr. House's mouth. Robert, he couldn't even bark back or defend himself no kind of way, cause in truth, at that time, he only knew one or two songs really good, and when he had played one of them two good ones he knew, Mr. House had said it was an annoyance.

After about thirty seconds of silence, Son House raised his hands to his hips like as if to ask Robert if he dared say anything in response.

Robert ain't said nothing.

Son, he ain't said no more.

What more need be said? You just been told you ain't shit by a man who is a master at the thing he told you, you ain't shit at doing. Standing there hands on his hips, and then rearing back and folding his arms across his ample chest, drawing up to his full six-foot-something height.

Robert smoothed down the back of his head, which didn't need no smoothing 'cause Robert kept his hair cut short, but, shucks, he felt like he had to do something besides stand there, nervously shifting back and forth, vainly trying to find a comfortable position.

Son ain't moved, could have been one of them twin oaks. Plus, everybody knowed Son House used to be a preacher and he knew about what was right and all that kind of stuff, so when he correct you all up in front of everybody, it made you feel small, but you couldn't rightly get mad at him, cause he was telling you right.

Besides Robert really, really admired Son House to the highest. Admired everything about him. How straight-backed he walked. How few words he used to make his point. How strongly he used those few words. Had a voice like what God must of sound like when he angry, like when he was cursing Ham.

It sure took a lot for Robert to bear up under Son House belittling him, which, in turn, told Son House that the boy might not be able to play but he was man enough to take a whipping without whimpering like a hurt puppy, and House, he admired mannish boys who was strong enough to stand being corrected in public without acting stupid, or cursing, or getting unnecessary angry. Or begging, or pleading, or acting any which a ways but like a man, stand there, take your medicine, don't flinch, cry, moan, or beg for mercy. Be a man.

So Son, he admired Robert for bearing up, so when Robert come to Mr. House, all humble like, and asked Mr. House to show him how to play some, well, Son, he had to sit with the boy.

Knowing how to approach people in order to learn from them was one of Robert's greatest assets. Robert was eager to learn, anytime, anywhere, up under any kind of conditions, and was willing to humble himself in order to learn something about music. Hell, Robert would study a mule if the mule's braying sounded like something Robert could use in a song. And on account of Robert always being ready to learn and always being willing to learn from any and everyone, Robert improved, and not only improved, Robert construction him a storehouse of ideas, ideas that come from every which a direction.

It was like Robert's head was a barn, full up with different approaches to music, and every time he heard something new or something for some reason that caught his ear, well, Robert would toss whatever it was up in there on the stack with all the other stuff he had already learnt, and some kind of way, whenever he needed an idea to play, he could kind of quick-quick reach up in his barn and just grab hold to an idea, just like your mama might grab hold to a chicken for Sunday dinner, if not that one, she grab the other one, and she wouldn't have to be chasing all over the yard like you do when she send you to catch supper, seem like she could just reach down and grab one without much botheration at all, and that's the way Robert was with music, he could grab it without no botheration, well at least once he learnt how to play the guitar, after he learnt to play then he could do that, just grab up some music, clean snatch it out the sun-shiny air.

Actually, even before he learnt how to play the guitar good, he could hear the music. And that's what separated him from most others: he didn't have to play it to hear it. On top of that, he could hear how he could use stuff that most other people would waste. Just like a good cook could take skins, and peels, and knuckles and grissle, and chicken foots and fish heads and make meals out of them, well Robert he could take any kind of sound and make music out of it. But all that was a long time coming, don't no acorn become an oak overnight. But on the other hand you had to know that Robert he started out what would seem unorthodox for a regular musicianeer, but since he was an ear-and-feel musicianeer and not no read-and-correct note playing, high faluting kind of musician, well, then his entrance into making music was not un-regular, cause the regular blues musician, leastwise most of the regular delta musicianeers they all come through a period of making they own instruments, or making up something they used as an instrument, or making up a way to play a regular instrument without no regular instruction, in other words they could make music out of rocks, and water reeds, and baling wire, and cigar boxes, washtubs, animal hide, animal bones, snake rattles, you know, whatever naturally was in they world, the kind of musicianeer Robert was could and would use whatever was in their world to make a world of music.

"Made me a didly-bow one time. Strung me a piece of wire 'tween three nails top and bottom what I hammered into the side of our house, took a rock and made the tension. Ginny, you ought to heard how good it sounded, like the whole side of the house was making music."

And Robert jumped up imitating the sound the didly-bow made. He slapped his thigh and bent over laughing like a mule laugh when he got plenty good corn. "Wang! Wang! Wang! Wang! Boy, that house was rocking."

Ginny, she just about bust open with pride listening to Robert sound like a house, and Robert he was smiling something powerful, twice-over proud, proud of what he was able to do and proud that he had someone like Ginny, a woman who wasn't jealous of his music.

Robert, he could talk with Ginny all day about his music and she would listen, or he could just play a new song and not say nothing more and she would listen, or he could just sit and look at a rock while he figure up a new song in his head, and she would just sit quiet-like and listen to him figuring in silence.

"Why you smiling at me like that Robert Leroy?"

"Ain't a man supposed to smile at his woman?"

"Yeah, I reckon. But you was just talking about making a didly-bow upside your house."

"Well, Ginny, you my house."

"Robert, I don't rightly know exactly what you mean, but it sure do sound like you mean something good."

"It is good. You a good house."

"Oh." Ginny smiled and looked down, feeling both complimented and embarrassed, "You know I can't hardly sing good, so I figured you was making fun of me not being able to sing none and saying I sounded like a house, or something."

"No, Ginny. I means you is my house," and he go over to her, bent down to where she sitting and place his hands on her shoulder, and bring his face down close to her's, and grin, and recite sort of like he singing, "You is what I lives in. You my loving bed, my eating kitchen. My resting space. My garden out back, the window my sun shine in. Ginny, you understand. You my house."

Ginny was just a looking at Robert, had her mouth hung open in wonder. She never knew how he could line his words up like that. Every time she wanted to say something pretty-like to Robert, her words would run every which a ways and she couldn't catch them fast enough to line them up. By the time she caught one, the other one she wanted to come next would be done slipped off somewhere down her throat and she would just be left standing with her mouth hung open.

And funny thing was, much as she loved to hear Robert sing and play and stuff, she didn't hardly hear him much anymore on account of what had happened a few weeks back at the juke and Robert saying he wasn't going to take her up in there no more. And, of course, at first she was worried and hurt—Ginny did not bear rejection well at all—but when Robert would return back directly from playing and would come in and put his earnings up in her hand and tell her keep the money somewhere or to buy whatever they needed: food supplies, feed for the chickens, or whatever, and wouldn't never even much ask her what all she was doing with the money, and she wouldn't never smell no other woman on him—cause you know she had to smell him, and she would've smelled another woman if Robert had ever got with another woman, but he ain't never smelled of no other woman, and he always gave her his money, and he always come home long before sun up, and she loved him.

Finally, Ginny thought of something worth saying, "Well, I wish you don't never get tired living in this house."

"Just like I ain't going to get tired of breathing, I ain't going to never get tired of loving you."

But loving her didn't mean Robert didn't love music. In fact, once Ginny thought about it, she totaled up that it was Robert's music that was his other woman. And that was one woman she just had to allow Robert to be with. Or something like that.

One Saturday evening Robert and a bunch others play for a picnic. One of the others was a visiting musician name of Son House, who some people say had just come out of Parchman behind shooting some man to death at a house party down near Lyon, Mississippi in 1928 but come out in less than two years when he got some judge down in Clarksdale to review his case, which go to prove it must've been self-defense and not no murder. Anyway, the function was being advertised as a special, end-of-the-season function. Peoples came from far as Memphis to hear what they call "The last cotton picking." Harvest was all done. And folk took a week of rest, culminating in this big picnic.

It was the best-est time Ginny ever had. Ever. They was gaming and funning and stuff. And all kinds of food, and special food too, not no every day food. Pies and cakes, and roasted pig with farmer Brown's secret sauce, and everything. And the last of the watermelon. And even some sweet sugar cane brought up from way, way Louisiana south. Oh, it felt so good to be alive and laughing with folk, and children running around, and mens chunking horse shoes, and womens circling and quilting for Sarah, who was expecting—some kind of way the heifer had got herself in a family way long before Ginny did even though she weren't hitched to nobody and Ginny was Mrs. Robert Johnson, but still it was nice, and still, since now Sarah weren't no longer no kind of competition, Ginny even lent a hand stitching on the blue and yellow and white quilt what had stars and crescent moons patterned all over it.

And, lord, when the music started up and all the dancing, oh lord. And Robert he was playing harp on account of farmer Brown and Mr. Son House was guitar playing. And when Mr. House started up, well, Ginny could see what Robert meant when he said how powerful Son House was. That man took to sweating music. She never seen nobody outside the church catch no spirit like Mr. House. Look like his eyes roll up all white and all, and his voice got raspy and wailing like he was a haint or something. And look like that sound was jumping out the side of his neck, through his bulging veins. Through his fingers. His trembling lips. The way he moan, he hoop.

You could hear his voice all up the road and cross the hollow. But he weren't just loud. He was powerful. And once he got going he was mighty, mighty strong winded. Plus, his guitar playing was so expert, sound sharp like hammer driving. Even fifty feet away you could hear every note on that steel body guitar he play with. He strummed that guitar like he was plowing with one of them new-fangled tractor machines, hit it with authority.

And his songs was about everything. Ginny really liked when Mr. House did that song about scriptures. Who's that's writing? John the revelator! Who's that writing? John the revelator! Talking about he wrote the book of the seven seals. And when he done "John The Revelator," Mr. House, he just use his voice. No guitar. No shakers or knockers or nothing. No fiddles. No nothing but his voice and his two huge hands clapping together. And he growl from deep in his stomach. In fact, when he growled like that it sort of affected Ginny a little something like the way Robert's music touch her. And that surprised Ginny, to feel herself responding to some other man like she was. But she comfort herself in noticing that she weren't the onliest one touched by Mr. House, cause it look like everybody had stopped whatever else they was doing to draw close-close to Mr. House, and everybody was lining out "John The Revelator." So Ginny guessed it wasn't so bad to be moved when everybody else was being moved too, and wouldn't nobody look askance at her for being moved by Mr. House.

Ginny hoped that Robert wouldn't be mad at her for liking Mr. House music so much, and singing, even though she really couldn't sing, but singing out none the less just like as if she could sing good. She reckoned Robert would accept her singing to Mr. House's music. She hoped so. Even at one point looked over at Robert with his harmonica in hand, standing behind Mr. House, responding right along with the crowd. Suddenly, like as if somebody come up behind her and covered her eyes and said "Guess who," suddenly Ginny realized that she never sang along to Robert's music cause when it was just him and her there wasn't no reason for her to sing along and the few times she was with him playing for some peoples she had been so busy paying attention to what womens was paying attention to Robert she had never much paid attention to singing along with Robert. Ginny wondered did Robert want her to sing along. Ginny wondered about that as she sang along with Mr. House, and it made her feel good to sing to Mr. House's music. But this all was peculiar.

Robert, for his part, wasn't studying nobody or nothing except Son House and how he was holding the crowd like a baby chick cupped in his two hands. That's the kind of power Robert wanted to have—he wanted everybody who heard his music to respond to it, to be touched by it. Robert wanted his music to mean something to everybody. Everybody.

Those were sweet days. Studying Son House. Loving Ginny. What could be better?

Robert remembered a year back from that moment. It was late 1928 and over in the juke he had heard Leroy Carr doing "How Long Blues." That's what had made him moved from harmonica to guitar. Robert liked playing harp well enough, but he also liked singing and he couldn't sing and play harp at the same time, although he could sing and play guitar at the same time.

One day Robert was going to make platters and have them playing up in all the jukes like Leroy Carr. Robert ain't had no victrola to play platters on, so he had to go down to the juke and pay a penny to hear the song he wanted to hear instead of listening to whatever Mule felt like playing. After a nickle worth of listening, Robert knew the song up and down. But still, he liked hearing it so much, one day Mule Mason give him an extra play, said he had paid for the record twice over what with all the times he listened to it.

"That record just like a woman to me, Mule. You know how, sometimes, you take to liking a girl. You don't rightly know exactly why you be liking her, but you know you be liking her. Well that's how I likes that Leroy Carr."

"Well, R.L., don't you want to study some other song. I got a good twelve or fifteen more up in there."

"No, sir. I hear all them others one time all the way through and I got them. But I don't never tire of this song here. Like I said, I don't know why, but I just likes it."

"I can understand that, but R.L. You don't play no piano, leastwise I ain't never heard you play no piano."

"Well the way I figure it, I'm going to play guitar."

"Guitar, boy, you don't play no guitar neither."

"I know, but I'm going to learn."

"Well, why don't you learn piano like Carr do."

"Can't tote no piano on my back."

"Carr doing alright, making platters. Got me buying them. Got you up in here paying to hear him."

"Well, I likes to listen to platters, but you know ain't nothing like making music with the people, you know, watching them dance whilst you be playing, that gives me more to make up just to keep up with them who be dancing, and I can take and tote my guitar to whereever the people is, so I believes a guitar be better to learn for me than a piano, just like you ain't got no piano up in here, so, if I was a piano player up in here I wouldn't be able to play for the peoples, so you see what I mean?"

"Yeah, R.L. I see what you mean. That figures up right to me. But I still can't figure how come you likes a platter with a piano more than you likes a platter with a guitar."

"It ain't the piano, it's the player. What he doing, how he singing and how he framing hisself, what notes he use. That's about the best I can explain to you. I just like it. I like what all he doing."

"Yeah, I guess it don't really matter if the cow is brown or black, long as it give milk."

"Here, I got another penny. Let me hear my song one more time."

"R.L., you just like a drunk asking for another drink."

"You don't want my money?"

"I'ma take your money, I'm just saying, I guess they got something every man get drunk on. Look like this here song is your special hooch."

One time Robert he hooked up some baling wire into a little frame to hold his harp so as he could play the harp whilst he was playing his guitar like he seen "Magic Magee, the one-man music band" do, except Robert ain't have no pieces of iron on his shoe bottoms like Mr. Magic had, so Robert's feet didn't click and knock-like, but still Robert was kind of a one man band, well, sort of, except even though the whole contraption it worked and all, it wasn't suited to Robert's style, cause Robert wanted his style to be like Son House style what commanded your attention before he even hit a lick on his box, just the way he sit or stand or look sideways down his nose at you, his loud silence demanding yours in return.

Ever since Mr. House moved to Robinsonville at the request of his good friend Willie Brown, Robert not only made up his mind to be a musicianeer, he also took Mr. Son House as a model for what kind of musicianeer he wanted to be. It was in June, right after Ginny's demise in April, right when Robert was feeling at his worst-est. When we weak is when we most open to influence, and Robert was lucky that in his weakness moment he had Mr. Son House, the strongest influence any musicianeer-man could ever want to hear.

The weight of House's music, that's what Robert wanted. Not to be no entertainer that got peoples to laughing and such, but a preaching musicianeer what delivered a message, a message people would remember, a feeling that get all up into their hearts and minds, in their blood, and not just in their gut tickling them to cackling a laugh, but in their memory spots so they would never forgets they had heard Robert Johnson sing to them. That's what Robert wanted and that's what studying up under Son House showed Robert the music was supposed to be about, which all led to Robert not fooling around with trying to play a guitar and blow a harp at the same time, nor even playing a guitar between his legs or behind his back like Tommy Johnson, even though Robert, he admired how Tommy could juggle his guitar and play it at the same time, could set it down, kick it up, twist it in the air, and still be playing a song on it, admired how he could ride it like it was Shetland, reach back and be playing it like as if he was urging the pony on with licks to its backside. Robert could see how all the peoples enjoy such showmanship, but Robert also saw how people ended up talking about the show and not much mentioning the music, and Robert thought the music ought to be the point, not the showing off, course Tommy he could play some music but seems it started to getting where Tommy, he was more showing off than making music, weren't at all like Mr. House, who didn't do no showing off and everybody whoever heard Mr. House remember they heard Mr. House, so that was Robert's baptism into being a real McCoy type musicaneer, a man what make sounds you remembered for the rest of your life.

-10-

ROBERT LIKED VICKSBURG BUT HE DIDN'T MUCH CARE FOR NATCHEZ, CALLED IT a whitened sepulcher on account of it looked real pretty, could have been a wall painting advertising what some white man thought heaven look like, but really it weren't nothing but a place what sucked all the spirit out of you like bats come at you at night, in fact, yeah, that was it, Robert thought: bats (and bats weren't nothing but rats with wings).

Natchez traded on being the magnolia of Mississippi, but good as they might smell when they bloom, magnolia trees didn't bear no fruit, leastwise not none that you can eat. Prettiness alone don't sustain nothing, and when you ain't got nothing to go with the prettiness, well that is misery. Plus, they was so puffed up and everything about being pretty said Jackson might be the capitol of Mississippi but Natchez was the capitol of the south, thereby discounting every other town, when from what Robert seen, there was pretty cities a lot of different places, that's just naturally how life is. Yeah that was it, cities was like womens and you had pretty women everywhere, weren't nothing special about being pretty, besides seem like vanity go with pretty, particular when pretty is all that a body got, and Robert, for his part, never did take to pretty women and his short time in Natchez kind of confirmed that tendency.

Robert, he passed through there once, a once he would never forget, try as he might. And what make it so bad is, he ain't had no special reason to be there, it was just kind of "there," down river from Vicksburg and Vicksburg had been sweet, and folk said Natchez was pretty, so not having no particular place to go, and since he was rambling, Robert decided to pass through just to get the flavor of the place, wanted to be able to say he done had a full taste of his home state. Well Natchez turned out to be one taste he spit out and hoped never to even so much as sully his mouth again by calling out the name of that particular jurisdiction. Just to say the word itself made his stomach queasy. The best way Robert could describe it ·vas to say the place taste like eating dirt off a murderer's grave.

Of course a woman was involved in the situation, although it weren't what most people who knew Robert would have supposed the situation was. What had happened was Robert was playing on the street that day, trying to raise a dollar or two and she come strolling by and stopped. Stayed listening for a good little while, maybe fifteen or twenty minutes, way longer than most people who would listen to but one or two songs, drop off a penny, maybe two, and then hightail it on off to where they was going before they come up on Robert. But, this real tall woman, she look like she had time to spend so she just stood there, off to the side a little ways, listening but not looking directly at any one thing, her face not smiling nor giving any indication she was even hearing the music. What made Robert take notice first was the hat she was wearing, it was not a work hat even though this was the middle of the week, but even so, he ain't paid the hat no particular mind on account of how her face was still as deep well water. Her fingers were not snapping, her toes were not tapping, in fact she was standing stark still like a scarecrow on a windless day. People didn't usually listen for such a long time and not give no indication they were taking joy in the music.

Robert did not take time to speculate on her because he was singing for his supper, and sort of concerned about making what he could make, so he was watching the folk who had happy feet, toe-tapping in time to whatever he was playing, which is when a guy come up with a harp and motions to Robert that he wants to join in. Robert, he looks down at his guitar case and sees he already got well over a dollar in coins and he only been playing a little lacking an hour, so he figures even if the guy can't play none, it won't hurt to let him do one number seeing as how Robert already had enough to eat today and tomorrow. So Robert, he nods yeah to the guy and the guy joins right in, no warm up, no hesitation, just jumps on in the saddle and gets to kicking right nice. Before they knew it, when they stopped to take a short breather, a whole hour and a half had passed and they had collected more than four dollars—well actually a little over three dollars before the lady come up, didn't say nothing, didn't look at neither one of them, and drops six bits in the case. Robert he noticed right away cause the coins was new and shiny.

Robert was intending to tip his hat to the hand of the woman what put the three quarters in the case but when Robert looked up she had already turned her back and was on her way, well, actually she weren't walking fast enough to seem like she was on her way anywhere in particular, and moreover, she weren't really walking, she was almost swaying like a willow tree do in the breeze of the cool, cool, cool of the evening. You couldn't help spying her hips and the curves of her figure, not that her dress was clinging or nothing, 'cause it was loose, but the way she move, and how tall she was, and how she plant one foot down before picking the other one up, and as she walked, she touched herself, on the shoulder, on the hip, the side of her leg, almost like her hand were a man's hand feeling on her or something. Damn.

"She look firm, but man that's quicksand," the harp man grinned to Robert.

"What her name is?"

"She spoken for."

"Man, what's her name?"

"Odessa. Odessa Rose Youngblood. They calls her Dessie."

"Dessie, huh?"

"Mr. I don't know you," the man said as he wiped his face with a red polka-dot bandana, "And you don't know me, but I got no reason to steer you wrong…"

"Ain't nothing wrong with looking."

"Some things ain't made for *us* to look upon."

The way he said "us" made Robert take extra notice, there was a warning there. Being experience at reading the wind, knowing the signs of a storm coming even when the sky is blue, Robert half decided to pull up stakes and move on down the line, sort of like when you fishing a spot and somebody come along next to you, they know it ain't neighborly to drop a line where somebody already got their pole stuck out, but they also know don't nobody own the river so you can't rightly stop them, and since they ain't got no manners, they don't ask you, and since they ornery enough to do what they doing without even a so much as "How you doing" or "Good morning," or nothing, since they wrong like that and demonstrating they don't mind being wrong, well all of that is signs that they would be trouble to traffic with, so you pick up stakes and move along, which all is how Robert looked at women like that tall woman, especial upon receiving an unsolicited warning like Jim Bob gave him, well, this all led Robert to forget about it. Every town had at least one extra tall woman who wasn't marked by trouble, so it make no sense to go promenading behind one who did have an unpleasant reputation.

Through with his speculation about that particular woman, Robert counted out a dollar and handed it to his new seconding man, but the old man backed away from the money.

"Naw suh, that's your money, mister. I should be paying you for letting me stand in your shadow, good as you is."

"You the one who good, better than what be blowing all a way up past Greenwood. How they call you?"

"Jim Bob."

"Well, Jim Bob, I goes by R.L. And I always pays my way. I had little over a dollar in the case for you come along. We got over three now. Way I figure it, half of what we got now less what I started with, balance out to the vicinity of two dollars. Now, half of two is one, and that's yours not mines, so here you go."

Jim Bob just look at Robert like he couldn't believe a stranger was giving him money.

Robert motioned with his head for Jim Bob to go on and take the money, but the elderly feller remained reluctant. Robert quickly shoved the money in the man's left trouser pocket. Afterwards, when Robert patted Jim Bob's pocket in a friendly sort of way, one coin come running down the man's leg and thunked onto the sidewalk plank. Robert ain't even hesitate. He bend down, pick up the coin and then, before Jim Bob could realize Robert's intentions, Robert borrows Jim Bob's bandana, places the coin in the bandana while motioning with his own leg for the man to shake a leg, which when he does, the rest of the coins come rolling down the chute for to be gathered up, which Robert promptly does, after which Robert wraps up the coins, ties a knot, and then deposits the gift into the man's trembling hand.

"Don't blow it all on no one thing, Jim Bob. Earnings is best spent in moderation and spread around like throwing corn feed to chickens," and then Robert makes a little harmless joke: he motions with his hand and goes "Cluck, cluck?"

Jim Bob still is not for sure that R.L. is not funning him.

"Say, Jim Bob, where would a man go hereabouts to have some fun?"

"What you mean? Hooch? Mister, we's dry here, they don't allow no drinking. It's the law."

"Well, yall must do something for fun."

"This the middle of the week, mister. We works. Maybe on Saturday over to…"

Robert had just about made up his mind to leave, first thing in the morning. "What about a place I could get some grub?"

"Miss Annie sell beans."

"Chicken?"

"No. Beans."

"I mean do she sell chicken with the beans."

"No. Just beans."

"Well, do she have rice with the beans?"

"That's extra. Rice extra."

"How much extra?"

"Five cents for beans, I believe, and two cents extra for rice."

"Well, come on, let's go."

Robert finished packing up. As he hoisted his sack cross his back and grab his guitar case in his other hand, he wished it wasn't so late in the afternoon, or he would strike out right now and try to make the next little town, but, hell, he'd just have to wait until first light when it would be much more safer than trying to travel in the dark.

When they started off to walking, Robert noticed that Jim Bob had a heavy limp and wondered why he didn't have a good walking stick to companion him along his way, but being his naturally standoffish self, Robert rejected asking about it.

"How far Miss Annie's place?"

"'Bout half a mile."

"I appreciate you taking me there, but if you headed somewheres else, you can tell me which a way to go and I reckon I could find it."

"No sir, I takes you."

"What kind of works you do, Jim Bob?"

"Well sir, whatever."

"Whatever?"

"Yes, sir."

"You mean like, whatever you can find."

"Yes, sir. Whatever needs fixing."

"Yard work, broke machinery, house repair?"

"Yes, sir. I fixes things."

"Good with your hands, huh?" Jim Bob didn't see the joke coming, "What they call you: handy man?"

"No, sir. They calls me Jim Bob."

That's when Robert come to a full realization that there weren't too much humor in these parts. Except for Jim Bob speaking to people they met along the way, they slow walked in silence. At first Robert felt uneasy, but then decided he was just spooking himself. There was no reason to be afeared or anxious.

Annie's place was a house with a sign posted inside made of a plank-of-wood what had "Annie's Café" writ large in white cursive letters on it. The big front room had two tables and three empty chairs scattered around. A couple was sitting at one of the tables eating cornbread and drinking coffee. For some reason (maybe it was how they was looking at each other like there was nothing else in the world to look at), the couple directly put Robert in mind of breakfast with Ginny, which didn't cheer Robert none, in fact, it kind of brung him further down.

"You eating or you just wants to sit a spell?"

Robert looked up. He hadn't even heard the woman come over. "Yes, mam, I takes beans and rice, less you got something else."

"Mister, tough as times is, we fortunate to have beans and rice. You want cornbread with that? We got coffee. We got water. That's about it."

"Beans and rice and coffee. I thanks you. Jim Bob you want something too, don't you? I stake you."

The old man stood there, hat in hand looking down on Robert sitting at the table. "A little coffee, thanks to you."

"No vittles?"

Robert watched the man hesitate. "Bring us two plates of beans and rice, two cups of coffee. How much that be?"

"Seven cents for a plate of food, I guess a nickel for the coffee. Coffee don't come cheap long through here."

Robert fished out a quarter and gave it to the lady.

"I bring your change when I brings the food."

Wondering why she was even worried about bringing him back a penny, Robert waved her away, "You keep the change."

The woman was shocked that this stranger was giving her a six cents tip, but quickly said, "Thank you much," and started to waltz off before the man changed his mind.

"Aug, Miss Annie. You is Annie, ain't you? I don't mean to be calling you out your name."

The woman paused. She was right to be wary of strangers bearing gifts, "Yeah, I's Annie." She knew it! Don't nobody be giving that much money to somebody they don't know. This was depression and times was tough.

"Well, Miss Annie, I'm a musicianeer traveling through, looking for accommodations. Be gone in the morning. You happen to know of any place reasonable."

"What you mean reasonable?"

"I mean clean, dry, and won't cost me more than six bits."

"Mister you give me six bits, you can sleep here tonight and get cornbread and coffee in the morning."

"Well, that's right kindly of you. Done deal." Robert tipped his hat to Annie. Annie turned around and smiled her way back to the kitchen.

When they finished eating, Robert reared back. The food was good, the coffee was real coffee, not none of that mix of sassafras root with a teaspoon or two of coffee trying to stretch it out. With nothing particular to do until it was time to light out in the morning, Robert decided to make the best of the time, so he reached for his guitar and commenced to playing "Sitting On Top Of The World."

The couple look over at him and smiles. Robert he smiles back. He likes them. They young. Look like young 'uns in love and all. Had dirt on they shoes, dust in they hair. They hard working. They deserves to enjoy each other.

Robert plays an extra-pretty chorus of nimble finger picking, looking over at Jim Bob while doing so, but Jim Bob shakes his head "No," which Robert takes to mean Jim Bob don't know the song, which don't surprise Robert none on account Robert know a lot more songs than the average person who only play country dances and who probably don't listen to no platters and not much to the radio, which listening to the radio Robert believes is kind of necessary if you wants to musicianeer up and down the country side, which put Robert in mind of "Down In The Valley," which he commences to pick, and when he looks over at Jim Bob, Jim Bob he shake his head "No" again, but the couple seem to like it, they still smiling, which kind of nudge Robert to go right into "When You're Smiling," and Robert even took to whistling some on the song, Jim Bob, he don't know this one neither, but by now Robert enjoying himself so much he no longer pay no mind to whether anybody else is keeping up.

Music can be so much fun. Robert whistling. The couple smiling. Miss Annie come dancing out the back, and even though he gimpy, Jim Bob take to dancing with Miss Annie.

Some kid come in, say his mama sent him for some cornbread and that if it's ok, his mama will pay Miss Annie in stamps later on when she get her government allotment. The kid, he see Miss Annie and Jim Bob dancing, he look over at Robert playing, he peep back around to the couple who laughing out loud now, and the kid, he start into dancing too, and go to slapping his hands on his lil' thin thighs keeping time with a kind of raggity hambone, which all, of course, gets Robert into the mood to play more better. And you know, Robert, he was just getting warmed up good, he could do this for hours, though usually when he play that long somebody would be feeding the kiddy, but this was one of those funning times when the music was on account of just because, just 'cause they was alive and in each other company.

By now everybody was either laughing out loud or smiling so hard they might as well be laughing, even the lil' big-headed, snaggle-tooth kid who was alternating between giggling in delight and jiggling around in a circle while seriously grinning, all of which lead up to Robert going into "Shake 'Em On Down," which, of course, Jim Bob knowed and therefore was able to join in on his harp. Man, you would of thought Annie's Café was a sure 'nough juke. Which is when Dessie walk in and broke the spell.

The change was almost too small to see. She could a been a boll weevil burrowing in the cotton of their good timing. The couple stopped looking at Robert and turned back inward on themselves, kind of accidentally on purpose ignoring the woman who had just stepped in the place. Robert kept playing. Jim Bob he stopped. Miss Annie went back in the kitchen, ain't even ask the woman if she come for some food. And the little kid, he kept up a little jig, but it was subdued, almost look like he had to make a call of nature or something.

Dessie look directly at Robert. Robert look her full in the face but he don't smile at her as he finish "Shake 'Em."

"Mister, like to hire you out to play some for a small get together."

It got real quiet. Don't nobody say nothing.

"Well, me and my friends having a get together here. You welcome to join us."

"No, I can't, I got to…, I mean, we pay you."

"Well, you know money ain't everything."

"Would you take four dollars for about hour and a half of playing?"

"Normally," was all Robert said. He sense there was more than horses and hay up in her barn, and he wasn't really up for no surprises, besides he was leaving in the morning, and it was his experience that eager women come with a wagon load of extra somethings, and you never could tell from looking at the front what all extra somethings might be out back.

"Leroy…" Robert look around, wondering how Annie knowed his old name, but Annie was talking to the young boy, not to Robert. "…take this to your mama," and she give the boy something wrapped up in a rag.

The boy grabbed the bundle, said "Yes, mam," and lit out of there like a runaway from a chain gang. Annie turned and went back in the kitchen. Meanwhile, the couple gets up to leave, the young man taking the young woman's hand and nodding to Robert as they went out the door. Dessie doesn't even bother to look in their direction.

Well.

For a few seconds it was like a stand-off, dog and coon facing each other, neither one really anxious to tangle with the other. Then Dessie she did something strange, she reach over to an empty chair and pull it right up in front of Robert, and she sit down, cross her feet at the ankles, smooth out her dress, lean forward and ask him, "What will it cost then for you to play for us?"

There was that word again: "us."

"Who 'us' is?"

"It's a private get together, if you understand what I'm saying?"

"Lady, you don't even much know my name." Robert scolded himself for making the mistake of calling her "Lady," which implied that he was interested or at least listening to her offer. He tried to spook her, see if she would blink. "I could be a thief, a murderer, a cheat, and you inviting me up to your private function. Don't sound so private if you going to have somebody there you don't know nothing about."

"I take that to mean you going to play for us." She didn't blink those big, light brown eyes, nor look askance, nor even shift in her seat, or nothing. In fact, she leaned further into him, and goose down soft laid a hand on his knee when she said, "So is that a yes?"

Robert leaned back and uncrossed his legs, then leans over and sits his guitar in the case. Dessie stands up. Robert reaches over and plays with the empty cup the coffee was in. Dessie smoothes down her dress again, not nervous like, but instead so as to say, I'm ready, are you ready.

A little voice is whispering inside Robert when he figures out something. It was her hair. Her hair wasn't rough or uneven, it was well kept. Somebody was taking good care of this woman. He looked down at her shoes, they were clean. Back up past her hips, her bosom was small. When he got back up to her face, her eyes was waiting for him, looking at him with a directness that held no fear, no seductiveness, no pleading. Robert looked away, it was hard to resist a female challenge.

"Miss Annie?" Robert called out.

"Yes, sir." Annie walked in immediately, guess she was hanging there just on the other side of the door.

"Wouldn't be no imposition on you, would it, if I was to make a little run and be back here in a couple of hours?"

"Mister, I lives here. If you stays or if you leaves and comes back later, makes me no difference."

Sometimes something big be about to happen and you don't have any idea something big is about to happen. Other times, like now, you know something about to happen but you just can't figure out what it is. Robert was a wondering: yes or no. Yes. Or no.

"They call me Dessie. Everybody here know me. We need to go."

And nobody said nothing. That's the way it is at a crossroads, especially when you rambling alone. Robert stood up, moved his sack over to a far corner, and turned to see Jim Bob looking like he wanted to pee on himself. Dessie was already most out the door. Robert, he waved his index finger in the air, like he was begging the church permission to tip out.

"I'm right behind you," Robert said to Dessie's departing back.

There was a frightful silence hanging behind him, and Robert couldn't help but wonder what was so mysterious about this woman called Dessie —well, for sure, he was about to find out, and that was Robert's one big weakness, not women per se, but a stubborn belief that there wasn't nothing he couldn't look upon and walk away from. He was always a sucker for the promise of a new experience.

When Robert saw the Hudson sitting outside he knowed it was going to be a long night. The automobile was newer than the new money Dessie had put in the kitty earlier in the afternoon. It was too dark to see who was behind the wheel, but it wasn't too dark to see the gleam of newness surrounding the vehicle, the kind of depression-era newness that only rich white folks could afford.

Dessie walked straight up to the back door and held it open for Robert. It wasn't too late to turn around, but backing out was never part of the way Robert operated, he was sort of like a cow in that regard. Robert remembered hearing tell of the prank somebody had pulled at the Clarksdale courthouse. Two farmers was arguing over cattle, and somebody drug one of the cows up the steps to the second floor and couldn't nobody lead the cow down. They had to slaughter the cow up there. Once Robert started in on something, he never was one to back down.

Leather and tobacco, that's what the car smelled like. Not just any leather, new, well-oiled, kid leather, and not just any tobacco, rich, heavy cigar tobacco. When Dessie close the door after sliding in beside Robert, everything was clear, or at least enough was clear that Robert was clear he didn't want to know no more.

The driver started the car and they pulled off.

This was clearly one of those situations where you didn't say nothing unless somebody ask you to say something and wasn't nobody asking nobody nothing. They drove in eerie silence.

In two minutes they was cross the tracks.

The houses got bigger. And whiter. Trees seem to creep up to the edge of the street. Everywhere was shadows. Robert tried to look around without moving his head, not wanting to betray no nervousness or call no attention to himself.

"You know who I am, boy?"

"No sir. I ain't from round here. I don't know nothing."

"Good."

More silence.

They slowed down. Pulled to a stop. The driver got out, and after a very brief period, got back in the vehicle. Robert didn't look at the man figuring the less he knew, the better.

The car started up again. They pulled into what looked like a small barn except there was no barn smell when the driver opened the door and got out. Robert didn't move. Literally didn't even turn his head or shift in his seat, just sat up bolt straight and held on to his guitar case.

When the man closed the barn door behind him, they were sitting in the dark. After a few minutes of waiting that kind of reminded Robert of one time him and Shines was hiding from some patrollers outside the Jackson railroad yard. They was hid good but the patrollers was all over the place, so they just had to stay secret until the train was long gone.

"Come on."

Dessie open up her door. By now Robert's eyes was accommodated to the darkness but he still couldn't really see nothing.

"Come on!" Dessie was more insistent. Robert scooted over towards her voice and bumped into her hand with his forehead, instead of withdrawing, she ran her hand down the side of his face, down on cross his chest and grabbed his free hand. He was fully out the vehicle now, standing up and realizing that he was so close up on Dessie he could smell her. Rosewater. She pulled him closer. He shuffled a short step. She leaned against him—when he felt her body, Robert froze up, he weren't fool enough to touch this woman up in this white man's barn, which is when he heard the car door slam. Like to made him jump, but he controlled his emotions by gripping his guitar case while trying not to squeeze Dessie 's hand. Soon she was pulling on him again. And he followed.

They slipped out of the dark of the barn into the dark of the night. There was a lamp light on in the house, but the lamp was down low, all you could see was a faint glow through a window. Dessie pulled him up the steps and into the door, instead of turning toward the light, she pulled him toward some steep inside steps and they climbed upward. She still had his hand. What now? Would he be able to climb down out of this?

At the top of the stairs it was dark, almost dark as in the barn.

"Dessie tells me you a first class guitar player."

Robert was at a total disadvantage. He couldn't see shit. He didn't know where the hell he was at. Dessie had let go his hand. Robert mumbled a reply, "Yes sir, I tries my best."

"Dessie, take him in my study. Set him up, let me hear what we got here."

"Come on."

Dessie grab Robert's hand again and lead him on down a long hallway. They come to a stop, she drop his hand and open the door.

"Come on."

Robert wanted to ask her if she knew any other words, but then he heard a match scratch, smelled the sulfur and was near blinded by the suddenness of the flame flicker. Dessie lit a lamp and turned it down low, then she turned to face him. Robert was almost consumed by an urge to run, not out of fear but rather out of a strong feeling that he was about to see something he didn't need to see, didn't want to see.

"He want you to play."

"What he want me to play."

"Play what I heard you play."

Man, this was going nowhere fast. Robert ain't remembered what he played on the street except for "Shake 'Em On Down," which was the last song him and Jim Bob had played together as well as the last one he played back at Annie's, but he didn't feel like playing no "Shake 'Em On Down." he more felt like playing "Bottle Up And Go," which weren't really no song, but, given the conditions, he was sure he could make it into a real song, real fast.

Robert opened his case, sat in a straight-backed chair, and tuned up his guitar—actually the tuning up was a way of stalling so as to give him time to figure out what he was going to play.

Robert start into "They're Red Hot" and was singing full out when he realized the verse said the girl was long and tall, which Dessie was, "Sleeps with her head in the kitchen and her feets in the hall," but, shucks it was too late now.

"Sing that some more. That's a funny song."

Robert did not even look up at the sound of the white man's voice. He simply proceed to jazz up the licks, rapping his knuckles against the guitar face to make a knocking sound while he strumming. Robert did five more choruses, making up sounds something like Louis Armstrong had did on that "Heebie Jeebies" platter.

"Odessa. Come here."

Robert was trying to figure on what else to play and decided on "Phonograph Blues" only 'cause of Louis Armstrong, which had set Robert to thinking on how much he learned from listening to platters, which was what partly led to Robert writing "Phonograph Blues."

Odessa come back in the room shortly. She bare footed now. "He say, you know any Gene Autry songs?"

Robert launches directly into "T.B. Blues," which Autry had just come out with under the name Bob Clayton, but it really was a Jimmie Rodgers song what included yodeling, which Robert was tolerably good at doing, besides Jimmie Rodgers was from Meridian and all the Mississippi musicaneers was familiar with him, or at least had heard of him.

All they had to do was tell Robert what they wanted to hear and whatsoever it was, if it was on a platter or on the radio, chances are Robert could do it 'cause music was Robert profession.

Odessa was leaning against the wall, just listening, her head tilted downward and all of sudden she bend over and touch the floor and then stand back up straight and reach her hands way over her head, bring them down and put her hands behind her, rotate her head around like she a rooster stretching or something. Then without saying nothing else, she walk real slow-like out the room, not really walk, more like slink, her hips moving more than her feet. Robert see where her dress back all unbuttoned and he could see her bare brown skin. Beautiful brown skin. Smooth and shiny, like a saddle. Guess this was a private party.

Next Robert did "Stay Away From My Chicken House," another platter by Gene Autry, and then he done Autry's version of "Frankie and Johnny," which Autry platter said Jimmie Rodgers wrote, but which Robert know weren't true. "Frankie and Johnny" been around long as he could remember, plus, Mississippi John Hurt had him a platter called "Frankie," come out in '28 or '29, except it was Frankie and Albert, not Johnny, but it was the self same song.

When Robert finished with "Frankie and Johnny" he could faintly hear rustling coming from some where beyond the door, which Odessa had left open. Shortly she appeared in the doorway, holding her dress up in front of her, "Keep on playing. Play me something you come up with, you know, like you was doing down to the street. Just play. Keep playing. We be through directly." And then she slip off, not bothering to try to hide the backside of her fleeting nakedness, which Robert peeped although not in no staring kind of way, but, from what he seen quickly, her thighs was well formed and her butt sat up high with a pronounced "S" shape, what some folk calls sway back. Lord, a woman like that.

We be through directly, Robert repeated the phrase in his mind. Robert wasn't no stranger to whorehouses, but this was, this was, shucks, this was some sure enough dog shit. Robert couldn't hardly play and sing and think on this shit all at the same time, so he mostly concentrated on singing, but it was hard to concentrate on singing when he knew what was going on and it was, it was, well Robert couldn't even much find a word for what this was.

-11-

"He sleep."

Robert look up. Dessie stood leaning against the door sill. Robert, he study her while he continues to play and sing. Dessie, she study him back.

Robert weren't scared of this woman even though something was telling him he ought to be. Just like most of the male species, Robert was fascinated by a woman whose angles he couldn't figure.

In a teasing sort of way, Robert go to playing "Love In Vain Blues" talking about loving a woman in vain, catching a train, looking eye to eye a lover who don't love him. He singing low and slow. Dessie drop her head again, look like she like that looking down gesture, it sure do make her desirable, damn.

Robert couldn't control his mind, which is when Dessie turn her head sideways and look at Robert, and a chill shot through him, not so chilly so as to say don't, but a chill so as to say, you shouldn't, you shouldn't even be thinking about wanting this woman, but shit, a woman this mysterious had to be something worth experiencing.

And then Robert he thought something he really didn't want to think, really, really didn't want to think. Even though Dessie ain't look nothing like her, was much taller, and thinner, and three or four shades lighter-skinned, had nothing in common in their voices, even though there was absolutely nothing to yoke one to the other, Robert found himself thinking of his mother. Briefly. With a shock, cause of course he had never thought about fucking his mother, but that's just what he was thinking about with this tall-ass woman standing cross the door sill with that dress just kind of throwed on and for sure nothing on underneath it. Nothing. Bet there wasn't a button even much buttoned all up and down her back, bet, if she was to turn around, he could see all the way to china, see her butt all sticking out, what a turn-on it was: a flat-chested, big-butted, tall-ass, shameless woman who was intentionally standing in front you, teasing you with her profile.

Robert knew it, he knew Dessie was on purpose flaunting herself in front of him, daring him to touch her. Robert understood that much, what he didn't understand was, why him, why was she fucking with him, she ain't even much know him from nobody, but some womens is like that, they concentrate all their power on causing a disturbance in your mind, for some of them it just be a game, like sometimes you try and chunk a rock as far as you can just to see how far you can chunk it, see if you can hit the barn across the field, no that ain't it, well, whatever, for whatever reason, Robert was certain Dessie knew what she was doing, and just the fact that he was thinking on this was an indication that she was one up on him, she had achieved her aims with regards to arousing Robert's desire for her, and then again, maybe she didn't give a rat's toenail about him, weren't the both of them in some rich white man's house, weren't that white man paying for the both of them, paying for Robert to play for him, paying for Dessie to play with him, so she weren't really in charge of nothing. Damn, she quiet. Tall and quiet. Tall. Robert bet her bush was narrow, like a little strip of dark weeds growing up between the ruts of a well-used country road. Dark and tight hairs, curled up shaped something long and slender like an ear of corn…

"You can stop playing."

"What?"

"You can stop playing now. He sleep."

Robert intentionally kept on playing, but softly. "So, I was playing for him."

"No. You was playing for to help me take my mind off him."

Robert stopped.

Dessie pushed herself out the doorway and walked directly over to the desk next to Robert, bent over, turned her head sideways and looked at him with those flat hypnotizing eyes, big and a chestnut shade of brown with not even a flicker of warmth in them. While she was looking at Robert and Robert was looking back, she pulled one of the desk drawers open, took out a small box, opened it and pulled a long cigarette out the box, closed the box, place it back in the drawer, closed the drawer, and still looking him directly in the eyes, raised the cigarette as if to ask for a light. Robert did not respond one way or the other.

Dessie turned from him, went to the lamp, lifted the glass, stuck the cigarette in the flame, rolling it around slowly in the fire, and then raised the smoldering stick of tobacco slowly to her lips, took a long, long draw, folded her free arm across her stomach, tilted her head upward and blew a slender stream of smoke toward the ceiling.

Robert had never seen his mama smoke, had seen some old women smoking pipes, some of them whores over in Vicksburg standing around when the night was just about dead, but never had been real close up on no smoking woman before. Dessie walked over in front of him, took another draw, exhaled the smoke while holding the cigarette close to her lips and then brought the cigarette down, spun it around and put it firmly to Robert's lips.

Robert stood still as a hunting dog, didn't move a muscle, not even his nostril flared when he breathed through his nose on account of holding his mouth tightly closed.

Dessie continued to hold the cigarette to his lips.

Robert did not nibble. Did not open his mouth. Did not sniff. Did not take his eyeballs off her eyes. She straightened up to her full height, withdrew the cigarette and as she raised it to her lips with her right hand, her left hand, palm facing him, briefly touched his lips. She let her fingers slide downward from his top lip to his bottom lip.

When she raised up straight Robert caught his first wiff of funk waffing off her, the smell of the sex she had had with whoever that white man was, that unmistakable scent that fucking leaves in its wake, like when you crush a stinkbug. Dessie ain't used no damp rag to clean herself. Robert willed himself to ignore the familiar odor, the smell he always associated with night women.

When you be doing it, you don't notice how funky you be smelling, but when you come up on somebody who been doing it and ain't cleaned up, then you notice it right away, especially 'cause it be so strong, and Dessie funk (mixed with the white man funk), that was powerful funk.

Part of how come the scent was so strong was on account of how tall she was, Robert was sitting straight up and her hips was almost high as his shoulders, which meant that her stuff was close to him, closer than if she was a short woman, so the smell was strong. Powerful. Robert ain't never thunk on the smell of funk before, never gave it a nevermind. Ginny was always cleaning up afterwards, and other women, damn it, how would he know about other women, he had never been with no one particular woman for more than one or two days, so. So? So nothing.

Robert turned from her and began packing up his guitar. Searching for some way to avoid interacting with her. After closing his guitar case, Robert turned to look at the books on the shelf to his right. He stood up. Dessie was directly in front of him. Robert stepped sideways, crossing over his guitar case and went up touching close to the books. He pulled out one of the volumes, turned out to have poetry in it. What with the lamp turned down low, Robert had to hold the book up close to his face in order to read the words. It was a poem called Evangeline. Longfellow.

"Can you read that or is you just ignoring me?"

"You really want to know or you just trying to rile me up?"

Dessie didn't answer him. Robert put the book back, but he didn't turn around to face her. He heard the soft sound of her bare feet on the hardwood. He heard wood slide against wood, but he still doesn't turn around. Then he doesn't hear anything at all. He still just stands there. A whole minute passes. When he doesn't hear anything further, Robert kind of peers over his shoulder and doesn't see her. He knows she is still in the room. He would have seen her out the corner of his eye if she had walked out the room. When Robert turns around, Dessie is sitting at the desk looking at him. Where was the cigarette?

Dessie reaches into her dress pocket, "Here your money." she stretches a long arm out toward him.

"Thank ya." but he doesn't cross to her. "Leave it there. I'll get it."

"I'm not going to hurt you."

Robert was getting real tired of this woman trying to mess with him. "If a snake say it ain't going to bite you, would you believe it?"

"You saying I'm a snake?"

"Naw, I'm saying I don't believe you."

The air gets heavy, like when a storm coming and you can feel it, smell it. Robert didn't like his chances at that moment, caught between a evil-hearted woman and a sleeping white man, a white man that the hard-hearted woman sleeping with.

Dessie withdraws her hand, places the money atop his guitar case, gets up, and walks out the room.

Robert watches her leave and when she does not return immediately, he goes over and picks up the folded-over money. Four dollars all right. Robert puts the money in his pocket, then puts his empty hand in his left pocket, which is also empty, he ain't even much got a pocket knife. And then, admitting for the first time that he is tired, physically tired, but really mind tired, matching wits with a woman like Dessie is hard work, Robert yawns with his mouth wide open, his head throwed back.

In his mind, Robert go to questioning himself: so, I was playing so she could forget about being with him, or so she says, but that can't be. She ain't knowed I was going to even much be in this town, and for sure I won't be in this town tomorrow or no time soon thereafter, or later thereafter for that matter, or never no more. Robert kept thinking on it. Her story was touching but it sound like what the hook tell the fish.

When he straighten his head and open his eyes from full-out yawning, she standing there in front of him. Like to scare the shit out of him. Robert was tired of this, her sneaking around like a haint, rubbing up on him one minute, spooking him the next.

"I didn't mean to scare you. He gon take us when he get up in a minute..." There was that word again. He just roll into this town for the first time in his life and folks go to talking "us" talk to him. He don't know these people and, judging on what direction the river flowing, Robert is pretty sure he got no burning desire to get to know any more than he already know. Unfortunately for Robert, there is more.

Dessie had paused to give Robert a chance to relax before showing her full hand, which was a full house. "I wanted to say something to you before I wake him up. I feel like I can talk to you. Can I?"

One minute she want to fuck, the next minute she want to talk, and all this going down up in this white man upper room. Robert swore to himself, if I ever can climb down out this saddle, ain't nobody in this or any other lifetime every got to worry about me riding this here horse again, or should he say "mule," 'cause this wasn't racing, this was plowing, and the ground was mighty wet.

Dessie watching Robert's face, close, like she can read features, understands twitches and trembles that the lips make, hears ideas when they crease your forehead with worry lines, and such. And she patient, very, very unhurried, like a fat rat in an empty house.

Finally, unable to think of how to put her off without riling her up and thereby jeopardizing or delaying his departure from this particular sticky situation, finally, almost on the verge of wishing... Goddamnit, Robert had to pee, not bad-bad like he would have to let on to Dessie and ask her where to go when you got to go, but bad enough that he knew if he didn't get to let it go in the next ten or fifteen minutes, it was going to be a touchy situation.

Robert knew better. He should of went and relieved himself before he left Miss Annie's place, but he didn't and now that oversight was about to cause him some serious discomfort. Robert sat down, which was a mistake. No sooner his rump hit the hardwood, he realized that his sitting down probably looked like he was saying, we can talk. But still Dessie ain't say nothing, and then it come to Robert how he could put the shoe on the other foot. He lean back, cross his legs, look dead up in her eyes and ask her in a slow drawl whilst simultaneously folding his hands in his lap, "Talk about what? What you want to talk about?"

Dessie raised her hand to her shoulder, Robert took notice without letting on that he taking notice, he notice that shoulder touching thing was another gesture she favor.

Robert twiddled his thumbs like he ain't had a worry in the world.

"I want to ask you to help me." Although Robert immediately stopped twirling his thumbs around, he didn't say nothing. "But we can't talk here. We talk later."

And then Dessie spun slowly and walked out the room. Robert let out a low whistle, he was in way over his head. He ain't never dealt with no woman like this and he realized he should have followed his first mind, he should have been scared of her.

For most mens, there is at least one woman, usually more, but at least one he stand in wonder of—that usually be his mother, but it could be his grandmamma or his first love (which is way different from the first woman, or girl, he made love to), or could be somebody off in the distance he stand in admiration of, but whatever, regardless, there is some woman that got his number writ in the palm of her hand. This was the third such woman in Robert's life, his mother being the first, Ginny the second, and now this Odessa Rose child, and what all three of them held in common with each other, which commonness would not be apparent to most mortal eyes, but anyway what was in common was that all three of them had a certain mysteriousness about them, a mysteriousness that just wormed its way all inside Robert, and also held a grip on him that Robert frankly generally wished they didn't have.

Dessie was obviously spooky and he hadn't even much spent one whole night with her yet, still yet here she was, got him about to pee on himself while she playing him with a carefree finesse better than he play his own damn guitar, and even though Robert was not yet in possession of the teachings of the two-headed people, he was by now respectable and reputable as a git-fiddle picker, and, of near equal weight in the consideration around this matter, Robert was also considered somewhat successful as a lady's man, and here this woman was messing with him in ways he never before been messed with. He had to take his hat off—his hat, come to think of it, he was still wearing it, had been so spooked he never thought to remove it. Robert reached up and took his hat off, sat it in his lap. Robert reached back up and smoothed down his hair, which didn't need no smoothing down, and then again, maybe it did, who knows.

Anyway, Dessie was one. Ginny had been mysterious in a good kind of way. Robert never fully understood how she come in to be so expert at loving him while being as young as she was, and he did not mean just the physical loving, he meant how she understood him and was his especial companion—if she had not been so jealous, he sure would have loved to roam the countryside with her along side him. And then, of course, the other part of her mysteriousness was why she had to die, especially the way she die. Why? Robert had concluded long ago, he never would know the answer to that question, so in general he stopped even asking that question, and was only raising the question now on account of at this very moment, Dessie had him questioning a lot of shit.

Which brought him back to his mama, who was the first woman Dessie made him think on. When his mama first popped up, Robert had not understand what she had to do with the situation at hand, but now it was clear, every time he run up on something or the other that he did not understand about a female, he would think on his mother, the first female he loved but did not understand.

Just like it's a sad frog what don't croak about its own pond, it's a troubled child what don't love its mother—course there was some folk who did not know they mama, and even a couple of people who had no use for their mother, but, generally speaking, most folk had a powerful love and respect for their mother. Wait, that's not quite right, Robert's relationship to his mother was sort of complicated, no, not sort of, it was real complicated. Some would say that Robert was a troubled child but he did love his mother, it's just that his mother love was a troubled love. That's it, yeah, and not just with his mother, with all the women he loved, it was a troubled loving.

Julia Dodds nearly overshadowed Robert all his short life. One day when Robert look upon his mother's life, it almost made him breakdown. Like how she had ten children before she had him. Ten. And the man she hooked up with was successful, so successful the white folks got jealous and run him out of Hazelhurst. That man would be Mr. Charles Spencer, a man whom his mother had led, or was it "let," Robert believe was his father, when, regardless of whether it was led or let, she knew good and well that Spencer was not Robert's pappy, and she knew good and well that Robert thought so, and, well, at that time, being that he was a child, Robert couldn't do no more than accept things for what they was, accept what he was told, and believe, believe what the grown folks said, what his mother said, but, you know, when he got older, the story had to be re-told, and if not re-told, for sure, re-thought, from the get go. Everything had to be thought about again.

At one point when Robert was gazing backward, he come to a stump he couldn't uproot. A man make ten children with a woman and then he get run out, but when he leave he take some of the children but he don't take the children mother, and instead he take another woman and her two children, and then after suffering all kinds of hardships the woman she hook back up with the man, but in the between time she had another child with another man, which would be Robert and Robert's father, name of Noah Johnson. So why she went back to this man carrying another man child, and then she leave that child with the man who was her husband, you understand, your husband leave you, you find him later and bring him a child you done made with another man, and then you up and leave him this time (the first time he had left you, and now you leave him), and you leave behind the child you made with another man, and then you go off and marry somebody else. Goddamn, is that some kind of woman, or is that some mojo?

When he was young, Robert just accept it, but each year he got older, especially after Ginny die in childbirth, each year, Robert think on all this jumbleness and each year he get a deeper appreciation for and wonderment about his mother, what all kind of woman she must be, but he don't never totally figure it out, except to acknowledge that womens must know something men folks don't, and, damn Robert had to pee bad now, and, of course, weren't no way he was going to step outside the confines of this room at this moment, pee or no pee, and at the same time, weren't no way in the world he was going to pee on the floor or anywheres else in this room. Robert was in a fix, felt like a coon treed by a pack of hounds and the hunter coming with the gun, how in the world was Robert going to get out this fix?

At this point Robert was feeling so miserable and so frustrated and so, well, hopeless, which would not be an inappropriate word to describe the situation, indeed, hopeless might be the best way to describe Robert's feelings, when just then in comes Dessie. Now if you was Robert what would you do?

"Dessie, I needs to relieve myself."

Dessie turns around without saying nothing and goes out the room. Shortly she re-enters the room toting a night bucket. She sits it off to the side, not quite in the corner, turns again, and, as she leaves, says, "When you finish, we ready to go."

Robert picked up the partially filled bucket and sat it up in the chair 'cause he didn't want to splash nothing, not no where, on nothing in this white man's room. Whilst he was taking a long leak, Robert was thinking, and the longer he leaks, the deeper he think on his untenable situation. For sure Dessie had not forgot about talking to him, Robert was certain of that, but when was this talking supposed to take place and where, and more importantly how would this be done without incurring the wrath of whoever this white man was? Were no way no white man was going to let a black man talk to a black woman the white man keeping for his own, especially not all up in the white man house, and most certainly not talk to the woman alone, and if the white man was driving Robert back to Miss Annie's place, that same white man was not about to let Dessie get out and go with Robert, or go with no other man, be they black or white, late, late at night, off into some place he don't know where.

Robert finish, shake himself lightly and carefully, and then take the bucket down from the chair and put it back where Dessie had placed it. What a pretty little bucket this was, all porcelain and looking more like a kind of medium sized cooking pot than like a night bucket, and it had a little lift cover with a hinge on it so as it could be flipped open and then flipped back down when you was through accommodating yourself with it, that way the smell wouldn't be wafting up all over, smelling up everything, and it also had a little metal handle with a wood spool fitted on the middle of the handle for carrying purposes, well, a bucket had a handle too, but this night bucket didn't look like no regular bucket, didn't look like it had ever been set outside or was converted from doing regular garden duty and house chores and what not, no, this little night bucket look like it was original designed for to be just what it was, like somebody on purpose took to making a receptacle for a person's natural functions.

Something told Robert to look up and he saw what he kind of suspicion he would see: Dessie standing in the doorway. This woman must be kin to some kind of snake. Robert pick up his guitar case with one hand, hold his hat in his other hand, and pray a little hope to himself that he make it out of this mess alive. He wishing and hoping 'cause he know the night ain't over yet, he just don't know what the end going to be, and Dessie, who ain't saying nothing—look like she delight in acting all mysterious like— she walk all the way in the room when she see Robert lift up his guitar case, and she go to the lamp and turn it all the way down, lift the glass and quick-quick smother the tiny flame with the flat of her hand. Now Robert he seen peoples do that trick of knocking a fire light clean out with a quick smothering motion, he even tried it once, like to burnt a hole in his hand, asked one of his partners who was good at it what the trick was to doing it, and Buck, he said the trick was you had to do it fast 'cause if you did it slow the flame would bite you, but if you did it fast you could put it out before it could nip you with its heat, which reminded Robert of them people who could catch a rattle snake with they hands, just shoot right out and grab the snake just back of the head and not get bit all up, and so now, standing here in this dark in the same room with a woman whose hand was faster than fire, Robert held his breath, where was the white man? What was going to happen next?

"Come on."

The magic words again, "come on." Coming on is what got Robert in this tight spot he was in, hopefully come on would get him out.

Of course, dark like it was, Robert couldn't see much of nothing.

"Come on," her voice was more insistent now, like she was talking about jumping a train and you had to catch it now or miss it altogether. So Robert put his hat on and starts walking, taking real short, tentative steps in the direction he remembered where he thought the door was, when he hear some other door slam, he hesitated.

"Dessie, you got him?"

"Yeah," Dessie said, startling Robert. She was much, much closer to him than he thought she was. Dessie reach out and grab his hand directly, no fumbling around or nothing. Could she see in the dark? "I got him. We coming."

Some kind of perverse way Robert couldn't help thinking they was going to kill him. You know like they feed a hog everything they can in the weeks up before they fixing to slaughter the hog, and the hog, he be in hog heaven and then one day heaven turn into hell when they slaughter that bad boy, and the average hog he don't have no premonition he ain't in heaven, but is in fact just being fattening up for killing purposes, sort of like once they finish with you, they kill you, but you don't know they going to kill you, well, like that, that's how Robert was thinking, he was thinking maybe they was going to take him downstairs and kill him.

Robert don't know where this killing thought come from. Maybe it was the hard edge in the white man's voice when he say, you got him? Maybe it was the way Dessie douse that flame. Maybe Robert was just spooked. A thousand maybes, but for sure Robert knew where he was. He was in Mississippi, and white men would kill a colored man with no more thought than to swatting a mosquito or stepping on a roach, or... Dessie was pulling him forward now, and Robert's first impulse was to resist, to dig in and refuse to go, refuse to walk down that long hallway, and certainly refuse to climb down them steps where who knows what was waiting at the bottom. Look like she done forgot all about talking to him. She wasn't saying nothing now, leastwise she wasn't saying nothing to Robert. She was talking to that white man and although they was talking about him, they was talking about him like he was a dumb animal or something that didn't understand talking. Who knows what the two of them cooked up in that room when they was in that room fucking each other. Maybe they was plotting up on killing Robert. Hell, Robert knowed that two people who was fucking each other and liking fucking each other was liable to do anything to keep on fucking each other, use anybody for any which God-awful purposes. Robert knowed he would a done anything, anything, including kill somebody with his bare hands, for the chance to stay with Ginny, for to keep Ginny alive. Dessie and that white man ain't knowed Robert, they done had their fun with Robert. They could kill him right now and wouldn't nobody say nothing. Not nothing at all. They could say Robert broke up in the white man house and the white man, he caught Robert raping his maid. They could say anything they wanted to say. And Robert would just be dead. Dead. And there wouldn't a been nothing more said. Naw. Robert didn't want to go down them steps. If he was going to meet his death, he would meet it here in this upper room. Light the lamp and look death in the eye, but not being pushed down some steps or cut all up in that little barn with the Hudson in it.

Robert, stop thinking like that, is what Robert tried to tell hisself as Dessie pulled him forward, but even as he reluctantly followed, Robert couldn't help thinking he was on his last go round. Some times a idea gets hold to you and just won't turn loose. Sort of like this Dessie woman had hold to Robert. He knew when he first saw her on the street she was trouble. Real colored peoples always patted they foot if they liked your music and she had not moved even one toe. And when she broke up in Miss Annie's place didn't nobody say nothing to her, yet she claim everybody know her. If they know her, how come they don't talk to her?

They were at the top of the steps now.

Robert went cold.

"Can you see alright? We at the steps."

Robert couldn't see shit.

"Dessie, yall coming? Or do I have to let that boy walk back by himself?"

"We coming. He ain't used to the dark."

Dessie slowly descends the steps, leading Robert by his hand. Robert is sweating.

When they get to the bottom, Robert take a long breath. Dessie doesn't turn loose his hand.

"Come on."

And they head out to the barn.

Usually, Robert is pretty clear-headed about where he is and what's going on around him, but Robert had to admit he was spooked, really spooked. He had no idea where he was. No idea who this white man was. No idea where they was going, or where they come from. No idea about nothing. And for sure, no understanding of this Dessie woman sitting up close next to him, seem like that rosewater stuff she was wearing had turned to funk-water. Surely that white man smell the way Dessie smelling up his new car. Although it wasn't cold, Robert even took to shivering a little bit.

When they pull up to what he hoped was Miss Annie place, Robert liked to jump for joy, started to try to open the door and leap out even before they come to an all-the-way stop.

Dessie, she do jump out and come round to Robert's door and open it for him. "Come on."

If he heard her say that one more time, he was going to hurt somebody. Shit ceased to be funny now.

It felt some good to be standing on God's good earth. Robert breathed deeply, looked up at the stars. Thank you, lord.

Dessie go straight up the steps like she was going up to her own place, don't hesitate or nothing, knock hard on the door, and then turn around to face Robert, who was standing at the bottom.

"She come directly and let you in."

"Thank you." It sounded funny, but Robert really did mean thank you: thank you, lord, I'm safe.

"Who there?"

"Dessie, with that guitar fellow."

"Good, I'm glad he safe."

"He safe."

The women were talking through the door like one had found a lost little boy and was returning him home. Dessie starts down the steps and as she draws neigh to Robert she says out loud, not bothering to lower her voice or nothing, loud enough for Miss Annie to hear, maybe even loud enough for the white man to hear—the white man, Robert start to look back toward where the automobile was, but quickly changes his mind. Robert still has not looked directly upon the face of the white man and figured that now was not the time to start gazing thereon. Anyway, Dessie, she turns and starts walking away, while doing so she says out loud to Robert, "I'll be back in a little while to talk to you." as Robert is looking back at Dessie leaving, Miss Annie, with a lamp in her hands, opens the door. Robert doesn't answer Dessie, who is already climbing into the back seat of the Hudson, instead he scampers up inside Miss Annie's place like a land lover jumping down the gangplank after a particularly rough ship ride. Robert hears the Hudson pull off as Miss Annie closes the door behind him.

"Son, I'm some glad to see you ok." Annie sits the lamp on one of the tables.

Robert exhales slowly, passes his hand across his damp brow, and blurts out, "Miss Annie, yall got some accommodations I can use? I got to relieve myself."

-12-

PEOPLE LIKE THE MUSIC AND USES IT FOR ALL SORTS OF REASONS, SORT OF LIKE water and all the various ways in which water exists, well, the music is like water, it's everywhere, it exists in a lot of different ways from rivers to rain, ice to steam, spit to sweat, tears to piss.

Although not an authority on physics and the transformation of matter under various conditions, for sure Robert knew how the music could stir our nature up, had seen it do that. Seen it? More than just seen it, on the regular Robert been one of the major forces whipping people up, plenty of times making his guitar be like a big old loving spoon that he was dipping into people's innards, stirring up their feelings. Imagine if you will, if you can, just to put things in a kind of context, imagine a conversation between Robert Johnson and Sigmund Freud.

Now Mr. Freud come to the forefront of worldwide attention long about the same time as did the blues. Dr. Freud he use drugs and words to dip into people's personalities, the blues it used songs and rhythms. Freud, he talked about sexual repression, about the id, the ego, and the superego, them three levels of desire, the first unconscious, the second conscious, and the third socially controlled or something like that. The blues it operate on the real level of bridging the gap between what is and what a body wants things to be, and usually the gap be a loving gap. Which all is not to compare what they call psychology with the blues, but which rather is to put all these things into the relationship that existed in Robert's heyday, because, you see, all this was going down at the same time.

Could there be a connection between the appearance of Dr. Freud and Mr. Son House, or Carl Jung and Robert Johnson? Of course not, 'cause concurrence does not prove causality. But it is really, really interesting to understand that all these things come along at roughly the same time, plus trains and radio, electricity and recordings. All these things at the same time. Floods and migrations. World war and liberation movements.

Marcus Garvey and Mao Tse Tung. Robert did not personally know all these people, but Robert, like many colored musicians, was aware that the world was turning and not just the times, but the people too were a changing.

Robert had seen New York and Chicago, put both China and Ethiopia in the lyrics of his songs. Robert was nobody's fool, able to read, write, and figure, you might even consider him more educated than the ordinary world citizen during his time. But sometimes, no matter how much learning you got, reality remains inscrutable, something you canst not get a handle on, and on such occasions, you just got to bear with it and ride it out, which is what Robert was doing at the moment, while laying on a pallet on the floor in Annie's café.

Robert sat up, leaned back against the wall, hugged his knees, and then let his head go all the way back against the wall while wishing he had a cigarette to kind of help calm his nerves, not that he was nervous in the sense of shaking or feeling upset or anxious. No, he was alive, the worst was over, and when he look back on it, nothing really had happened. He got paid to play while two people was fucking, wasn't nothing unusual about that, they did that in whore houses all around the world, had piano players up in there, and with victrolas now, people with money would play platters, and what about the radio, all that while they were mating up, no it was not unusual, Robert told himself. So why had he been so spooked?

Them people ain't did nothing to him. Treated him right. Paid him four dollars, just like Dessie said. Everything went straight arrow. So why had Robert been bothered? Robert had seen all kinds of stuff in Vicksburg, that weren't nothing special back up the steps at that white man house. Robert kept trying to psych himself up. It wasn't really a half hour ago or howsoever many minutes back when he was in that upper room that he was concerned about, it was a few minutes from now, or whenever Dessie would come back. Supposed she never came back? Naw, she was going to come back. A woman like that, she like a high sheriff or a tax collector, sooner or later, she always come back.

Robert had never felt like this before, tied up in knots about he didn't know what.

When Dessie tapped lightly on the door, Robert said, "Shit."

She tap again, lightly but insistently.

Robert push himself up and go to the door. He do like Miss Annie done and said, "Who that?"

"You gon let me in or do I have to wake Miss Annie up?" which is when Robert fully realize how big a disadvantage he was at. Dessie knew all these folks, he didn't know none of them and none of them knew him, in fact he knew Dessie better than he knew anyone else in this town. Robert opened the door.

"Can I come in?"

Robert backed up a step. Dessie step just inside the door, moves to the side a little and softly closes the door behind her and then leans back against the door. She look him in the eyes without saying anything for about twenty seconds or so, and then she drop her head down, looking toward the floor.

She had on a different dress. Had cleaned herself up. Smelled like rosewater again. Had her hair tied back and a little scarf-like something wrapped over the top of her head like a hat with no brim and no crown, just a band. Robert had not noticed how long her eye lashes were, how small her ears were, how slender her neck, how...

"For some reason, I feel like I can trust you, mister. I don't even know your name and like you said, you could be a real bad man," and then she look up at Robert, "But what choice I got?"

Robert don't answer.

Dessie look around the room. When she sees the pallet by the wall, she stares at it, "This where you sleeping tonight?"

"Yes, mam."

"You probably tired."

Robert stays silent, figuring the longer he don't say nothing, the better off he'll be.

"Can I talk to you?"

She must have had a total other kind of definition for the word "talk," or at least for sure she meant something else other than what she was doing now. Robert start to say something, start to say, well, ain't we talking now, but he stays his tongue and waits, like when you hunting deer, you don't show yourself when a rabbit come along, you stay hid and wait for what you hunting for, except Robert didn't know what he was waiting for. Oh, yeah, he was waiting to find out what kind of help she wanted from him, waiting and half hoping she would change her mind, even though he was pretty sure, she wouldn't.

Dessie went over to the table, slipped into one of the chairs and put her head down. Robert rotated in the same spot, like a horse trainer do when he got a colt circling round him at the end of a rope. After a minute or so of silence, she sat up and looked at the far wall on the other side of the room. Robert did not move. Finally, she turned around part way in the chair and looked directly at him.

Robert examined the plain prettiness of her face. She was not what you would call real pretty-faced-it, although she weren't ugly either. Her big eyes would have been attractive, if they weren't so sad looking, which is when Robert realized, all this time, he'd never seen her smile.

Out the clear blue, Dessie asks Robert, "You know who your daddy is?"

Dessie is steady looking into Robert's eyes, before he knew it, Robert walked over to the table and sat down across from Dessie.

"My daddy name Noah Johnson, but I ain't never seen him. Never met him."

"My daddy a white man."

Robert almost asked, is that why you like white men, but once again held his tongue.

"I know who he is and he know who I am, but he don't recognize me in no public way. He send money, which make him more a daddy than most white mens ever be to they colored children."

Twisted up. Robert understood being twisted by what your parents done, and because he understood, he also knew it was better to avoid getting involved with people like Dessie. His life didn't need more twisting.

"Do who your daddy be make a difference for who you is?"

"What you mean?"

"Never mind. I come to ask you to take me with you."

Robert does not hesitate. He shakes his head no, very slowly but quite definitely, no.

Dessie turns her head away and soft, like she talking to herself, she says, "Seem like nobody wants a kept woman."

"You could catch a train and ride, four or five dollars take you a long way from here."

"A ticket ain't the problem."

"What's the problem then?"

She did not hesitate, stared straight at Robert, leaned forward and started to running down her deficiencies to him, "I can't hardly read. I can't figure much. I ain't never worked in the fields. I don't cook nothing but coffee and tea. I ain't good but for one thing."

Robert looked away. Dessie put both her hands on the table top. At first Robert thought she was going to try to touch him or something, but she just clasp her hands and continued talking. "My daddy kept my mama, and his younger brother, he keep me. But I'm tired, tired of being kept. I wouldn't be no trouble to you."

Robert drew back from the table. He didn't want any part of this. She read his body language, and judged that it was useless. She stood up suddenly, turned away and walked to the door.

"Wait." Robert didn't know where the word came from, why he was saying it. Maybe it was the father thing, but he felt like he wanted to hear her talk.

"Wait for what? What? You want a fuck me? You done already told me no. You want me to lie down with you thinking that doing so going to get you to change your mind?"

There was nothing accusatory in Dessie voice. It was flat, emotionless, matter of fact, could have been counting out bales of hay. Robert couldn't figure out what to say, couldn't even figure out why he had said wait, so he said the first thing came to his mind.

"I wanted to hear you talk some more. I guess you the first person I met who 'bout twisted up as me. For sure you the first I done met who willing to say so right out the gate."

For the first time Dessie smile a little, just a little beginning of a smile, but it look huge on her, and Robert smiled back.

"Just so's there ain't no crossed up understanding. I ain't taking you no wheres, I'm just saying we can talk."

"I lives down the road a piece."

"Ahh no."

"I ain't going to hurt you. You the man. I'm the one who should be afeared."

Robert chuckled. Dessie smiled some more. Robert found himself liking her little, infrequent smile.

"I'm leaving here in the morning."

"You can leave from my house. The street I live on go to the road too."

"So you want me to lie down with you," it was Robert turn to make fun of Dessie, "thinking that doing so going to get me to change my mind?"

"No. I told you I want to talk. Seems like I been holding all this in for years. I feel a need to talk, to talk to somebody who'll listen to me and not ask me for nothing, and will kind of understand what I'm saying. You understand? I know you understand."

"Yeah, I understand. I was just funning you?"

"I know you done already seen how nobody round here don't talk to me even though everybody know me, know who I am, who my mama is, my daddy and what all."

"Yeah, I know. So, yeah, I guess I could shove off from your place."

Robert went over to retrieve his guitar case and then his crocus sack and started toward the door when he stopped.

"Hold up, let me leave something for Miss Annie. She been right kindly to me." Robert put a dollar atop the pallet, and then him and Dessie snuck out the door like they was young folk running off somewhere secret.

Robert had pulled the door closed behind them and hoped that nobody would break up in Miss Annie place. He told himself the neighbors wouldn't disturb nothing. Dessie, for her part, wasn't even much studying Miss Annie front door being left without no key turning or no latch from the inside. Dessie was just almost overjoyed that she finally had somebody she could talk to, and she didn't care that she'd probably never seen this somebody ever again in life, no matter, 'cause he was a listening now.

Dessie started talking as they trod down to her place and just kept talking. Told Robert everything she could think of, and everything she felt behind saying all the stuff she was thinking about. And Robert listened, patiently at first, but then with great interest. Unbeknownst to Dessie, her talking was helping Robert untwist some of his feelings.

When they got to Dessie place, at first Robert thought it must have been some white man's house, but Dessie laughed at him and told him, "No, some of us, we got money here in Natchez. Doc and Mr. Tidwell, the undertaker, they got two automobiles, a brand new one and ones what a couple of years old. And quite a few more colored own automobiles and businesses and such."

When they got inside, Dessie turned a light on. She had electricity. This was a whole new world to Robert, which is when he saw Dessie's radio. It was too late to listen to anything now, but maybe tomorrow morning before he left town, maybe then he could listen for a hour or so. It had been almost a week since he had heard a radio. Robert was excited, which is the way any self-respecting musician would be.

"You tired?"

"Yeah," Robert answered truthfully, "But I ain't too tired to hear your story telling."

"Yes, you is. You just making nice to me," and then she smiled again, like she getting used to smiling.

Robert put his things down. Dessie said, "Naw, put 'em in here," and she stepped into her bedroom, pull on an electric wire to make another light come on, and pointed to a big cherrywood armoire. Robert did as instructed.

He saw she had a big brass bed with a pretty quilt on it. When he turned the key that was sitting in the latch of the chiffarobe and opened the door, the strong sour-sweet smell of cedar wood filled his nostrils. She must have had ten or twelve dresses up in there, plus other pieces of clothing and hats on the top shelf and a couple of boxes of stuff sitting on the bottom, but even so, the cabinet was so huge there was plenty room for both his crocus sack and his guitar case. When he turned around, closed the door and locked it back, Dessie went over to him and removed his hat from his head.

"You can wash up in there," Dessie said pointing to a door. Robert opened the door and Dessie was up breathing close behind him. She reach round him and pull another electric wire. She had more 'lectric than most folks had lamps. Dessie back out the room and close the door.

When the light had come on, Robert's eyes like to popped out his head. He saw a water basin sitting on a counter with little, small spigots on it. Directly in front of him was a big, long, white metal trough like rich people had for washing they self. To his left was a little, stone looking, chair-like something, which when he lean over and inspect it closer, had a hole in the middle of the seat with water in it. Robert believe it to be a commode, which is what he once heard tell of but had never sat upon before, just like he had never been up in a rich colored folks' house before. Not like this. There was a little rack with towels hanging on them. A hand mirror. Combs and such. Damn, Dessie had quite a place here. It was hard to believe she wanted to leave all this behind.

When Robert come out, Dessie was sitting indian-style on her bed, which was a whole lot of legs to be folded up under herself like that. She must be limber like a slender willow branch what you could twist up into a circle without breaking it.

Dessie had on what looked to Robert like a cotton shift of some sort but it was smooth and not coarse, sort of medium weight, not flimsy but not no sack material either, and it was blueish colored with white polka dots and a little lacy collar with two string hanging down. This woman sure did have a lot of clothes.

She hardly poked out much in the front. Robert wondered what size her breasts really was, maybe big as his fists, which was substantial 'cause he had long fingers.

"I ain't got but one bed."

Robert wasn't sure if that were an invitation, a trick, or a trap. He had never been caught betwixt wanting and not wanting a woman so much, he guess what was bothering him was him wondering whether she was just using him or if she had real feelings for him? Robert was clear that he wasn't clear. He was wading in muddy water, had no idea what all was up in that pond nor how deep it was, plus even with all this light a burning he knew he really was kind of in the dark about Dessie. Sure she had told him about herself, but all that she told him was also kind of an indication of how much he didn't know. She was tall though, and probably knew how to use them legs. But so what if she did know legs trickeration, cause if she knew that, then what else did she know?

Robert knew he didn't know as much about what was going on as she knew, so he was at an extreme disadvantage, and therefore what he ought to do is be cautious and take the long way round, now wasn't no time to be taking no short cuts, crossing no unknown fields.

"I'm used to pallets."

"It'd be better if you slept in here. On the floor or up in here," she said patting the bed, "Makes no difference."

"If it makes no difference why not out over there," Robert said pointing to the front room.

"'Cause if he come by I don't want no trouble."

Dessie didn't have to tell Robert who the "he" was she was referring to. Robert hesitated and looked around. Trouble, huh? There was no window and only one door. Maybe he should have stayed over to Miss Annie's. It sure would have been safer.

"I don't want no trouble neither. I believe the floor'll work out fine."

"Suit yourself, Robert."

And she lean forward and push herself up, reaching for the electric, which is when Robert got a good but slightly obscured view of her body. The light was outlining the leanness of her body inside that shift she had on, he was right about the size of her breasts.

No sooner she turn the light out, she turn it back on. "Here." she threw a pillow to him, and flip the quilt back and pushed it with her feet over toward where Robert was standing.

He had not moved when the light went out. Tell the truth, he were thinking on climbing up in that bed with her, and thinking on if he did climb up in that bed whether he would sleep with his back to her or whether he would reach out, and desire was telling him what the hell climb up in there, she done already told you to come on, and common sense was telling him when a deal look too good to be true, it do really be too good, or leastwise it don't be true. So he was still standing there in the dark when the light come back on.

The way she threw the pillow at him, told him something. How she kick at that quilt. Robert could see where she had childish ways. Look like she was getting upset on account of things were not going the way she want, but, on the other hand, it could just be that she was used to being by herself, so there was no other way for things to go but the way she want since she ain't had to live up in this house with nobody else, which is when Robert was reminded of how hard it was for him to get used to living with Ginny and minding another body's ways, which, in turn, led Robert to resolve that it would be best to bed down on the floor and forget about sucking on this woman titty.

Robert left the pillow on the bed but grabbed up the quilt and laid it down on the floor between the bed and the armoire. He ain't had no night clothing to change into. Usually he slept in what he wore for the day or else, if he was with a woman, he slept naked.

The light went out, again. If he was going to sleep alone, on the floor, he could have stayed up to Miss Annie, but then he never would have seen no washing room and accommodating chair. Hell, what difference did it make? He would be gone in the morning, and all this would be behind him. All this.

"What you like for breakfast?" Dessie's voice disturbed the dark.

"Don't matter. Whatever you got."

"I don't got nothing much, but I can go get whatever you want?"

"Dessie, why you trying to make so nice to me? You…"

" 'Cause I don't usually have nobody around me to make nice with."

There was so much pain up in her voice when she said that, it felt like she was about to cry, even though Robert was for sure that she weren't going to cry, still, it sounded like that.

Shortly she continue in a real quiet voice, "It feel real nice to have somebody to be nice to."

Much as he wanted to ignore her, he was also flattered by her. Lingering manly desires nibbled away at the restraints of his common sense. Robert reposition his head on the side of his curbed-up arm and responded more out of manners than out of conviction, "Well, I appreciates you being nice to me. Thank you."

Robert couldn't never be for sure when she was being teetotal honest with him and when she was telling him stuff she knew would blind his vigilance, but he was used to seeing card sharks and whores at work, he ain't mean to think of Dessie as a whore, she didn't seem like the kind you find up in what they call a house of ill repute, or nothing like that, and for sure she wouldn't be showing herself on the street, but she was a kept woman and, Robert was for certain, any kept woman would do whatever she had to do to keep on being kept, and, worser than that, any kept woman what been kept for any substantial time usually done had time to get expert at keeping the keeper happy enough to keep on keeping her, and that all was just too much keeping for Robert, too much to have to think about, to have to deal with. Naw, Robert liked the simple life. It must be a powerful worriation to be liking on a woman like Dessie, no matter how tall she was or how thick her thighs was to say she was so lean. Robert felt like he'd like to look again to make sure his eyes weren't tricking him: she was tall, she was lean, and she had thick thighs. That was an unusual combination, attracting to him, but unusual none the less.

There was a couple of minutes of quiet before Dessie ask another question.

"When you used to go to sleep with Ginny, what you said to her before dozing off?"

"What you mean?"

"I mean what you tell her."

"Weren't no one thing."

"I mean, you know, how people say 'sleep tight' and what not or 'dream on the good so tomorrow be better'? Like that."

Robert had not intended to tell Dessie about Ginny. It had just come out whilst they were making the long walk from Miss Annie over to here, and now here this strange woman was with Ginny all up in her mouth like the two of them had been best buddies.

Robert had been lying on his back, but Dessie calling out Ginny name made him turn over on his side and draw his self up like a doddle bug and start to feeling quietness overtaking him. When he left Miss Annie place, Robert figured he'd get him some nookie and be gone with the sun. While he was walking here, listening to Dessie tell her story, Robert decided he wasn't going to fuck her 'cause she been fucked with enough and was just looking for a helping hand and not another man to take advantage of her. Still yet, for a minute when he was looking at her switch that electric, for a minute while he was staring at her leanness, he had felt a jolt of desire for her, a real strong jolt, but now, in this dark, on the floor this woman house, all balled-up and thinking on Ginny, well hell, that was it, Robert was through wanting Dessie. All he wanted was to get some sleep and get to stepping away from this sad town, and, you know, in order for a town to be considered sad in Mississippi, it had to be powerful sad.

"Robert?"

"Mam?"

"I wants to say something to you."

"What, Dessie?"

"I wants to say I hope you always have somebody to listen good to you the way you listen up on me while we was walking here. And I appreciate you ain't bothered me in no kind of way. You was just willing to listen to me. You the first man what ever treated me kind like that. So I hopes you always have somebody to be your ear."

Robert didn't say nothing. He was just glad all this work out for the good.

"Good night, Robert."

"Good night, Dessie."

–13–

ROBERT FLEW DOWN TO HAZELHURST. HE WAS HOLDING HIS HAT DOWN ON HIS head with his left hand and holding the neck of his guitar in his right hand (actually it was not his guitar, it was that national steel that Son House like to play cause it loud strong sound, cutting-loud, and not the warm-loud like the tricone model, Son's box (a duolian metalbody, 12 frets clear of the body, single cone model) was especial good for playing round them levee camps and saw mills and what not where loud was considered better and there was no provisions for the musicianeer but possibly a chair, though most often it would be a box or a barrel to sit upon whilst playing. They say Son bought it shortly after release from Parchman, costs him $32.50 hard currency.).

Now this national steel guitar what was so beautiful loud sounding when you struck upon it, it was also shiny new and was reflecting the sun like do a piece of broke bottle glass sitting in the grass. The hat, on the other hand, was for Robert, a bad black felt, high-crowned hat, which, however, Robert did not yet own, and was not to actually buy until some years later in San Anton (which is the way Robert and most other ramblers call the name of San Antonio), or was it Dallas, anyway, it was one of them Texas towns, but since it was not none of his at this moment in time, Robert did not recognize the hat (although anyone who has seen the suited-up portrait of Robert, which is one of the two pictures that Robert had took of himself so peoples everywhere would know and remember what he look like, anyone who has seen that sitting cross-legged with his guitar across his lap picture would immediately recognize the hat, especial on account of the way the front brim is broke down and ace-dueced to the side).

Robert pass up a flock of ducks heading south for the winter, they was green-head mallards and particularly fine of feather, but they was no match for Robert's cleanness, which was close to immaculate, and being clean was R.L.'s reputation. Even walking dusty Mississippi roads, he stayed clean, cleaner than a hundred pound bale of freshly ginned cotton. The mallards quack at Robert acknowledging his presence as he speed by them, you see they was in no particular hurry, but Robert had a date with destiny. He was going to meet up with his pappy for the first time in his life and, for that matter, for the first time in his pappy life, no, wait, his pappy had seen Robert when Robert was a baby, but almost immediately thereafter had made himself scared. Robert did not remember that occasion and, it is said, that Noah Johnson, for his part, did not want to remember the occasion, but don't nobody really know 'cause Noah ain't never talked about it to nobody. In fact, none of the throng of white mens who, years and years long after Robert gone, combed up and down the delta looking for any which scrap of information about Robert they could find, and they found bits and pieces all over the place, talked to everybody whoever even much heard the name Robert Johnson, anyway not a one of them was ever able to find even so much as one somebody who ever acknowledged even knowing Noah Johnson. Now, of course, Noah Johnson had to exist 'cause Robert existed, and Robert could not have existed if his father had not existed, and at the same time Robert do realize that this search for his pappy could be a wild goose hunt, 'cause you know even though it for sure that Robert had a pappy, it ain't for sure that his pappy was some man named of Noah Johnson as Robert's mother, Julia, had said, in fact sometimes Robert even took to wondering whether Julia was really his mama, he knew she was but sometimes when he tried to fit all the pieces together and had a whole handful of life puzzles that didn't match up, at them times things was so a jumble and so confuse-a-ting, that he felt like he himself was something made up in a confusion factory where stuff come out with the wrong labels intentionally writ on the side, at which times, Robert would just sigh and think on some music or something and keep on walking regardless to how blue he be feeling. Part of his walking was to forget about all this stuff and part of his walking was to find out about all this stuff. For this particular flying south, he was on the specific mission of finding out the origins of his existence, so that's why he was going down round to Hazelhust, Mississippi where he was told he hail from, that is, where his mama claimed she conceived him from the seed of Noah Johnson.

Robert was quite a sight, he had a black jacket on. It was not buttoned but it was not flapping in the breeze neither, just straight and staying flat up against his body. And he was singing "When you're smiling," even though he weren't smiling. It was a sun shiny day, kind of cool though, which was why he had that black jacket on.

When Robert got to Hazlehurst, he walk up to the gallery where the mens was sitting, playing checkers, and lying, and such. It must have been a Saturday, had to be a Saturday evening, otherwise so many of them would not have been congregated on the gallery, front of Breedlove's feed & grocery.

"How do?"

They nod to Robert but keep to talking amongst themselves, almost like Robert ain't standing there.

"December woman, that's what I works best with. You know that girl, Mabel, come from round Tunica?"

"Now, Amos, I know you trying to sell a mule for a horse now, that girl been married going on twenty years. Fine, upstanding church woman what wouldn't be caught dead in your presence."

"You see that's what I'm talking about. You's born in February, bet you is. No matter what somebody say, you going to contradict. Somebody say the sky blue, you say, naw, not at night. At night the sky black."

"Well, Amos, you mean to tell me the sky ain't black at night."

"No. I'm just saying contradict is your nature, you was born that way."

"You know good and well, right is right and being right ain't got nothing to do with what month you was born in."

"Yall see? Yall see what I'm talking about? He can't help but to contradict. He contradict right there 'cause he can't stand that I'm right when I tell him 'bout hisself. But, let me get back to what I was saying, cause that's one thing about them February people, if you don't watch them they throw you off whatever you was to be doing. What I was saying, before brother contradict here try to throw cold water on my fire, was that I were going with that girl sister, Amy Louise, we called her Amy Lou. December born. Fun loving. See me, I'm March born, so I get along with them December born womens."

Robert was watching with shine-eyed fascination and listening like a hungry calf for its mama's mooing, the conversation was stimulating his memory. When you go into loving somebody, you don't start off by finding out what month they is, so what difference to it make, if you love somebody you love them regardless to when they born, except that Robert also knew there was no road that was strictly left to chance, somebody built the road, and even if you was to cut through the woods, you made the decision to cut through the woods and whatsoever you was to find up in them woods, or whomsoever you was to come across on the road, well, part of that was a result of your decision to travel there, 'cause for sure, if you weren't traveling you wouldn't never come up side of them, and maybe loving women was like that, you love who you love 'cause in your travels you searching for that kind of love, or, at least, expecting, or hoping, to find a particular love you can live with, so maybe you do pick the kind of love you looking for, and then again maybe there is something about us that attracts certain folks to us, and something about certain folk that attracts us to them, maybe birthing month do have something to do with what all happen in the long run. Attraction was a powerful subject for Robert to think upon, which is part of the reason Robert was content to listen before asking the question he had come down to Hazelhurst to ask one and all until he come upon a satisfactory answer.

"Amos, what borning month got to do with who you gets along with?"

"There you go again, mister contradict!"

"Naw, a question ain't a contradict. Don't you know no grammaticals? Contradict is when you point out a wrong. Question is when you find out what's right."

"I believe Rufus got a point there, Amos."

"And guess what, Amos? Rufus telling you right, and Rufus ain't none of February born, so you can't say contradict his nature."

"Rufus what month you born? No, wait a minute, don't answer, let me guess. You June born? They all up in the air, whatsoever which way the wind be blowing, that's the way they go."

"I May born."

"Head or butt?"

"Butt? But what?"

"Is you born when May sticking its head in the door or when May was carrying its ass out?"

"I born twenty-fifth."

"Well that's the same as June born."

"Whoa horse! How May the same as June."

"It ain't."

"You just said it the same."

"No, mister contradict, I said being born in the butt-end of May is the same as being born in June. I ain't said nothing about May and June being the same. Tomorrow morning when you get up and wash your face, stick your finger up in your ears and clean them out too."

"Amos, my ears clean, I hears you good. You got a mouth malfunction is what all it is."

"Pardon me, yall. I'm passing through here on the look out for a Noah Johnson what used to stay round here twenty years or so gone. He was friendly up with Julia Dodds before she left here."

Nobody said nothing. Robert stand there a whole minute in silence. Still nobody said nothing. Robert tip his hat, "Well, thank you for your help."

And that's the way it was every which a way Robert turn. He say he looking for Noah Johnson and nobody say nothing to him. Nothing. He stand outside the country church the next day, asking round. He say, "Noah Johnson," and they say nothing. Robert ask fifty-eight different peoples. Each one of them say the same thing: nothing.

Robert got so desperate to find his pappy he even go to asking white folks if they know of a colored man go by Noah Johnson. They say nothing. The sheriff, he say: nothing. The judge: nothing. The gin man: nothing. Straw boss with the labor camp (and he know more negroes than any white man fifty miles around), he say: nothing. Nothing. Nothing. That's all Robert find: nothing.

At one point Robert took to asking a mule he saw in a field he passed, two ducks swimming in a pond, and a crow that was cawing on a fence post. The mule just look, but don't say nothing. The ducks, they swim away and quack, they quacking sounding like they was laughing at Robert. And the crow, he keep cawing like he was cawing before Robert come along, except now the crow's cawing sound like he stuck on one word: " 'cause, 'cause, 'cause."

On the third day, Robert give up and start to walking away, going he don't know where, which is when a voice come to Robert.

"What you looking for me for?"

Robert was tongue-tied. Now it was his turn and what he say? Nothing.

"Even if you was to finds me now, what difference it make? You growed."

Finally Robert catch his words up, but he don't speak them out loud. He say them in his head, even so, the voice hear the words and answer back just like as if Robert had spoke out loud.

"I want to know where I come from." Robert paused his trodding, he wanted to clearly hear what the voice answer.

When Robert stopped walking and waited for a response, the voice didn't say nothing, but soon as Robert start in to walking again, the voice re-commence to sounding, responding to Robert's statement about wanting to know his origins.

"The dirt. The air. The hot-ass sun. That big muddy river."

Searching for something more substantial, Robert asked the voice, "And where you come from?"

"The same place you come from. All us, all peoples, everybody from the same place."

Robert don't bother looking for the voice. There was only open road before and behind him. Open road. And on either side of him, cotton fields, stretching far as the eye could see.

Who that boy people is?

Suppose you never know the people you come from? Suppose all you know is what you been told and you ain't never been told much? Would you recognize your birthing spot even if you was to stand thereon? Do you have a home town, if you never had a home?

Who that boy people is?

And with that question, Robert woke up. Confused at first as to where he was. In front of him was dark wood and he was sleeping on a quilt, and then it come to him, he was up in Dessie 's place and it sound like it was raining outside.

Robert closed his eyes back and hoped his ears were tricking him. He had to get out of here. Today.

Unfortunately for Robert, it was raining steady and would be raining for most of the morning.

Dessie was already up and about, sitting in her kitchen, drinking coffee and smoking a cigarette. And now she had on a different dress than from the one she was sporting last night when she come to get him from Miss Annie place, and it was also different from the one she was wearing when she brung him over to that white man's upper room, and, come to think on it, it was also different from what she had on when Robert first saw her on the street while he was playing, which is what made Robert next remember seeing all them dresses up in that big chiffarobe she had.

You know it's one thing to see rich folks from a distance, but it's a horse of a different mule to be seeing them all up close, close like seeing them last thing at night and first thing in the morning and be all in their house, and able to reach out and touch their personables, like Robert just done in that water-closet room, which is what Robert thought to call the room where the accommodating chair was, somewhere or the other Robert had run across that word: water-closet, which, when he was up in there this morning, after taking care of his body functions and such, he had spent some time up under the electric examining and touching Dessie 's comb, smelling her washing cloths (they smelled pretty, like roses, she must own a rose garden out back the way she have rose fragrance following her, or maybe it was the white man who own the garden, course, it could be the white man who owned this very house Robert was standing in), and turning the spigot four or five times just to watch the water start up, and even much figuring out how to pull on the string what release the water into the middle of the accommodating chair, which all set Robert to wondering a wagon load of questions, like:

The accommodating chair was nailed down to the floor, leastwise it didn't move when he push on it, so how you get the night bucket out from up under the chair to empty the bucket?

And if there was no night bucket up under there, where the night water and other excretions go? Surely not up under the house, that would raise up a powerful stink and Robert didn't smell nothing stinking up in here, not even the water closet room.

Thinking on which, how come in them books Robert read he ain't never read no description of an accommodating chair and how it work?

Seem like something that a body used all the time like that, seem like it would be important enough for somebody to set down in words how it go.

Another question was: where electric come from and how it work?

It was a great thrill for Robert to close the water closet door, stand there in the dark, count to five, and pull on the electric. It feel a little something like you was God making the sun come up. Of course, Robert had seen electric on a many occasion before, but still, it was thrilling to make it work for his own personal use.

A more easy question to answer, or at least it seemed more easy to Robert, was who make soft soap like the soap sitting up on Dessie counter, smelling all like a rose petal?

That soap weren't rough or nothing either, just real smooth with teenie-tiny, real-soft bubbles.

Well, those was just some of the questions inhabiting Robert's head as he walked out the bedroom, into and through the front room, and turned around in a semi-circle like wheeling a hay wagon up into the barn when you coming from the back side of the barn. When Robert walked on up into the kitchen where Dessie was sitting, Robert wondered, how come somebody would want to stay up in a house this big all by they lonesome?

Of course the first words out of your mouth to somebody first thing in the morning don't be no bunch of questions and stuff, Robert do have manners, so he stands in the doorway until Dessie look over at him and when she do, he say, "Good morning."

She say, "Prove it."

He say, "Prove what."

She say, "Prove it's a good morning." and then she take one of them extra slow drags on the cigarette, the kind of drag when your jaw cheeks sink in and you make a sucking-in sound, and she let her eyelids slide most ways down, half covering them big old eyes, and she lower her head, blow smoke out her nose, like she a bull or something, and then look back up at him, waiting to witness his proof.

Robert don't say nothing. He know it's that fish and hook thing again. If he don't open his mouth, he won't get hooked.

So what Robert do is turn on his heels and retrace his steps back into the bedroom, goes over to the armoire, unlocks it (which is a strange, strange thing to Robert, it being locked, when don't nobody but one body inhabit this house, who or what she locking the chiffarobe for? Plus, even more strange, if you going to lock something up, why leave the key in the lock, that render the lock kind of useless, don't it?), anyway, he unlocks the thing, opens the door, reaches in, and pulls out his guitar case, lays the case on the bed, opens it, takes out his guitar, lays the guitar on the bed, closes the case, and puts the case back in the chiffarobe, closes and re-locks the door (he does all this on account he has noticed that Dessie is real, real orderly about her possessions, seem like every little thing has a spot of its own, and since he don't want to mess up nothing, he do his best to leave everything exactly like he found it).

When Robert come back into the kitchen he still don't say nothing. He sat down in the chair and hoisted up his guitar, which is when he noticed that during the short time he been gone, Dessie done poured him a cup of coffee and got it sitting on the table, which immediately put him in mind to play something inviting for Dessie but he couldn't think up nothing like that right quick, so he had to fall back on something slow and mournful-like, 'cause actually, you know, Robert really, really wanted to be on the road by now, but here he was sitting in front of a cup of coffee in this sad, tall, woman's kitchen and it was raining outdoors. Now them what know Robert may suppose this is where his song, "Come into my kitchen because it's going to be raining outdoors" come from, but Robert had not yet written such a song, what he was doing right now was simply fooling around searching for a flavor what would compliment the feeling that was in the air.

"I got to go / but I sho / might like to stay / i'd like to talk / but I don't know what to say / so I guess I'll play this little song / and if you of a mind / join up with me and hum along / ummm hummm hummm / ummm hummm hummm / hummmm hummmm, hummmm."

She don't join in.

Robert smile up at her.

She don't smile back.

Robert repeat the humming part, asking once again for Dessie to join in.

She don't join in.

Robert stop smiling. Robert stop humming. Robert stop playing. All in a slow one, two, three order.

"Why you don't join in?"

"I can't sing."

"Well, at least you can pat your foot and keep time."

"My auntee in town."

Robert was, of course, throwed for a loop by that. What was she saying, or meaning to say by saying that? Dessie could see that he didn't understand, so she go to him direct, "My woman monthlies done come down."

Robert don't say nothing, but start back into random picking. Ginny was good about that, wouldn't never be snapping at Robert or nothing behind that but, at the same time, would be kind of standoffish. Robert understood that different womens approach this kind of subject in different ways, and since he weren't a woman and neither had he studied up on this particular topic, he felt it was best to tread lightly and give her a lot of space, sort of like circling way, way around a cantankerous bull, which amused Robert to think like that, comparing a woman to a bull, it got the point across but it didn't make sense, so Robert smiled to himself, which Dessie would have wondered why he was smiling if she had bothered to look up at him, but she had not bothered. Robert was not on her mind at that particular moment.

What was on her mind was going to meet her keeper. He would come later on today and she would go with him, and be forced to... she didn't really want to think on it.

"Soon as it stop raining, I'm gonna shove off."

Dessie don't say nothing.

Robert reach down and sip on the coffee.

"This a good cup of coffee. This some of that last drop coffee?"

Dessie don't say nothing.

"What they call that Maxwell House coffee, name it after that hotel over to Nashville." In one of his ramblings, Robert had hooked up with a whore what was from Nashville and she told him all about that special blend, said she used to trick a man what would stay at that hotel when he come to town, and plus she knew another man who work up in the kitchen there. They swear it was president Teddy Roosevelt himself what said that thing about that coffee being good to the last drop. Robert pull up short in thinking on that, now why he thought of that woman as a whore, she weren't no street walker or work up in no brothel or nothing, in fact she were a fine lady with two little ones, but she was poor, real poor, and pretty, and shapely, and colored, a pleasing kind of brown-skinned, well, leastwise white mens found her pleasing, sort of like they probably look upon Dessie and be pleased, though Robert for his part do not think of brown-skinned women as being more magnetizing than black-skinned women, in fact, Robert was of the mind like Son House whose song "My black mama" was a praise song for dark-skinned colored womens. Robert loved that song, loved to sing "My black mama," and most certainly loved the women that the song was describing upon.

What Robert was thinking was that this was 1931 depression time, a very, very hard time to be a poor, black, pretty woman, a time when rich white men was taking advantage of both they whiteness and they money (not to mention they man-ness in a man-made world), which all was a powerful advantage, especial over colored womens. So, no, Robert guess he would not call Dessie no whore, neither that Nashville woman, they was just born during hard times and doing what they had to do to survive, or at least that's the way Robert choose to approach the topic, maybe some other body see it different.

"Somebody must a told you about James."

While Robert don't know what Dessie was talking about, he pretty certain she don't know that he don't know, so Robert don't own up to not knowing, instead he play possum, don't say nothing and wait to see what Dessie going to say next.

"Is that why you won't take me with you?"

Robert pick up the tin cup and commence to slow sipping the coffee.

"People blame me for what they done to James. They shun me. Nobody talk to me, like it was me who hung James, but I loved him. Don't nobody understand how much I…"

Dessie broke off talking, got up and went to the back door. She opened it. It was still raining sort of hard, and she closed it no sooner she opened it because the rain was a coming in the kitchen. But she don't say nothing more. Nothing.

Robert found himself wanting to know what happened but not wanting to ask Dessie.

"You ever bury a man they strung up, and burned up, and cut up. The flesh all chared up, blacker than…, blacker than anything you ever seen. They burnt up the only one somebody who really love me. The whites lynch him and burn him up and the colored blame me for him getting burnt up. Robert, I don't know what they told you. I don't really care no more."

Through all that talking, Dessie never once look upon Robert, instead she ramble on like she reciting out loud trying to memorize her times table.

Robert wished it would stop raining so he could go.

Robert thought that Dessie might feel better if she could cry.

Then Robert thought that she probably all cried out.

Next Robert thought about the last time he cried. Holding Ginny. If Dessie felt worser than Robert felt when he was holding Ginny, then she must be an empty grave waiting to lay her body down.

Which all is when Robert thought he understand Dessie, but was persuaded otherwise when a pole cat crept up in the chicken coop.

Dessie turn her flat eyes on Robert. Her face rigid like a pond froze over.

"That's why you was scared to touch me, huh?"

Robert remained closed-mouthed.

"They told you any colored who touch me, gon die."

Robert legs start to itching real bad, his feet telling him run, but his head is curious and his heart is crying behind likening what he felt like behind Ginny to how Dessie must feel behind that James man.

After a minute or two of nobody saying nothing more, Dessie reverse herself and go off riding in a different direction.

"You ever lay with a woman when her way come down?"

Robert know he ain't got to answer, she going to continue whether he respond or not. Worser than that, by now Robert convicted she would be steady talking even if he, or nobody else, was up in here to listen to her.

"He like to make me, you know, do like he ice cream or something."

Dessie looked at Robert and then after awhile turned and looked out the window, but Robert don't notice that, he got his head down, his eyes closed. Dessie continues after pausing to count eighty-seven raindrops. "Or he make me turn around and come at me in my behind. You ever come at a woman behind? You a country boy. Sheep and such, ain't you? Well even if you ain't, you know about it. You know what all I mean."

Yes, Robert knew what all she meant, but it were not something Robert generally think on. He had heard tell of it, even knew of a feller who say he done it. And to tell the truth, which was hard for Robert not to do, which is how he got into the habit of being quiet, 'cause sometimes it was better to stay quiet than to tell the whole truth, but to tell the truth, a whore or two had sucked on Robert but he had never come up from behind on no woman, and for sure never up behind no sheep or some such.

Robert ain't ate nothing yet, but he started to feel like he feel when what he ate want to come back up.

This woman was ruined, flat out ruined.

Robert had to go.

Robert look up, Dessie was looking out the window at the rain. All the time she had been talking to the rain and Robert thought she was talking to him, or felt like, or, shit, he had to get out of here. Robert he step backwards real quiet so as not to disturb Dessie. Let her stay up in that window.

While Robert was securing his sack and donning his hat, a small part of him felt like he was betraying Dessie by not staying and listening to her, and doing what he could to help her, but, hell, Robert was not ready to die, and now that he knew for sure that those long legs had got one man kilt, he was not about to be number two.

She was standing in the middle of the front room watching him when he come out the bedroom. But Dessie ain't said nothing.

Robert he paused for a couple of seconds trying to figure up on what would make sense to say.

Nothing.

Nothing would make sense.

So Robert look at Dessie one last time, mentally shook his head as he wondered what had even much made him interested from the jump, she just tall, that's all, was what he lied to himself at first, trying not to confront the way he really, really feel.

He standing there. She standing there. Nobody saying nothing. Before he could come up with some diplomatic way to say goodbye, Dessie turned her back on him.

Robert bit his bottom lip, torn between telling her something unpleasant about herself and the nagging uneasy feeling that it was like they was really close cousins—close in consideration of the fact that they was both intimately involved in contributing to the death of somebody they really, really loved. So, despite his drawing back, his desire to get away, Robert also understood Dessie and when he shook his head at her turning her back on him, he was also shaking his head at himself turning his back on her, shaking about the two of them, who probably understood what each other was feeling better than most anybody else each of them had run into. The two of them was so near to each other and at the same time so far away, like as if they was standing on either side of a not so wide, but still yet powerful deep, deep river, standing there seeing each other but not having no boat and can't neither one of them swim.

To the average eye, they might of seem like they had nothing in common, but Robert knew they was connected by death. Death. Robert's old friend was visiting him again, this time in a way Robert would never, never have been able to foresee in advance, but in a way he recognized when it come, and certainly would never forget once it gone.

In the awful quiet of that tearing apart, the drumming of the rain provided an ancient rhythm of melancholy, Robert slow walked around Dessie, giving her plenty space. When he get to the front door, he twisted sideways so as he was facing her and opening the door at the same time. He was sort of scared to turn his back full on her.

"I thought you was different, but you just like all them other mens."

Robert heard what she said. She meant her words like throwing dirt in his face, but even so Robert knowed something she didn't know: he really was different than them other mens.

He had not tried to touch her not out of fear—well, maybe fear was part of it, actually, yes, there were some veins of fear running through his feelings, but nonetheless, the main reason he ain't tried to touch her was because he didn't want to be another boxcar on the freight train running her down. He ain't touched her 'cause he really come to understand her situation, or, to put it more bluntly than he would openly admit to her or to himself, he ain't touch her 'cause he care about her.

So here was death again mocking Robert, twisting up a situation he involved in. Robert was not trying to contradict Dessie, rather, as he flinched before leaning away from Dessie, that little head shake was both a recognition of his own failures, his own disasters, his own intimate dealings with death, as well as an acknowledgement that death, like a bloodhound that don't never get tired of tracking you down, death ain't nothing to fuck with.

As he cross the sill and slipped out into the warm rain, Robert blinked his eyes like he was trying to wake up from a bad dream.

He pulled his black jacket close, hunched up his shoulders, adjusted his sack cross his back, picked up his guitar case, put his head down and trudged on up the muddy road. It really wasn't raining that hard. He might stop if he come to a general store or something, or come up on a big tree roadside, and then again, he might just keep walking 'til he was clear gone from this particular jurisdiction of sadness.

There was no looking back. He didn't have to. He needed no picture to remind him.

Robert knew some things you should let go, forget about, and some things, try as you might, it is impossible to disremember them, to bury them. Such feelings is like a wound that won't never fully heal, a wound that not only leave a permanent scar, it also stay tender to the touch when poked in a certain way. Dessie was that certain way, a sharp stick jooged into his deepest feelings, another woman he always going to recollect, and, once again, that was not a good thing.

-14-

WHENEVER ROBERT PLAYED HE ATTRACTED WOMEN, AND LOOKS LIKE EVERY TIME he played it was a different woman he would end up with, so few who knew him ever would of thought of him and just one woman, and anybody who didn't know him over a long period of time would have never seen him with the same woman more than once. But like they always say, you can't tell how far a frog'll jump while he sitting on his rump. The truth was that Robert had jumped into marriage. In fact, the whole truth was Robert was married twice. The first time short. The second time longer. The first time for love. The second time for convenience. And, no, he never went back to Sweetwater. Sweetwater, she got over Robert on account of Tanner, who, in one of his many moments of utter honesty, told her, without even a hint of a stutter, you take care of the kitchen, I gots the garden. Whatever you need, I'll grow, we ain't go'n never starve and we going to always have pretty flowers to smell.

Tanner's rough hands was so terribly tender whensoever he touch Sweetwater that a couple of times her eyes water over thinking on how extra special he treat her. Tanner would spend hours expertly plaiting her hair. Sweetwater never heard tell of no man with a touch like Tanner. Got so they walked to work together, arm and arm. And walked back home, her arm looped in his like they was youngsters experiencing an extended bout of puppy love. Never had no children though, just the two of them. Arm in arm. Inside. Outside. Kitchen. Garden. House. Yard. Sweetwater never told Tanner about Robert. Tanner never told Sweetwater he saw her go off with Robert. Tanner figured they both had water under they bridge, so what mattered was they was together on the other side of whatever was back there in their past. What mattered was now and tomorrow, and now and tomorrow was good to the both of them. So Sweetwater and Tanner was like a big placard advertising the joys of marriage, and Robert, he was the initials on the side of a railroad boxcar rambling through town after town advertising nothing but its own existence.

Robert seemed predisposed to be a loner, could spend days with just himself for company and not feel lonely, and yet he never lacked for female attention, which attention he was good at cultivating, especially the attention of plain women, females who never thought they had much of a chance with him, he would row on up to their landing and gift them with more attention than they ever got in their entire life from all the menfolk they knew added up together. Robert was powerful persuasive that way and while he was with them, he was with them. He had learned from Ginny, if you don't give a woman reason to be jealous, she'll give you everything she got. Second rule was: don't never lie to them. It ain't necessary, especially seeing as how there was no intention on his part, nor any real expectation on their part, that he would be a permanent part of their lives.

"Why you talking to me?" Maryemma asked with a soft country shyness as she addressed a man known to travel from town to town. She was sure it was a mistake that he sat down next to her after getting up from playing and having everybody dancing and hooting and hollering and whatnot. Maryemma was plain-faceded, just like the majority of the women what work up in them fields sun up to sun set, ain't never had no fancy dress, she smelled of the earth, didn't know what perfume was. Had never been outside the county. Had two, three children by age eighteen. She was fully aware that her life was limited, that she was part of an endless cycle: be born, grow up, have children, work hard, die, or should she say, be born, work some, grow up, work harder, have children, work harder than before, die working? Don't you get tired of working, working hard so them who don't work hard can get more rich than they already is?

Unless you been held down in the Mississippi dust all your days, you can't know how mesmerizing shiney, how magnetic attractive new shoes look on a music-playing man passing through town with a beautiful sound and a dazzling smile.

For his part, Robert first of all gave Maryemma his attention. When she averted her eyes, he understood and looked over by the door, like he was looking for something, which he wasn't, he was just giving her the opportunity to look upon him full-faced without being flustered by him looking back upon her, and then he would turn and face her and tell her something she never expected to hear, "I'm a traveling man stopping in your area looking for some companionship whilst I'm here."

Maryemma, predictably would draw back from that. She was not about to get used by some slick talking songster playing with her affections. At this point she would not know what to say, would not know how to get away from something she wanted to be up close on. Robert knew that the reason she was in the juke was to have a good time and the reason no man was hanging on her is 'cause either she weren't attractive enough for a man with means to go after or she done turned down all the field hands seeking a quick roll in the hay.

Typically at this point in the ritual, the woman would try to retreat, which is what Maryemma halfheartedly did, "I gots to go."

But, of course, an expert at the two step, Robert was waiting for that move, "I knows you do, but I'm working here, I can't leaves now. I gots to play a little more." and then Robert would thrust out his hand to her, "Pleased to be talking to you. Would be powerful happy if you was to stay and listen for just a little bit more. My name Robert, they call me R.L."

Her hand would be limp in his, or sometimes almost firm, and usually rougher-skinned than his, 'cause it had been years since he picked cotton or did any other kind of regular labor that would callous-up all the insides his palms and crack up the skin on the dark-hand side. And she would feel the difference in their hands because he would hold her hard hand in his soft hand, his long, spider-looking fingers caressing the pulse spot on the inside of her wrist—even the burnished tips of his fingers, made solid from years of string plucking, even them would feel powder light as he touched women with a dexterity kin to running up and down the fretboard of a Stella guitar (which was one of the brands Robert favored). And if she didn't respond with her name, like this particular Maryemma didn't, then Robert would patiently continue stirring the pot without missing a stroke, "What your name is?"

"Maryemma."

"Maryemma," Robert said rising up out of his seat, "Please wait for me to finish playing. I sure would like to talks to you some more."

Before she could answer he was gone, back to the chair by the wall, grabbing up his guitar and was singing, "I'm a stranger here, could somebody please give me a drink. I ain't looking for no whiskey, cool fresh water is what I crave," and before you know it, Robert done made up a little song continuing the conversation with Maryemma.

Some of them Maryemmas been done left by then, but if this here Maryemma stayed, well then Robert would've knowed everything was going to be alright. And if she didn't, well, there was always more than one woman in every location he visited. More times than not, this was all it took: a little time, a little attention, some soft conversation and Robert would have a companion to complement his stay in whatever location he was in.

Maryemma went with Robert that night. He was staying in a room somewhere and in the morning he walked her back home and no matter how her people tried to shame her about laying with that rambling man, Maryemma was proud to have wrapped her arms around somebody who was more myth than man.

Some times the myth might roll to a pause for a whole week, occasionally a month or two, but for sure when the seasons change, he gone. Playing country towns during harvest time, railroad camps in the spring and summer, winters visiting bigger cities. He had folks up in Commerce, round Robinsonville where his mama and Dusty was staying. A favorite half-sister, Carrie, up in Memphis, a special woman over in Helena, Arkansas, across the river not far from Tunica. And some distant family plus his second wife down in Hazelhurst and nearby Martinsville. So he was constantly up and down Mississippi.

In his birth spot of Hazelhurst, located east of Natchez, Robert had him a good time for a sweet little while. It was there that a foursome walk in the woods with an 18-year-old girl, Vergie Jane Smith, and with a friend of hers, Eula Mae Williams, who was coupled-up with another fellow, well, all that led to a pregnancy and a son, Claud (born December 16, 1931). However, shortly after the boy was conceived Robert married another woman in secret. And right there is where another Robert story get so twisted, it's hard to make heads or tails, except to say, that many, many years later, an October 15, 1998 court case would establish paternity and yield another one of those mythic stories that people like to tell about Robert.

According to the court record, during pretrial questioning by attorney Victor McTeer, Eula Mae described what might have been the moment of

Claud's conception.

Q: All right, so you walked off the road, correct?

A: Right.

Q: And you started to kiss and do whatever people do?

A: M-hm.

Q: All right. Now, when you started that, what was Vergie and —

A: Doing the same thing we were.

Q: How do you know? You were sitting there watching them while you were -

A: We was both standing up.

Q: Oh, so both of you were standing up in the woods?

A: Sure, we was standing up out there in the woods.

***

Q: Excuse me, I haven't finished yet. Vergie and Robert, were they kissing and standing up?

A: Right.

Q: Was there ever a time when you were not looking at them?

A: Well, yes.

Q: I see. Did you at any point in time remove your clothing?

A: Well, had to.

Q: Okay. Did you observe them remove their clothing?

A: Sure.

Q: You were sitting there watching someone else do this?

A: I done told you.

Q: Well, let me, let me share something with you, because I'm really curious about this. Maybe I have a more limited experience. But you're saying to me that you were watching them make love?

A: M-hm.

Q: While you were making love?

A: M-hm.

Q: You don't think that's at all odd?

A: Say what?

Q: Have you ever done that before or since?

A: Yes.

Q: Watch other people make love?

A: Yes, I have done it before. Yes, I've done it after I married. Yes.

Q: You watched other people make love?

A: Yes, sir. Yes, sir.

Q: Other than...other than Mr. Johnson and Vergie Smith.

A: Right.

Q: Really?

A: You haven't?

Q: No. Really haven't.

A: I'm sorry for you.

Q: Well, I appreciate that. And perhaps I need the wealth of experience that you have. But share with me this. Did you actually watch them engage in the act? You actually watched that?

A: Yes.

Q: When they were engaging in the act, was your husband (her boyfriend at the time) watching, too?

A: Sure.

Q: Okay. Did they watch you?

A: Sure.

Q: And you watched them watch you?

A: Yes.

Robert didn't stay around to be a father to his son by Vergie. What was Robert thinking? He knowed the worriation searching for Noah Johnson caused him, why then afflict such a torment on his own off-spring?

Who knows? Every fact we know only begs more questions. And besides what facts do we know? Did anyone truly know Robert Johnson? Indeed, one wonders, did Robert know himself?

In 1931 nobody had any indication that a then twenty-year-old Robert Johnson was going to become a legend, after all, he was just one of many, many musicianeers trying to make a living playing the blues on the streets and in the jukes in the Mississippi delta and elsewheres.

On February 16, 1929 Robert had married Virginia in Penton, located in Tunica county, in northern Mississippi. On May 4, 1931 Robert secretly married Calletta "Callie" Craft at the Copiah county courthouse and took up residence in Martinsville, Mississippi, a lumber camp located a few miles south of Hazelhurst. Virginia was 16 when she died in childbirth in 1930 and Callie was 30 when Robert married her in 1931 and Robert could have been as young as 19 or, like the 1931 marriage license said, he could have been 23. Who knows.

Callie, for her part, don't ask Robert nothing about where he go or what he do—most times he declare he been over to Ike's learning up on some music. Sometimes he stay gone all weekend, other times he come back the same night. You never could tell. Callie, nor nobody else, could figure out when Robert was about to leave, nor could they tell when he would show back up.

Course Callie had plenty of practice understanding the ramblings of men, seeing as how she been married twice times before Robert, plus she had them three kids to take care of, so she was sort of expert at giving Robert all the slack he need. And though she was almost old enough to be his mother, she liked kicking up her heels to Robert's playing, which he liked to see 'cause her moves moved him.

Her moves. One time, early one morning—or was it late? Come to think on it, even though it was for sure in the morning and Robert was just stirring, most likely it weren't very early 'cause, of course, Robert ain't had no labor camp to go running off to, anyhow, Callie, she had come prancing up in their bedroom buck naked except for a tray of breakfast food which she sit up in his lap after she done woke him by soft sucking lightly on his member. She was an experienced woman and not at all afeared to expression her affections like that, and too in other ways that less accomplished people might consider, what was that word they had for them crazy people what did all kinds of biting heads off chickens, swallowing glass and some such? Geeks, yeah, geeky, that was it. What others might consider geeky, well far as she was concerned it weren't nothing but having fun with somebody you loved having fun with.

Callie was well aware these wonderful Hazelhurst mornings was a tasty treat that you had best enjoy today since most certainly, just as sure as a cute little chick what done grown into a plump hen inevitably going to become somebody Sunday dinner, seems like nothing that grows up, goes undevoured in Mississippi. But she didn't care about tomorrow, why should she? From what she seen, tomorrow would not be nothing but what Mississippi tomorrows had always been every since she could recognize the difference between now and later, tomorrow would just be more toil and trouble, so since she had some good times in hand, she was going to savor them, sucking up all the sweet she could, yes, lord.

And yeah, the Hazelhurst area was good to Robert too, was a place where he could of set up a little kingdom, well, at least as much kingdom as a poor black man could have in Mississippi in the thirties, which, admittedly, wasn't much of a kingdom, in fact, such a kingdom wasn't really a kingdom, 'cause in Mississippi the white folks weren't letting no black man be no kind of a king. Soon as a colored man rise up good and start to stretching to his potential height, they cut him down, much like they done to Charles Spencer, Robert's step-daddy, but Robert, for his part, he had done figured out something: ain't no ax could fell the tree, if the tree had swift feet, of course, that also meant the tree had to forsake its roots, which all is what standing tall meant, standing tall mean moving from place to place, 'cause a tall black tree standing stationary was always going to get cut down in white Mississippi.

Down in Hazelhurst and Martinsville, Robert was hundreds of miles away from Robinsonville (which was only twenty or so miles below Memphis, Tennessee on Mississippi's northern border). Even though times were depression tough, there was plenty work down Hazelhurst way. WPA was building roads and the lumber camps were in full swing.

Moreover, Robert was not looking for no work. He made his living off of entertaining working people who had small, but significant, sums of hard earned money they were willing to spend for a real good time, such as was provided by Robert and his buddies like Ike Zinnerman, who became Robert's new mentor.

"Robert you good, but you know what you got to do to get gooder?"

"I don't reckon, but I'm a certain you gon tell me."

"Naw, I can't tell you how to play no music, but I can show you."

"I'm looking, I'm listening."

"Naw, not now, not here."

"You call it, Ike. Tell me the time and the place, I'll be there."

"Over to the church graveyard, midnight tomorrow."

Robert scratch the side of his face like he got an itch or a couple of ingrown hairs, which he never had 'cause he had Indian blood and ain't had much facial hair, but anyway, Robert he scratching like he do, which all was Robert way of stalling.

Ike throw his head back and laugh.

"What's the matter? You scared of haints?"

"I don't know, I ain't never seen none." and then Robert kind of lifts his hat up a little and pass his hand across his scalp, patting down the top a little.

"Me neither and I been playing in graveyards for neigh on to ten or twelve years." Ike slap Robert on the back of his shoulder, clamping down like he throwing a saddle on Robert back. "You know what I likes about the graveyard?"

Robert, with his aversion to death, could not think of one good earthly reason to sit up in a graveyard at midnight playing on a guitar. Ike seem to take joy in Robert's discomfort.

"What I likes is how quiet the peoples is. Nobody be talking while I'm trying to play."

Robert laugh along with Ike, just he don't laugh so loud or so long as Ike do.

The next night when Robert approached the bone orchard, he could hear Ike clear as a dinner bell long before he seen him.

Ike was sitting on Ludlow Thomas' headstone just picking away like as to he was up to turpentine alley at a juke.

On account of his bad left eye, Robert was having some difficulty making his way up over to where Ike was sitting. He kept stubbing his feets on rocks and such set down in the weeds to mark where a body is. Robert, he don't want to be walking on nobody grave, but he can't really tell what all he stepping on, especial since the moon weren't nothing but a slender silver sliver barely lighting the night sky.

"Robert, I'ma give you some notes, you give 'em back to me."

A couple of times, Ike trick up Robert with chords Robert ain't never before had fall upon his ears, but most of what Ike play, Robert could play right off. What interest Robert was not particularly figuring out how to play any one or two chords, but instead Robert wanted to figure out how to use the new chords he learned, how to incorporate the new sounds into his old sound, which was a particular thing that stood Robert out from the rest like an old cypress towering over pines in a swamp. Everybody else hear something new and want to play like that, Robert hear something new and want to fit that into what he already know.

One time Ike told Robert, "R.L.," which is how folks was then calling Robert, "R.L. teaching you notes is like planting seeds. You suck it up and before you know it, your tree dropping rich fruit. I knows more notes than you, but you knows more ways to use them notes than me."

"Ike, what all I know would not be as much as whatsoever it is, if you had not showed me what all you showing me. I thanks you for that."

At first, Robert would be all the time standing up while Ike would be sitting on Ludlow's headstone. Robert standing 'cause he can't bring himself to sit in no graveyard. In fact, one of the reasons Robert catch on so fast is 'cause he want to hurry up and get out there. But Robert desire to learn be stronger than his dread of death, so he continues his cemetery schooling.

Well within two months Ike is repeating himself at the graveyard. By three months they be dueting. Four months gone they dueling, and a couple of weeks later, Robert cutting Ike's head.

They was under a yellow moon when Ike says to Robert, "R.L. I can't learn you nothing more. Look like now you know more than me."

By then Robert was comfortable enough in their makeshift open air classroom to sit on a headstone. He nod to Ike without saying nothing.

"R.L., you ever hear tell of them two-headed people?"

Robert don't hesitate with his reply. "They teach you how to wrap your fingers twice around the neck of a guitar and be able to play any note you can hear."

"Yeah, that's them. So you heard tell of that?"

"Yeah."

Robert don't say what he thinking though. He used to think Ike was one of them two-heads on account of playing in the graveyard, but instead all Robert say is, "Folks say you got to go down to Louisiana to get fixed that a-ways."

Then Robert stopped his random picking to listen to Ike talking about a dream Robert been nursing for quite awhile.

"If a body had a mind to, you could walk down there in a week from here, or catch a train in the morning get there 'fore sundown."

"You been there Ike?"

"Naw, I was born in Grady, Alabama," which is not what Robert asked. Robert is a good listener, he catch that Ike don't answer him directly.

"I'm going down there one day."

Which is when a hoot owl commenced to commentating. Robert could a swore the owl was talking directly to him, asking "Who" you is? "Who" going to Louisiana?

Ike keep playing like he don't hear the owl. Robert use his slide to make his guitar give out the owl's notes. Ike liked to jump up and run off when he hear that hoot echo coming from Robert. Robert was getting too good.

After hearing that owl call to him, instead of going straight back home, Robert walk for about five miles or so toward Louisiana before turning back and making it in just before sunrise. He was almost ready, almost strong enough to face whatever was at the end of his road, and, just like most peoples, although he had a strong hankering to know his future, he just wasn't quite ready to witness what his end gon be.

-15-

USUALLY, WHEN YOU A CHILD AND YOU WANT TO KNOW SOMETHING YOU ASK your mama, ask your daddy, your grandmama, or what not, but then you grow a little older and you turn to friends and maybe aunts and uncles, or others you feel close to, but then there come a time when you want to know or understand something about your parents, which, this wanting to know something, generally don't happen 'til you get experienced enough to have to figure out how your parents done what you trying to do, or dealt with what you trying to deal with, and then it get truly deep when you wonder and really want to know who they be, know them as peoples, as men and women with feelings like your feelings, and then you realize you really must come to understand them if you ever going to fully understand yourself, but how you going to do that without talking to them, talking to them in a big old heart-to-heart way where y'all discuss stuff people don't usually discuss with their parents, like why you had me, how you hook up with him/her, why you stayed/left, here/there, why, you said you stayed with them, again, and took them back, again, let him come back when he old and ready to die, and even more intimate questions, and you usually don't ask your people none of that, not directly, maybe indirectly, or keep your ears open at funerals when people be talking deep reminisces, or peeping bad family arguments when old shit get slung around, but even that still don't get it all, sort of like a child grown to an adult don't ever tell their parent everything they done growing up is the same way a parent don't tell they children everything the parent done as a grown-up.

Whenever Robert get drunk and don't be playing music, he start thinking about stuff that ain't got no answer, at least not in his life, maybe other people got answers for them kind of questions, but Robert don't. And it be powerful frustration to think upon questions for which you can't never find no answer, especially when they be questions that all the time be coming up, like why the sun come up every day, you know it's going to come up, and you know when it going come up, but you don't know why it come up. Or, that major question: why white people the way they is?

Robert ain't nobody fool, he know he don't know the answer to certain questions, but he also know that it ain't the questions that's the problem, and it ain't not knowing the answers that's the problem, it's the conditions that's the problem. Like white folks. Them being white ain't the problem, and him not knowing why they be like they be, that ain't really the problem either. The problem is that they got the power to impose they will, how-so-ever and where-so-ever they choose, and colored ain't got no power to challenge or resist that. That's the real problem and that's the problem that lead to drinking 'cause if you drink enough, then you won't care nothing about the problem. So that's another reason Robert drink. He drink 'cause he ain't got no power over conditions that happen whether he drink or he don't drink, at least while he drinking he feeling better and he can forget about the prob... shucks, there ain't even no sense in thinking about it.

Robert turn around on the rock he been sitting on, cock his ear up and listen to a woodpecker going about its business. The tree is bigger than the woodpecker, but the woodpecker going to keep on pecking 'til it knock a hole in the tree. Robert likes that. And if somebody come along and disturb Mr. Woodpecker, well, Mr. Woodpecker, he just fly away.

Mr. Woodpecker set Robert to thinking about the time one Saturday over to the courthouse in Hazelhurst when Robert was playing for nickels and pennies—and some quarters too! Can't forget them quarters. This white man come up to Robert, his face pinched all up like he bit into a spoilt apple.

"Where you from boy?"

"I'se born here, sir."

"Where you work?"

Robert was so tired of them trick questions. Robert knew what the man wanted to know was whether Robert was up under some other white man or was Robert roaming free.

"I works the road crew over to Madisonville, sir."

"How come you ain't over there now?"

"Mule mess my foot up, boss. Yes, sir. They laid me off 'til Monday, say I weren't pulling my weight. But I gots three children and a great big woman, and they eats, eats a plenty. I gots to make some money so we can eat. Captain sent me home but I comes out here with my box and tries to collect some pennies so as my babies can eat. Captain John says he gon let me work Monday, but we all can't wait 'til Monday to eat. I could go, boss, I could go three, even four days on just cornbread and coffee, but my babies, and I believes they mama, she might be in the way again. So here I is, boss. I thanks, God, Jesus helps me pull these box strings so as I can feed my babies."

Robert was hating every word coming out of his mouth and every time he think back on it, he get mad and sort of sad, somewhat angry, and even a little bitter.

"Boy, I don't believe Jesus would direct you to be singing them devilish songs."

"No sir, he don't. I just sings what-so-ever the peoples pays for."

"Well you best start singing some Jesus songs."

"Yes, sir."

"In fact, you best move along. We don't need no colored standing around listening to devilment."

"Yes, sir."

Without another word, Robert had bent low, picked up his hat with the coins in it, and quickly placed it firmly on his head so as the coins were caught up at the top of his head beneath the crown of his hat. Robert grab his guitar case and don't even bother putting the guitar up. He scramble away like a crab caught on land scurrying to make the water's edge. Robert don't forget about his mule lie and as he leaves, go to fake limping just like as if his foot busted up.

A pretty normal 1931 incident.

And that was the problem, what happened was normal. It was normal to be humiliated. It was normal... Robert had thought... Oh, why even think about what he had thought? Life had been normal for as long as Robert could remember. Which all is when Robert was for certain he was going to leave here. Robert knowed that sooner or later if he stood in Hazelhurst he was going to run up some white man with a saw in his mouth, some white man what was going to trying and cut Robert down just 'cause the white man saw Robert standing there. Some white man.

In general Robert try to avoid drinking by himself, it ain't healthy, he end up drinking too much, and besides drinking was already a part of the condition of being a musicianeer who be playing up in them jukes, 'cause you see a lot of time the pay was six bits and all you could drink, so if you didn't drink you wasn't getting your full pay. Robert didn't know any musicianeer who ain't drinked, that's 'cause every musicianeer wants to get paid for they work and since part of the pay is liquid, they drink they pay. So Robert know all them rumors and such about him being an alcoholic is a misunderstanding, what was he supposed to do, leave his money sitting in the bottle?

Course, sometimes them juke owners take the shit too far. Robert was up in St. Louie and a juke man wanted to say that Robert and the other mens had drink up all they pay so he ain't had nothing to give them. One feller said, ok, of course he was drunk, well, Robert knew he ain't hardly drank none and when he did drink, his St. Louie kid-lady what he just this self-same night met, she was taking care of him, and Robert Jr. (talking about Lockwood), he wasn't drinking much, same glass all night, so it wasn't right what the juke man was saying, and when Robert Jr. ask for a reckoning of what all they drank up, the juke man pull out his gun and put it on the table and said, I reckon by this, I don't owe yall no money. Well, the feller who was drunk turned out not to be so drunk after all, 'cause he come up with his long, long forty-four and laid it on the table and said, I drinks but I ain't so drunk I can't count. The way *we* reckon (and he pat his forty-four), *we* believes you owe us two dollars each, what come to six dollars, which is when Robert stand up like he reaching in his pocket and before he could come out with his pocket knife, Robert Jr. had done come up with a little thirty-two derringer and laid it on the table, well by then the juke man, he soft talking now and explaining about maybe there was a little misunderstanding and he reach in his pocket and put some bills on the table and end up laying down seven and thanking the band for a good night of music. They left St. Louie that night, hid out in the rail yard 'til a north bound come through. That's the kind of thing make you disinclined to be too trusting of people, which is kind of why some musicianeers come across as sort of selfish to folk what don't understand the working conditions, and, of course, even with a mean streak and a six-shooter, there still ain't no guarantee you gon get all you supposed to get, in fact, the guarantee be that you ain't going to get what all you owed 'cause they start off short changing you from the jump, which all if you think about it, will lead you to drinking, or leastwise lead you to more drinking ('cause you already drinking if you making music) like Robert was drinking at the moment. He through playing, he ain't got nobody to go with, he don't know nobody in the juke, he never been up in this area before, so what else he got to do but make music and drink, and he through making music for the night.

Finally, Robert make up his mind he going to leave Callie soon. But it wasn't soon like the next day or nothing, in fact, Robert ended up going up to Clarksdale with her—he shouldn't never have carried her with him up to Clarksdale, should of left her in Hazelhurst, but she cried and shit, we married now, so what that mean, that's what Robert told her, and she saying it mean where you go is where I go. Callie ain't knowed him like that. Robert don't never take anybody everywhere he go. Nobody. Only Robert know everywhere Robert go, and he done forgot some of them places long time ago.

Anyway, Robert had started to drinking heavy and was gradually making up his mind to leave that very minute, just pick up his guitar and walk on down the road, see if she could follow him with them three kids in tow what with it being between midnight and daybreak and the kids sleeping, shit, he could be gone before she could even wake all three of them up, besides they wasn't none of his.

Robert was tired of Hazelhurst and Martinsville. The money was ok, but money weren't everything. They had money every place else, besides he weren't going to never get knowed good if he didn't travel round so folk could see him. The only other way was to get on the radio or make some platters, but it was hard for colored to get on the radio regular and most of them platters was hard to make since the depression come, wasn't like back in the twenties when lots of peoples was making platters and record companies was recording everybody they could find.

"Robert, I goes where you goes, but I thinks we do better here than up in the delta. Up there cotton fetch ten cents a pound, pork chop cost forty-five cents, we can't eat good up there as we eats down here, but if you think it best, I guess we can tough it out."

Womens never understand if you stay in one place, ain't nobody going to pay no nevermind to you. Everybody want to hear somebody from some place else, don't nobody want to listen to somebody they can hear all the time. Home always take you for granted, but see when you be passing through, people pick up on you 'cause they don't never know if they get a chance to hear you again. Which is another reason to drink, to fight off the loneliness of being unknown, ain't no drunk worser than a taken-for-granted musicianeer.

"Robert, you hear me, I intends to stick with you, where-so-ever you go, I'ma go with you."

Robert look away from Callie, she think she making him feel good insisting on being with him and bringing three children with her. She think he feel good about that? She think that make him want to stay with her? That's like offering a runaway a ball and chain to carry. Robert could climb out the window right now, at least he feel like leaving quickest way possible and Callie saying she going to go with him just make him want to leave when she ain't looking.

"Come on to bed, Robert, I can make you feel like staying."

How come a woman think she the only one got a pussy?

"Robert?"

Don't she know the only reason she seen him in the first place is 'cause he was on the road traveling from place to place, if he'd a stayed up in Robinsonville, she never would have seen him no way, so now that she seen him he supposed to stop traveling. Traveling is by what he come and traveling going to be by what he goes.

"Robert, why you sitting in there looking at the wall?"

In his mind Robert know why he looking at the wall. He looking at the wall 'cause he used to looking at walls and at the side of a number ten tub when he was a baby and Julia put him in the empty tub when she go out working and Carrie the only one would pick him up if he cry, but she weren't hardly much, much bigger than Robert, but she would try to help him. Robert spent a lot of time looking at walls. When you drinking, a wall can be interesting. A wall can tell you things. Can tell you what your pappy look like. A wall. A wall with no windows and no door and you got to bust through it to get outside. Mississippi was a wall, if you inside it, it smother you, give you the heebie jeebies, make you want to leave it far, far behind, but if you leave it then you don't never see no wall look like it and you miss your wall. Robert love him some Mississippi wall, he just don't like looking at just one spot on the wall. The wall got a north. The wall got a south. A east, a west.

"Robert, I hate it when you don't say nothing when I'm talking to you."

Robert hate it when Callie don't be saying nothing when she talking to him. Sometime he sit at the table, put his head down and sleep off the pay he drunk. And in the morning find himself in bed, all undressed and everything. Callie must of put him to bed. And when he wake up, she have food waiting for him, he ain't even got to get up, hardly, except to swing his feet down to the floor so he can sit on the edge and use the night bucket, and then Callie come and take the bucket out, and he swing his feet back in bed and go back to sleep. And while he sleep she wash his clothes, and clean his shoes, and dust off his hat.

"Catfish and grits Robert, you wants eggs with that?"

Sometimes Robert don't never get up while the sun shining. He sleep and he dream, and when he wake up, he turn over and think about his music, call for Callie to bring his guitar if a song come to him.

"Here your Stella is."

Callie really do love Robert, but love don't stop the walls from closing in. Pretty soon the whole town feel like a cemetery, feel like he buried alive, living in a graveyard. Especially when he drinking.

The longer Robert stay someplace, the more he start drinking to forget he staying, but generally he don't drink too much, 'cause he don't stay too much, but he been down here a long time and he thinking about Clarksdale, about Vicksburg, about Greenwood, about maybe even going back to Robinsonville, see his folks, maybe even go see Carrie in Memphis, really, he want to go to Louisiana but he sort of scared to go down there. He need to go to Louisiana. The moonshine talk him out of going. Ike don't teach him nothing no more. There's only so much good time to be had here. He like dancing with Callie, but they can dance somewhere else, any place else. They ain't got to dance here.

Robert know if he go north, he ain't going to go back down to Louisiana. Why he scared to go? Womens go down there and don't never come back. You don't never hear from them no more. Robert ain't never been outside Mississippi. He love Mississippi. Later he would travel all over, but right now the moonshine is better, and he making it alright here. Can't make no platters here though. Can't get on no radio here.

Ike say go.

Callie say stay.

On one day, the bottle say go, on another day, the bottle say stay. The wall don't say nothing. Damn, them kids getting big and starting to call him daddy, but he ain't they daddy. He ain't nobody da… No, wait, yeah, he is. Vergie say Claud his baby. That make Robert drink more. Vergie don't say much of nothing to Robert no more, but Robert know Vergie want him to stay. Robert drink some more. How he going to stay here with Callie and her three and same time be with Vergie and Claud, who she say is Robert baby, how he gon stay with two families in one place? Shit, that's what Spencer done. Robert he hate Spencer. So why he doing what Spencer done? Hate is a powerful attraction. So is Callie supposed to be Julia or is Vergie supposed to be Julia?

Why Vergie name had to be Vergie? She could of been Sue, she could have been Jane. She ain't Ginny, so why she got to be Vergie? Is that why he fuck her? Is that why he make her pregnant? Now Vergie done had a baby. If it was his baby, why she ain't called it Robert, Jr. His daddy name must be Claud. He ain't none of Robert baby.

Everytime he stop drinking, he hear Louisiana calling. But he also hear Callie and hear Vergie, and all them children. And them same songs.

He making enough money to live, but he ain't going no where. He singing the same songs. He ain't going no where. He ain't making no platters. Ain't no radio place for him to even try to get to.

Suppose he can't find them two-heads. He can't expect to just walk up on them. How you ask for them two-heads? That's like a deacon asking for Jesus—hey, man, you seen Jesus?

Money ain't everything.

One night when Robert had truly drink up all his pay and his pockets was empty, Robert he come stumbling home and he hear two things. He hear that hoot owl and he hear that night train. Owl. Train. He hear 'em, even though he kinda drunk, sort of, he still can hear, even if he can't hardly walk.

Robert sit down a minute, right in the middle of the road. He sit down. He tired of not living in one place and not walking from place to place. If he was walking he wouldn't be tired. He wouldn't be drunk. If he was walking he wouldn't be sitting here in the middle of the way. He sitting in his own way. Robert would crawl home but he can't carry his guitar and crawl at the same time.

Home? Why he call where he staying at now, why he call that home? Hazelhurst ain't his home. Hazlehurst just where he was born. Even when he had Ginny, that wasn't his home, that was Bessie and Granville place. Home? Robert ain't never had no home. He can't crawl home. Even if he ain't had the guitar to carry. Robert couldn't crawl home 'cause he ain't never, never had a home.

The train sound like it crying. Sound like it lonely. Sound like it saying, I'm lonely Robert, come with me. I carry you. All you got to do, Robert, is jump on me and ride. Ride. I'm lonely, Robert. Them other mens don't mean nothing to me, I just takes them on whilst I'm waiting for you. Come to me, please. Come on. Robert. I'll take you places. Louisiana. Wherever. I'm lonely. Robeeeeeerrrrrrttttttt.

It's a foolish man what believe a train.

Now that damn owl is laughing at Robert. You just an old, drunk ass, guitar player what can't play nothing new, ain't doing nothing but collecting pennies, making babies and fucking women, that's all you doing. Dessie was right. You just like them other mens. When you die you ain't going never have existed. Won't nobody even call your name. You ain't no musicianeer. You's a nigger. A Mississippi nigger. That's why your ass drunk. That's why you sitting in the middle of the road, scared to go home, scared to go to Louisiana. Scared. You's a scared nigger. Is all. Shit, even Wille Brown made a platter. You think you better than Willie Brown. You think you play better than him? Huh, nigger? Huh, Hazelhurst, nigger?

Admit you a nigger, nigger!

The hoot owl talking to you, asking you "who" you? Who you is? Who? Who?

-16-

WHAT LED ROBERT TO WANT TO FIND THE TWO-HEADED PEOPLE WAS NOT JUST THE music, there was also Robert's fascination with women, and the rumor was them two-headeds knew all sorts of secrets about womens and whatnot, about fucking, about talking to womens, about making it so that nobody could resist you and nobody could harm you, some even said once you became two-headed (how-so-ever that process go), but once you achieve that state then nobody could ever fix you or bring no harm to you, and you would live as long as you wanted to live.

The living forever part was not the real interest for Robert, he ain't had but two deep interests in life: music and women, and though he do enjoy the both of them to the highest, he really don't understand womens no where near as good as he understand the music, or at least think he understand the music, 'cause when he really think on it, there be music he don't understand either, but he understand songs way more than he understand women, he know that, and he want to understand, he really do, he want to understand why he love music so and why he love women so.

Music and women just seem so powerful to him, and the conclusion, or really the position, that Robert had come to to tell the difference between his two loves was that he could make music but he didn't know diddley about what all it take to make a woman.

His mama had eleven children. His first wife couldn't even have one. His second wife had three children for somebody else and for Robert she had none. Vergie, who he mated up with round the same time he married Cassie, Vergie gave him one son. Which all do not even take into consideration women like Dessie or Wilma Mae (who you has not yet met). Or you remember that poor, confused child Eula Jean? And don't forget Sweetwater, and the many more whose names were mere moments, some of them not even seconds, on the watchface of Robert's life.

Still to come was Estella Coleman, Robert Jr.'s mama. Robert would stay hooked up with her for most longer than any of them others. And Carrie, his most beloved half sister, who he loved stronger than most any other. He give Carrie his pictures, all two of them. He send Carrie postcards. He write to her. Why?

And this woman thing is deeper than Robert can even imagine at this point. Some white mens, of that period (and still yet, for that matter) believe that African peoples is feminine, they assign to us what they perceive as a weakness. They figure femaleness is weakness. And that women was made to be conquered by men and that women will harm men, somehow lessen men, hurt men if men let women influence them. Hence their mythology, their Adam and Eve.

What was Eve's great crime? All she did was offer Adam a chance to know life and who did Eve listen to? She listen to the snake, or so they say. The serpent. They say Eve disobey God, but was not this God she supposedly disobeyed, was not this God-the father, the male principal? So when a woman don't do what a man say do, then she evil?

Robert did not know about all of that. Of course, when he was a child he had heard the word, been up in churches, read the Bible and all. But this women thing was deeper than just going along with white men and Christians. In his bones Robert was revolting the best way he knew how, he was walking. Walking away from everything they told him, everything they was doing to hold him down, except there is good in everything, there is even good inside evil, and vice versa.

Robert had been using arithmetic but figuring up required some calculus, some understanding of algorithms and negative numbers, differentials and integrals, this was a bit beyond ten fingers and ten toes, which didn't meant that Robert couldn't get with it, it just meant until he was taught it, what was required to fully deconstruct and reconstruct his situation was not within his grasp. Still yet, Robert's beauty that he was steady reaching, intuitively understanding that there was something else out there for him other than the madness of Mississippi, the dumbing down that was the general order of his day, the using you up and throwing you away like you was a chicken bone after all the meat gone.

And vice versa, Robert's ugly side was that the Robert who was reaching for something more, something different was also the Robert who had been shaped by the very thing he was trying to escape, so while

Robert was searching for a different kind of future, in his searching he was carrying a yesterday that sometimes made him exactly like what he was striving to put behind him. The complexity of the issue is what makes cynics out of a lot people, even when they don't know what cynicism is or know that they themselves are exemplifying a general disbelief in the ability of folks to be better than they usually are.

Plus, no matter how sad the situation, it is not a good thing to reject everything, or even to reject the whole of a thing because part of the thing ain't right, in fact, what is right anyway? Action got to be separated from essence, what you do with what you is, but being and doing is different even though you become what you do, still your essence do matter. Or some such as that, is what some believe. See right now, it was all jumbled up in Robert's head, which is why he had to get with the two-heads so they could give him some way to think on these matters without falling in with the cynics, so he could understand that virtue was a striving and not nothing fixed for all time.

But this all becomes too complicated to figure out in one lifetime, especially one black Mississippi lifetime.

All Robert know is that women is not only necessary for life, they is essential to being a human being.

Robert ain't knowed nothing about all fetuses starting life as female and some of them getting washed over with testosterone in the womb and thereby becoming male. He ain't knowed he started life as a female. Ahh, but what Robert had, was an inclination, an inclination he ain't understood but an inclination he nevertheless could not deny, an inclination to cleave to womanhood. Robert had no way to think on all of this, no words, no ideas to help him figure has way through the thicket, and it was this inclination that was impelling him to search out for something he didn't even know whether it really exist.

Like something you hear when you walking by yourself down the road. You don't see nothing but road and fields, earth and sky, birds and four-leggeds, and what not. You walking along and you hear a sound, and it don't be the sound of your mind thinking, you know what your mind sound like inside your head when you thinking, so it don't be that voice you hear, it be another voice. Where that voice come from? Do it come from inside you or do it come from outside you?

At that moment Callie come in the bedroom and sit the tray of food on the empty side of the bed. So Robert shove away all them thoughts he wondering about things he don't understand, which is sort of interesting you know: a delta blues musician contemplating the philosophy of cynicism in 1931.

"Where you going, baby?"

Callie turn around at the door and look back at Robert, she pause but she don't say nothing.

"Crack the shutter. I can't hardly see."

Callie goes and throws the shutter open. The wind blow the little piece of light cotton serving as a curtain and the blue cloth dance back and forth in the breeze. Sunshine spill into the room like a puppy playing in the back yard. Moving back to the door after leaving the window, Callie figure Robert must be planning on getting up soon. He look so pretty laying in the bed with all that sunshine snuggling all around him. Callie smile. She can't help smiling. What woman wouldn't smile to have Robert Johnson all up in *their* bed.

"Callie, I been thinking," and he bite into the pork chop—at least once a week she try to feed him pork chop for breakfast, especially on a Saturday morning when he going to be juking later on and probably will be doing plenty drinking before he really eat again. Callie hear her babies—all three of them walking now, Robert get after her for calling them babies, he say they eat almost much as he do, anyway, Callie hear the children laughing and messing around and all, while they eating they grits in the bowl. She had poured the pork chop grease with some fried onion on top they grits and they was delighted to be having such a special breakfast, and, God, she wish things could stay like this.

Callie waited patiently for Robert to stop chewing and finish what he had started to say.

Robert sucked his teeth. Callie know that mean he really enjoying the food. Good. Now he sucking on the bone. Callie knowed she had seasoned them chops good, salt and black pepper and them sweet red onions and she had cooked them slow so all the flavor could seep into the bone so when you suck the juice out the bone it be savory. Robert sucked his teeth again and waved the pork chop bone at her.

"Callie, I gots to admit, I think you right about stuff being sweet here and all, but I still believes I got to go back up country, Jackson maybe, or I was thinking Clarksdale, on account of I can't get to make no platters down here and I powerful want to make me some platters, so, what I'm thinking is maybe in three, four weeks or so, if you of a mind to, we head on up the highway."

Callie heart flip over a couple of times and she smile brighter than that morning sun streaming through the window.

"Robert, when you ready, we ready."

Robert teeth-sucked again.

"Yeah, I believes so. I believes that's what we do."

Robert turned his attention back to the pork chop and the last of the scrambled eggs. Callie turns away too 'cause she hears her children tumbling about, they must be through eating, but before she can fully leave the room, Robert calls to her again.

"Callie, baby?"

"What, Robert."

"You feel like dancing?"

Callie does not immediately turn back around when she hear his question. She hold her breath and close her eyes. Could he really mean he want her to go juking with him tonight? Callie sort of put her hands together almost in a praying way, well, really she do pray in her mind, say, please, Lord, let that be what Robert be saying, and then she interlace her fingers and kind of rub her hands against each other sort of anxious like, God, she sure hope he want her to go dancing while he playing. They been arguing so much the last week or two, well not really arguing and not a lot, just sort of at odds with each other about little things, and she could see that he sort of getting restless, and she sorry she ever said anything against traveling on up to the delta, indeed, when she had first give out her words contradicting his, she had knew she had made a grave mistake, and for the last four or five days she had tossed and turned whenever he was gone, never sure he weren't really gone, that he had not taken off and she would never see him again. And how long had it been since they went dancing? Two weeks and six days—of course, Callie knew exactly how long it had been since they danced together last.

Oh, to dance with Robert. That was how Callie had won him over in the first place. She knew she wasn't the best looker and she sure wasn't the youngest, but she could dance.

Instantly, in her mind, Callie journey back to the juke for that first coming together. He was playing and she was dancing, but she weren't dancing for him or nothing, she was just dancing, in fact she was behind him, but she was dancing so good and he was playing so good, and the gooder he played, the gooder she danced, and the crowd took to urging the both of them on, hollering at her and hollering at him, and she remember when he change the song up and she just flowed with the change, and she peek over at him and see him putting the eye on her and playing little rhythm figures and her responding to every figure he make. He hit a chord, she hunch her shoulders, he do a little run, she switch her hips side to side, right in time, he holler "whoa," she bend at the waist and stick her butt out, he go to singing about shake it, she show him what shaking really is, and by then everybody was clapping and look like everybody done stop doing whatever they was doing to pay attention to Callie dancing to Robert's playing.

Callie remembered it. Lord, how could she ever forget. Even the young girls stood in a circle clapping and keeping time and laughing. And then Robert, he stood up in front of her and went to playing real hard trying to shake her, but at that time he don't know Callie, he don't know how Callie was the dancing-est somebody in all of Hazelhurst. He might can play gooder than most them other songsters, but wasn't nothing he could play that Callie couldn't dance to. He tried but he couldn't lose her, her hound was following his hare which ever twisting way it choose to go.

Standing in their bedroom door, her back to Robert, just like her back had been to him in the juke, standing there now, Callie felt like she was back in that juke when Robert had stood up and started to hollering at her, getting happy behind how she was shaking, and everybody was clapping and laughing and shouting, and Callie was just plain a dancing fool that night. A teetotal dancing somebody and then came the moment Callie never in life would forget, Robert stop strumming his guitar and reach into his pocket and pull out his harp. Robert start into blowing his harp and dancing with her. And, Lord, such a loud merriment went up from the juke. And Callie ain't never seen no man dance up in a juke good as Robert danced. He small, he light on his feet, and he steady blowing that harp, and seem like the whole floor was shaking on the beat because by now peoples was stomping time with their boot heels and such. And, oh, my Lord, by then Callie had her pride on the line. She ain't had never been out danced, not by nobody in, around or passing through Hazelhurst. Everybody knowed Callie was top shelf dancer. And now it was Callie facing the new songster in town. Who was going to take down who?

Robert, he was good. Callie remembers how she had to dig deep. She was used to winning but there was a new horse on the track now and she had to run extra hard to stay up with him. She never been challenged like the way Robert had challenged her. Callie closed her eyes, savoring the rememberance of that first dance with Robert. She almost beat him that night. In fact she did beat him, 'cause he pull up to a stop first. She had done caught her second and third wind and was prepared to dance until she drop dead. She had been convicted, she was not going to let him out dance her that night. You know when you good at something, really, really good and you run up on somebody else who good, and you got your whole reputation on the line, and this the onliest thing in the whole wide world you really good at, well, you know how when such a butting of heads happen, you make up your mind you going to win or die trying, period, bottom of the sack, that's just the way it was going to be. When Callie put her mind to it, there weren't nothing she couldn't do when she was doing something she knew how to do.

Robert, he was good. He twirl, he dip, he cross his feets. He shake, he shimmy, he buck and wing. But everything he done, Callie she did and more. Did back at him and then added a step or a slide or a shake for him to think on. Robert got serious, he stopped blowing his harp and just concentrate on his dancing. By then everybody standing in the circle hooting and hollering, most of the mens was rooting for Robert but was dreaming of being laid up somewhere with Calllie and having her shake like that with them, and all the womens was doing the same thing, rooting for Callie but wanting to lay up with that little man who could move like that, or at least that's the way it had seemed like it was to the best of Callie's recollection. Most everybody do that when they see somebody who can really dance, most everybody want to be loving on such a body, that's only natural, especially if the body you desiring can really, really shake that thing.

Robert, he was real good, but he done met his match when Callie kept on stepping to him, not backing up an inch, not even when Robert he squat down low, prop his hands on his knees and be like a bulldog jumping a poodle. A lesser woman might a quit right then and there, but Robert ain't knowed who he was juking with. Callie, she had something for him. Without so much as a second thought or a bit of hesitation, Callie had throwed her leg up atop the table next to Robert, planted her heel on the table edge, bit her bottom lip, let her eyes drift skyward, and went to sucking in air, uh, uh, while her hips was gyrating in a wobbly circle, her skirt hiked up past her knees. She ain't' cared who saw her bloomers, they was clean, damp, but clean, which is when Robert had throwed his hands up, shouting to her bouncing bosom, "you too much for me, mama, I gives it all to you, you got it," and he slip his harp down her top up between her breasts and walked back to where his guitar was, picked up the guitar, sat down, took his hat off and started in to using his black hat to fan himself like he was too through.

Could this be true? Callie was almost scared to respond to Robert's question about dancing, less she spook Robert with her enthusiasm, so she tried to be calm as she turned to face him.

Although she was trying to be extra careful, still her personality was such that her being careful was like another body being bold. Callie unconsciously lifted her hands and put one hand on a plump hip and with the other hand gripped her apron front just above the knee, "Robert, you knows I loves to dance."

In fact that was the self same thing she had said to him that night in the juke when she had handed him his harp back. The little instrument was still warm from his hot breath and had felt like a sun-warmed shirt nestled up close to her skin.

Robert, he stood in that juke and stared her up and down, literally, started with her eyes, and worked his way all the way down to her feet and then back up slowly, looking hard at her, and she had stood there and felt him look at her, and felt everybody looking at him looking at her, and, of course, felt all them sideways stares from friends and them that didn't known no more than that she had just out-danced that new guitar player and now was standing there bold as Cuff, and all the peoples was waiting to see how Callie was going to handle up to the pressure of being examined all up in the public juke spot. Some peoples was waiting for her to break or at least bend, but that was them what ain't knowed her, they thought she was a willow but she was a fully growed oak and she did not flinched or nothing, just withstood all them stares, gloried in it even, pushed her breasts forward, spread her legs a little, took a fighting stance, and then firmly put her hands on her solid hips. Since he had wanted to look, she had gave him two eye fulls to look upon.

"Baby, I don't knows your name, but I sure loves your dance." Robert tipped his hat and complemented Callie while simultaneously wondering whether she could dance as good laying down as she had just done on her feet.

"I loves to dance," she said, her hands still planted on her hips.

"Is that right?" Robert replied while staring at Callie with as raw a display of lust as he had ever layed on any woman.

"Yeah. Dancing is what I does," Callie was responding as though she was reading his mind. Two husbands, three children, and a double-handful of miscellaneous lovers was more than enough education to enable her to discern what Robert was thinking while he was standing there sort of panting after Callie like a buck ready to rut with a doe, even though Robert, for his part, probably would have said he was just catching his breath from dancing so hard.

Callie knowed she had the upper hand at that moment and, taking special joy in her victory, real prideful like, Callie stood her ground and responded loud enough for all to hear, for all the mens to look upon in google-eyed wonderment and all the womens to have their mouths gape open at the joyful forwardness of this dancing fool, "mister," Callie cooed like as if she was singing an especial song, "and you know what? I'm good too."

"You don't say."

"You just seen me, ain't you?"

"Yeah, I seen you." Being experienced as he was, Robert had immediately picked up on her invitation and without no hesitation, had lightly reached out for Callie's elbow and guided her toward the door.

"Mama, my name is Robert. They calls me R.L. You most done wore me out. Let's step outside and get us some air while we talks to each other."

And now, many months later, married to him and all, here she was in their little cabin, her eyes shining like new money, her deep voice turtle dove pretty, Callie answering, "Robert, you knows me. You knows I loves to dance. You ain't even much got to ask me none of that."

Robert smiled at Callie as she stood in the doorway, teasing him with her hips. He too remembered that first time, especially that thing of using her hand to call attention to her hip, that stance of leaning back on her left leg, her left hand firmly mated to her hip, her right hand gripping the front of her skirt like she was going to hike it up to step 'cross a ditch or such.

"Reach me my trousers there, baby." Robert said, pointing to the chair next to the door where Callie stood.

When she went to hand the pants to Robert, he put the pork chop bone down on the plate, reached out to her apron and wiped his hands, and as she held the trousers up before him, he retrieved two bits from one of the pockets and offered it to her.

"Gets one of them Edwards girls to watch them young-uns tonight, take them over there, 'cause ain't no telling when we get back and what all we feel like doing when-so-ever we do get back."

-17-

Sometimes Robert wonders did he ever really go to Louisiana. Well, no, not really wonder about Louisiana, 'cause he know he went to Louisiana, played down to Baton Rouge and Bogalousa, and round there and all, but what he wonders about is his hooking up with the two-headeds. Robert wonders, did that really happen.

Sometimes Robert's memory is foggy, like a misty late winter morning when you stand in your backdoor and can't even much see the barn out back. And if you step off into the yard and walk out that way, soon enough, you catch sight of it but once you walk past it and look back, you can barely see it, and if you keep walking out into the fields, the barn disappears, well that's how it was, as more and more days passed, Robert became less and less sure of what had happened. He is certain something happened but is not sure about what that something actually was.

Sometimes Robert is confident he met them, but then again he woke up in an old, empty shack, not even a spider or a roach, or a nothing, just Robert, a dirt floor, four bare walls, and a broke-ass door hanging open. And ever since that moment he is not sure, not really sure, that what he remembered is something he was actually remembering, or whether it was something he dreamed. It all could of been a dream.

How had it started? How does anything you can't really remember start? Memory is essential, but it's unreliable. Robert had been laying up with Callie, in fact he was all up in her, deep in her when it hit him that at that moment he should be some place else, which is a frightening thought to think when you all up inside somebody, and you be knowing it's not them, not the other person, it's you that's the problem.

"Come on, baby."

Had she felt that he wasn't feeling it at that moment, even though he was going through the motions of feeling it?

"Come on."

It was funny that he would think about leaving while he was in the act of trying to come, but that is what had happened.

"Robert, what's wrong?"

Yeah, that is when it had been. Then, when Callie asked what's wrong. When Robert rolled off Callie and lay on his back looking up into the darkness covering them, separating them.

Although she stopped talking after that first question, even in her silence, Robert could clearly hear her many questions.

It was a most unsettling moment for the both of them as Callie lay there respecting whatever it was that was happening with Robert that had him not staying hard even while he was all up in her.

Callie is nobody's play thing, nobody's girl child who just getting used to being with mens. Callie know men. She knows that when a man like Robert gets tired of doing it, well then it wouldn't be long before he be gone and, of course, that made her sad, and full of a deep fear that she would not be able to go through this loosing-a-man thing again—she had been hurted up too many times before. She was thirty, old, almost too old for twenty-year-old Robert, yes, this was the last go round, or at least it felt like the last go round, felt like *do or die*, a real do or die, not no just saying it like it's just a saying but saying it like it was fate, like that's the way it was going to be: she was going to do this or die, was going to hold on to Robert or else let go of life.

So even though there was no crying, no deep anxiety up in her voice, even though she were caressing his chest, her voice real soft and low like as if she was telling him how much he move her, even though one of them platter making machines would have only picked up a turtle dovey-dove sound issuing from her, and even though Robert was so preoccupied with his own torments at that particular moment that how she said what she said did not register, and for that matter what she said hardly seeped into Robert's awareness, even though Callie's mouth was right up next to his, right where she had just kissed his cheek in a reassuring way when she asked "what's wrong?", even though all of that, still and all it was a long time quiet, like spitting down a dry well, you drop a rock in it and you don't even hear no plop, not even no sound of it hitting bottom, you don't hear nothing. Nothing. For a long time after Callie asked her not-so-innocent question, she didn't hear no answer.

Of course, very, very few men will outright tell a woman what's wrong when she ask him what's wrong, especially if she ask him that while they was trying to fuck and it wasn't going right. Men is sensitive about that, about how they do what they do with a woman. Real sensitive. And even though Callie was aware of that, aware that if it wasn't happening in bed, it was going to be hard for it to be happening out of bed. Not for her, but hard for him. Women used to making do in bed, but men, especial a man like Robert, who done had plenty women, plenty experience, well, he liable to base his satisfaction mainly on how the loving going.

Therefore, like a many woman who desperately want to hold on to her man, Callie was willing to do anything to keep Robert. Anything. What made the whole thing so horrible was the secret fear worming all inside Callie, the fear that somebody done fixed her, done made it so wouldn't no man ever stay with her. Don't care what she did. Don't care how she treated him. She could clean, cook and give him all the nookie in the world, it wouldn't matter. Nothing would matter if she been hoodooed.

It had to be hoodoo, 'cause if it weren't hoodoo, it meant Callie naturally weren't worth shit. Not nobody, nobody at all, likes feeling worthless, which is how she felt in the dark of their bed. Felt like she was laying on the tracks waiting for the 3:19 to come along and end it.

"Callie, you treats me as good as any woman could take care of any man. Better, I do believe, better 'cause you understand I'm a musicianeer, and you takes near as much pride in it as I does."

Robert stops talking. Callie holds her breath and waits for what Robert going to say next. She know he going to say "but." She pray he don't say "but," but she know he going to say it.

"But...," he pause again. She close her eyes, might as well, she can't see nothing anyway. "Callie, there's something I got to do, someplace I got to go."

"Go where you got to go, Robert." God, how she hated to say that, but she tried to disguise her voice and sound cheerful, sound like she sending him off to pick flowers for her or something. "We be here when you get back," as if there was a coming back in Robert's going away.

Though she mostly used to the dry land of not caring anymore about a particular man, Callie found herself thinking hard on how to cross this swamp of holding-on-to-Robert feelings, being extra watchful for water moccasins, them cotton-mouth snakes would rise up silent out of the water and bite you, most poisonous as a rattler except they water snakes, and they be waiting in the low water for you to come along trying to make it to wherever you trying to make it to, and you don't be meaning to disturb no snake, but just being out in that swamp you do disturb the snakes 'cause the snakes live in the swamp and you just passing through, just trying to go in through they front door and hoping to make it out the back.

Hell, they were at the critical days immediately following the second week, usually two weeks was the extent of a casual thing. Robert was going on four weeks now and Callie had started back to church, praying and what not for Robert to stay, which most of the church folk looked askance at her the first Sunday she showed up on account of Callie having already had two husbands, and got them three kids and no daddy, and now laying up with a blues playing sinner, but Callie she know what she feel, and she know what she know, and she feel like God know her better than she know herself 'cause he made her, and therefore God, he must know how awful much this Robert man mean to her, and so she prayed her deepest prayer, and just like she was willing to do anything to keep Robert, she was also willing to promise God anything if he would fix it so that Robert stay, which is what some of them too righteous folk was all tight-faced about: Callie praying to God to fix it so she could keep on living with a stone fornicator. Which is when God gave Callie an answer she was not ready to hear but which she heard loud and clear: if you want a man bad enough and he want you back, then you should be married, otherwise you wouldn't be nothing but a fattened frog up in the mouth of an evil snake, and you surely would burn in hell on account of it—the hell part did not really bother Callie, she weren't even sure there was a hell—well, there was a hell 'cause this life was hell, she wasn't sure there was no eternal brimstone and fire and such after you died, wouldn't no real God send you through Mississippi and then send you to hell, that would be what they call that double jealousy stuff, how can you be tried twice for the same crime of having to live once—no, what bothered her was the other part, the part that went: have him right or don't have him at all. Of course Callie ain't never mentioned none of this to Robert.

But was this what Robert was feeling when he was up in her and went soft even though he ain't shot off yet? Was Robert touching on a resolve

Callie was wrestling with: how in the world was she going to get Robert to marry her? Can a man feel when a woman be thinking on wanting to get hitched up? Was this what was wrong?

No, Callie wanting Robert to stay was not wrong.

Robert wanting to go was not wrong.

What was wrong was they was at a crossroads, meeting up for a minute but heading in different directions.

And in truth there was something else wrong, something that neither one of them could see at that moment, something further on down the line that kind of hog tied their futures.

But before their marriage ran its full course, they had to be raised up high so they could be dashed all the way down.

And then once they had rejoiced up high and despaired down low, that's when the marriage would meet its end and it would be so twisted up, you could not tell whose fate was more terrible—the one who survived or the one who died.

The way it happened was Robert, he did come back, and when he come back, he come back fundamentally changed for all time.

When Callie got home, Mary, her oldest, told her, "Mr. Robert up in your bed, sleep. You know that guitar man."

Callie kissed the bearer of good news that evening, kissed the child plop, right in the middle of her forehead. Callie could barely contain herself as she crept into the dim light of her darkened room, her one and only sanctuary, the spot where all three of her children knew never ever in life to go up in unless Callie told them "come in," especial not to go up in there if Callie weren't there, and all it took was one severe ass-whipping to convince little Mary to respect Callie's private space and to keep the other two from roaming in there, anyway when Callie crept up in there, she stood in the doorway, leaned up against the sill and just peered down upon Robert fast asleep in her bed, resting on his side all curled up, more like a child than a fully-growed man. Callie slumped against that sill, dropped her bag and just looked there upon, and big old, silent tears rolled down her face.

She closed her eyes for a brief spell and then blinked two or three times while wiping her eyes with the back of her hand, and each time she did so, when she finished blinking, finished wiping, finished closing her eyes and thanking God, when she finished any of that, all of that, Robert was still there soundly asleep.

God had done his part and brought Robert back, now it was time for Callie to do her part and get Robert to marry her. Callie gathered herself up. She did not go further into the room. She just back out the doorway, ran up in the kitchen, reach down the tin from the top shelf, picked out some coins, and sent Mary off to get some syrup and a little bit of butter. All she had in the house was an old bonnet full of pecans, a big bag of cornmeal, some fatback, and a pot of rice that Mary had already set to cooking.

"Mary. Mary."

"Yes mam," the child answered. Mary was already down the steps, almost gone.

"Here another quarter, fetch some coffee. Grind it up yourself."

"Yes, mam." After dashing back up the steps to get the extra money, Mary spun back around and skipped off, singing a little play song to herself. Mary loved cornbread with pecans in it, especial with dark corn syrup running all over it. Yeah, huh. Cornbread. Cornbread. Cornbread with pecans and syrup.

Callie had made a quick decision. She had them pecans up in there. She was going to make the sweetest cornbread Robert Johnson done ever put up in his mouth. Slow cooked cornbread with pecans in it, with some Karo on top, and some steaming fresh coffee. That was going to be the desert to the onion-smothered fatback and rice she had already planned to serve for dinner.

Before she knew it, Callie was dancing round the kitchen, humming "Shake 'Em On Down."

The children was fed and sleep before Robert woke up. Callie was sitting to the table, her head down. Really she was half sleep too, when Robert ease up long side her. The smell of coffee wafting up from his cup roused Callie. When she rear up, Robert smile at her.

"Callie, I got something I got to tell you."

He sounded so serious, she was sure it was nothing nice. Couldn't it wait until in the morning, let her at least have this short moment of full out joy without it being all marred and marked up by whatever serious something Robert had to say, surely he had not come back to announce to her he was leaving, but what else could it be?

"Callie, my music is all I got." And then he pause to take a slow sip of coffee.

Callie couldn't resist correcting Robert. She mumbled, "you got me."

You got me, was she a treasure or a torment to him?

"Well, that's what all I'm trying to get to saying to you."

Callie reach up and wipe back that one tear trying to jump out of her left eye.

"I done decided…"

Callie held her breath. Why didn't he just come on out with it, all at one time? Why he was drawing it out like a cat birthing nine kittens?

"What, Robert? What you done decided?"

This was just like Robert, gone for a week and two days, come back, go to sleep and wake up talking about what he done decided without even so much as a hello, or I'm home, or nothing. Supposed she had decided some things too, some things that didn't include whatever all Robert had decided? Callie fought back the urge to get angry. Sometimes it was best to hunker down and ride it out rather than to rise up and get blowed away.

"Callie, I done decided, I got to make serious about my music. I done learnt everything from Ike. I been down to Louisiana and learned that my music ain't nothing to play with."

Was this all that Robert was so serious about? Callie already knew Robert care for music more than anything. This was not new. This was not something he just decided, no matter that's what he saying, the truth is he was dedicated to music long before he come down to Hazelhurst.

"And, I…"

Callie knew there had to be something else.

"I… well, I done learned the importance of going back home with what brung me to the dance."

Callie had to wipe that leaking left eye again. She had to force herself to be quiet, to listen for the end before she judge the middle, but still and all, it sounded like he was saying he going to keep on dancing with her. That's how she got him, that's how she was going to keep him, by dancing to his music, what-so-ever he play, she'd figure out how to step with it and keep on dancing.

"Robert, I got some pecan cornbread warm up in the oven and some Karo dark to pour over it."

"You knows me, huh? You knows I likes yellow cake." That's what he calls sweet cornbread—yellow cake. And yes, Callie knows how much he likes it, especially when it's baked like a cake inside the oven instead of cooked top of the stove.

"Robert, I loves you, and I ain't afraid to tell you that or tell anybody else who might want to know how I feels."

"Well, Callie, that's what I'm talking about."

"What?"

"What you said."

"What, Robert?"

"What I'm saying is I been thinking. I been thinking on how you took me in and care for me and give me time to study up under Ike and not have to worry about nothing. I go down to Louisiana and I come back and you ain't mad or nothing. You fix me yellow cake, you don't disturb me whilst I sleep. I knows you love me, knows how strong your love is, and I powerful appreciates all that. You's a kindhearted woman, and what-so-ever come of me, whatever all I gain in this world, part of it is on account of you, and I wants to fix it up so as you never have to worry about that. You know what I'm saying?"

Callie didn't know. All she know is he didn't say *I love you* back to her, but that was alright because at least he say he powerful appreciate her, and that's a long ways down the road toward love.

"I think I know what you're saying, Robert. I think you're saying you likes what all I do for you."

"I'm saying more than likes. I'm saying I wants to make our partnership legal and all, so as you won't never have to worry about nothing between us."

"Legal? What you mean? You don't mean..." Callie wanted him to say it, so she open the window, but he was going to have to wave the flag hisself.

"Callie, you understand. This going to be between me and you. This ain't for the world to worry over."

"Robert, what you saying?"

"I'm saying, we go over to the courthouse and regist our partnership legal like, but it got to be kept between me and you. If something happen to me, you'll have the papers and all, and you get whatever I got. Whatever.

But I wants it just for us to see."

How does one laugh and cry all at the same time. He was willing to marry her, but not willing to tell nobody they married. What kind of marriage was that?

"Callie, I'm leaving it up to you. You can marry me and keep it quiet, or you can not marry me and tell all the whole wide world we ain't married."

And with that Robert stood up, drained the last bit of coffee down his throat, and started slow walking toward the bedroom.

"Come on, baby, we can talk better laying down."

Callie undressed slowly in the darkened room. When she lay down, her stomach was all a jumble. Robert reached out and softly laid his hand on her thigh, she flinched and before she knew it, the words were spilling out almost as a challenge.

"Robert, what you want? What you want with me?"

"I done already told you. I wants us legal and I wants us quiet."

"Why you wants us quiet, Robert?"

"I don't wants people bothering you about what all I be doing when I be away from you. I'm going to be away lots of times. You know that. I know that. I don't want nobody throwing that all up in your face."

Laying flat on her back like she was on a cooling board, Callie wrung her hands in the dark.

"Really, I just wants to pay you back for what all you been doing for me."

"Robert, you don't owe me nothing. I'm doing what I'm doing 'cause I wants to do it, 'cause I love you."

"And I'm doing what I'm doing 'cause I understands what you doing."

He wouldn't say it. It was like he couldn't. Right then, Callie would have settled for a lie, just to hear him say it would have brought satisfaction, even if he took it back later, but for him not to say it at all…well.

In the midst of the silence, it come to her. God done answered her prayer. Robert is back, but the deal was, if they stayed together, it had to be as man and wife, well now he was offering to marry her. Callie knew it would be ungrateful for her to hold out for him telling her he love her and for them to be married all up in the public. God done give her exactly what she bargained for, nothing less, and, unfortunately for Callie, nothing more.

They were married May 1931. By the spring of '32, they move up to Clarksdale. If Callie would have really thought about it, she would have peeped something distressing about Robert. Callie knew about Vergie and Claud, and even if she didn't know if Robert was slipping round to see Vergie and the baby from time to time (he wasn't, but she didn't actually know he wasn't), what Callie did know was that when they moved up to Clarksdale, neither Vergie nor Claud journey up there with them. So if Robert leave his baby and his baby's mama behind, why would he stay with Callie?

It seem like everything he do for her, every gift he give to her come with a ton of torment. She get what she want from him but the cost be so high she find herself sinking under from the weight of somebody who supposed to be rescuing her. She had wanted to go with him to Clarksdale, but now that she was up there, she found herself all alone without nobody she knowed to help her out, and ain't no lonely like the lonely wife of a musicianeer sitting up in some place when he gone and she don't know no one.

She wanted to be married, huh, well now she not only married, she might as well be a widow, he gone so much, so often, so long. She wanted him. She got him. And now even though he there, he stay gone. She wanted to be in the game, well she find out you spend more time in the field and sitting on the bench than you does in the batter box, even though it's the thrill of hitting it that you crave.

And when he there she be trying so hard for everything to be right that she don't get nothing right. All the pecans she brought from Hazelhurst long since gone. The pecans up here in the delta don't taste the same sweet soft like the ones down to Hazlehurst, up here it's all about nothing but cotton plants. Cotton plants. And cotton seeds ain't at all tasty up in no yellow cake.

And Callie be hating to see little Mary come back from the fields, her fingers all pricked up from pulling at them cotton bolls, her little legs all scratched up. Sometimes all Callie can do is grab hold to her little brood, hug them all to her bosom and pray for better times. Pray. That's all she can do, especially when Callie start to feel poorly herself, a couple of days too feeble to head out in them fields. Where Robert? It's been seventeen days this time. Where Robert? Two weeks gone. Where Robert? A whole month, thirty-eight days since she seen him. Where Robert? Where Robert? Robert, where you is?

He always come back with a pocket full of money, full of coins. But it don't last. No matter how much he bring, whatever number it be, the money always run out after he leave and before he get back. Callie she try putting something by for when he gone, but soon as provisions running low and she let him know, he say he going to go out and earn some more, which mean he going to go off somewhere again, and it just start (cough), it just start (she cough again, coughing more regular now), the grinding start over and over again. And the light going out in the children's eyes. Mary don't smile no more. Never skips or plays or dances... dances? When was the last time Callie dance. Robert don't even play no more when he home. Home?

Callie finding out the hard way, a musicianeer ain't got no home. So what that make a musicianeer wife? Huh, Robert? What that make me when you gone? Don't nobody care about no musicianeer's kept woman. Especially not the musicianeer. Huh, Robert? If you didn't love me in Hazelhurst, ain't no way you going to love me in Clarksdale. Huh, Robert?

Callie look around the house sometimes and there ain't nothing in the house, not a goddamn thing (COUGH) to say Robert live here. Nothing. No hat, no shoes, no clothes, no guitar. No nothing. (COUGH) A hound dog could walk up in here and not catch no scent of Robert Lonnie, or Robert Leroy, or whatever-the-hell his name is. (COUGH! COUGH!)

Strangers see Robert more than his wife do. Women he never before seen in life dance with him more than his wife do. What's the use of even trying to hold on, for what? So he can leave again? Hold on so he can go? Be there when he get back so he have some place to leave? Why? What for? What does it gain a woman to marry a man, if he ain't never there?

The delta is no place to be alone. One lonely somebody can not survive that particular corner of purgatory, and that's what it feels like. You works and works. And then you works some more. And some more. Again. You get enough to scrap by but never enough to get ahead. One or two climbs out by stepping on the backs of all who they leave behind. If you ain't got no kin, you ain't got no wind in your sails. You ain't going to make it.

Like you take: what you do when you sick in the delta and ain't no doctor around for miles? And even if a doctor was around, ain't no way to get to him or for him to get to you, unless somebody go fetch him. And even if you get him to come out to where you laid up, you can't pay him to look at you, to poke your stomach and peer down your throat. That's why so many folks be all bent up and broke down in the delta, they been doctoring on theyself, been setting bones wrong, been swallowing goose grease and turpentine to fight off parasites and who know what all viruses. Been praying to God, when what they needed was some medicine, some clean water and sewerage, some un-starchy, un-salty, un-sweetened-up, some nutritious food, some not having to spend twenty-seven years bowing down to cotton plants, which you can't even much eat. Some cuisine other than rabbit, squirrel, coon and possum, when you lucky enough to get that. Something other than the daily unrelenting grind of hard times in the delta.

If you been up in the delta you done seen a thousand Callie's. Colored womens trudging down the road, their young bodies prematurely old, squared-off and made box-like by toil, most all their curves gone or else deeply diminished into crooked outlines, they got that look that cattle standing in the rain got, that sadness of spirit that make it take an extra effort to smile, and when you do smile it be a crooked smile, a tight-lipped smile, not showing the bad teeth, the missing teeth, covering the mouth with hands that ain't been soft since early childhood, early, early, childhood, the grimness, but then too, to be truthful to who all they are, one most recognize that there is a beauty to them also, dirt-caked faces that somehow display a near saintly beauty that soft glows like fireflies in a summer dusk.

And that's it, their beauty is the spirit of survival, the way they scoop up the good moments of their lives like those few minutes was a floppy-earred puppy that you delights in holding, or the way everywhere you go even the roughest field hand will tenderly hug a baby child. The beauty of these Callies is not just in survival but also in how they manage to take scraps and quilt up extraordinary prettied-up moments, an unmatchable and extraordinary loveliness crafted from the will to survive no matter what it take, except for every one that swims on there is two or three others what go under, that break up like a building caught in the flood waters of a river overflow.

Probably, other than her three kids, probably didn't nobody take no special notice when Callie began to splinter and then finally cracked, 'cause down in the delta, when you crack, be you young, old, single man, married woman, whatever, who-so-ever you is and how-so-ever you go over the edge, whether you lept out from a high branch when you just plain got tired of holding on or whether some night riders shoved you over the edge off some high up riverside bluff, it didn't really matter, 'cause when you crack in the delta you, you just another cracked negro.

And from these bending and breaking moments was distilled a proverbial song: you gon need somebody on your bond. Yes. From time to time, we all need somebody to come and see about us, come and provide deliverance.

One night Callie calls back down to Hazlehurst. She has not seen Robert in two months. She don't know where he at, what he doing. Things are desparate for her and her children. Do Robert care? Her health done broke down, could somebody come up and get her? Please? Yes, she know she shouldn't of never left in the first place. Yes, she know Robert weren't no good when she got with him. Of course she lucky she ain't had no more children with him. No, it ain't news to her, she know he got a baby down there in Hazlehurst. Could you just please come get me? She know it be a long, long, long-ass ride up to Clarksdale and they had to find somebody with a car. No she couldn't take a train down, she had too much stuff to carry on a train, besides she would have had to buy four tickets when she ain't even had the money for one. Could someone please come and get her? And send some money. No, Robert don't be sending no money no more. Yes, he should. No, he don't. No, mama I don't know why. Yes, daddy I know no real man would be acting like that. Please come and get me. Please. Please. Come.

Within two years of that phone call Callie is dead and she never told nobody that she and Robert was married. Never. Dead. Who knows what all she died of.

That day she dance with Robert she shoud of never crossed her legs. Should of never shook her shoulders in front of him. Should of slapped him when he shove his harp down in between her breasts. Should of pitched that low-down, little piece of an instrument out the window. But she didn't and now she dead. Not only is she dead, Robert ain't never come see about her, never even come visit the grave. What does it profit a woman to love a man who can't, who don't love her back?

Where was Robert when he find out Callie dead? Might have been over in Greenwood, or was he down in Hazlehurst? Yeah, it was Hazlehurst. The second and last time he saw Claud. No wait, that couldn't be. Claud claim he remember Robert coming to see him when Claud was seven years old. By December 1938 Robert been dead almost six months. Knowing Robert, it is possible that he was still making his rounds from the grave, but more likely it didn't happen the way Claud claims to remember. So who knows?

Robert is just a hazy memory and 29 songs he done recorded, some of them with a second version. Was it worth it? Was Robert music worth Ginny and the baby dying? Was it worth Callie going down slow, and eventually going under? Bobo? Was Robert worth…?

Ginny family hate Robert. Callie people would kill him if they could catch him. Vergie's folk just feel if she stepped in dogshit 'cause she was too dumb to watch where she was stepping, then that's on her, even though they do believe for sure that Robert is some sure enough dogshit.

Robert slip through Hazelhurst and nobody he seen the last time he was there see him this time he there, and by the time folks that used to know him try to catch up with him, Robert gone.

There is plenty people, womens and mens, what would spit on Robert grave, but even that ain't possible 'cause years, years after Robert done passed on, ain't nobody sure where he buried. They got a headstone in one place and a big old monument in another, and nearest some knowledgable folks can figure, Robert probably buried up in a field in a different place altogether.

Which is why folks keep that story going about Robert selling his soul to the devil to play music. Some say it was just a story. Some say it was the whole story. And a few say Robert ain't sold his soul to the devil, 'cause Robert, he was the devil.

Who else but the devil would do some of things Robert done, treats kindhearted people cruel the way Robert done, especially the way he done Callie? Some folk say that one of them first songs he recorded, "Kindhearted Woman," was a song for Callie, but they just talking, 'cause they don't know.

Who knows? Who really knows what Robert thought about all this, how Robert felt about being Robert. Nobody ever heard him even much mention Callie no more. In fact nobody ever knowed Robert was married to Callie—well, the clerk of court know 'cause the marriage liscense was right there in the big book, but hell, what can anyone say? What can be made of Robert and Callie?

Wherever he was when he hear tell about Callie dying, Robert took it as a sign—the hounds of death were still on his trail, still killing up anybody who get close to Robert. Sooner or later them hounds was going to corner Robert. Sooner or later. What else could Robert do, but keep moving, keep on moving? Rain. Shine. Drunk. Sober. Good times. Whatever. Just keep moving. Keep moving. Keep on moving.

-18-

EVERYTHING HE OWN, HE COUD CARRY ON HIS BACK, IN HIS SACK. TWO HATS. A pair of walking shoes. A pair of playing shoes. His guitar, of course. A change of clothes. And that was it. There was literally nothing else he own. When you saw him, you saw all of him, all that he had to his name, all that he had to offer to anyone.

All he really had was music, so if he did make a deal with the devil it cost him far more than his soul. It cost him everything. Two wives, a stillborn baby. A daddy he never knew. It cost him. Who? Who in their right mind would ever want to live with Robert Johnson? Be married to Robert Johnson? Be a child of Robert Johnson? Be Robert Johnson? Who?

1932, just south of the Louisiana-Mississippi border, Robert is walking and thinking, thinking and walking. His health is good—you know how doctors say walking is good for you? Well, that make Robert be in excellent health. Averaging about fifteen miles a day, not including catching a ride here and there in a passing vehicle, or hopping a freight when he wanted to travel a stretch. And he had stamina. Walking in the sun does that for you. Builds up your fortitude. Which is how come Robert can play for so long without a break and not feel in no ways tired. Ain't none of them book trained musicianeers can keep up with Robert, he play them softies 'til they fingers hurt, they tongue be hanging out, and they be talking about they got to get home. Robert laugh.

He play all night and walk all day. Music is his profession, fitness his extra benefit. Walking up and down Mississippi ain't no joke though, besides being fit you gots to be smart, be able to read signs, understand a look, hear a train and know which way it going, see birds perching and know some rain coming, decipher the fear in field hand eyes and recognize that you best keep moving on, and most of all avoid evil white peoples, which is most of them, especially when it's more than two of them in any particular location, 'cause then one of them always trying to prove who the king of the hill is.

Robert don't usually have no trouble with white folks 'cause he avoids them just like he avoids rattle snakes, not that he's comparing white folks to rattle snakes, that's a discredit to the snake, 'cause see if you don't mess with a rattler, it won't mess with you, but you take Mississippi white folks—at this point Robert don't know too much about white folks what ain't from Mississippi, so he can't rightly say how they is, although he willing to give them the benefit of the doubt until he see for his self, of course, Ike swears a Alabamy cracker got a Mississippi peckerwood beat by a country mile when it comes to plain old being mean and onery—but still, you take Mississippi white folks, they some of the meanest spirited creatures what ever walked the face of God's good earth. Up in the delta, Sonny Boy swear to god and all his angels there was a white man what didn't want nothing black on his farm, horse, mule, cow, chicken, whatever, nothing. When they was born if they came out black he would sell or give 'em away if he couldn't sell 'em. Now, that sound like some gallery fat mouthing to Robert, but he did know a man what would shoot crows for sport 'cause he say they screeching remind him of niggers singing and he hate to hear all that racket.

Some people wonder what make white folks like that. Robert don't, just like he don't wonder what make the rain, it's just part of life in Mississippi. Besides if you get all bitter about white folks it will end up turning your whole life sour, 'cause there wasn't nothing you could do about them, and besides they had the upper hand. So Robert tries not to ruminate on no white folks, ain't no win in it. You come to a losing proposition every time you tries to think your way pass their meanness.

Robert can't help for thinking, so what he try to do is direct his thinking onto things he can do something about, which is why he was headed south, feeling good, with a smile on his face. When he saw a red wing black bird light down on a fence post and then, as Robert pass near by, the bird takes off heading south, Robert is relieved and tickled. He know he doing the right thing.

Pretty soon Robert thinking on how the road makes lots of musicianeers kind of sour tempered. Lots of folk don't understand what all it mean not to sleep in the same place, around the same people. Hell, sometimes not to really sleep, not to mention cold ground and rock pillow. But it's either guitar or hoe, walk the lonely highway or be up under some white man command. Pick a tune or pick cotton. Robert know where is heart is, know what his head say is right for him to do, and he smile because he's content with the life he has chosen.

Good health and good disposition. Ain't nobody who knowed Robert, ever thought of him as mean spirited or hard to get along with, in fact most folk found him charming, which accounted for why every stop of any size and respectability had a house with a kitchen, a bed, and a woman Robert was welcomed to share.

When Johnny Shines traveled with Robert he noticed that Robert never chased after the pretty ones or the young ones, most of the ones Robert liked were older than him, some much older, and plainer than him, some even what you might call homely, but Robert he was way ahead of most of the part-time musicianeers, who mostly played around their home area and only traveled occasionally. Robert was never out there chasing after what they call a fling, his tastes ran toward something more substantial notwithstanding that most of his stays were mainly stopovers.

In small doses Robert was a wonderful manly companion for a lonely woman. After Callie no woman got a sustained taste of Robert Johnson, even though there was one nest he frequented more than any other, or more precisely, more than all the others put together, and that weren't even in Mississippi. It was over to Helena, in Arkansas. But that story comes later in the saga, in fact right now Robert is south of, rather than west of, Mississippi.

Yesterday he had mentioned to Callie that he thought he wanted to go see Ike again, but when he got a few miles down the road instead of cutting cross the tracks and making it over to where Zinnerman stayed at, something told Robert to stop putting off what he knew he had to do. He had to go to Louisiana for to get fixed.

Now Robert ain't knowed what all was entailed in getting fixed, or even if he could afford to get fixed—he only had five dollars and change secreted down deep in his sack.

Although every now and then he might take his sack when he hiked over to Ike's place, usually he just took his guitar case, and this time, without even giving it a second thought, he had grabbed his traveling sack and had left twelve dollars under the pillow for Callie. Even though he was not willing to all-the-way open say so, Robert had an inkling that he was going to be out for an indefinite stretch.

Since he ain't never knowed nobody who had been fixed, he couldn't ask nobody how long it took to get fix or how much it cost to get fixed. Maybe he should have only left seven or eight dollars with Callie, after all she had over five dollars in jiggling money up in that tin she keep on the top shelf, and that five plus his twelve that was almost twenty, and on top of that whatever all she made washing and whatnot. Suppose it took more than five dollars to get fixed.

Robert smiled. He always smiled when he was going somewhere. In a way rambling was as much Robert's profession as was musicianeering. Couldn't nobody ramble like Robert. Robert had perfected the art of moving from place to place. Like he had certain habits and regulations he kind of stuck to.

Never roll up in a juke looking tired or raggity.

Don't play in dirty shoes or with dust on your face. Paying peoples don't cotton to supporting tramps.

If one night be good, it's ok to do two, but never three in a row in the same location. Go to a different juke or whatever. When you does more than two in a row, you wears people out and becomes something they get used to—you wants people to remember you, to want to see you, to be looking forward to seeing you again.

Never tell nobody when you leaving—that make 'em come out for you extra 'cause they don't know whether they going to get another chance to see you.

Always play for the dancers, the drinkers don't care what all you play 'cause they ain't listening no way, ah, but the dancers, see the dancers be the ones listening to you, or at least feeling you, and usually where-so-ever you finds dancers, you finds womens, but see them drinkers, they usually be nothing but mens and they'll drink 'til they fall out and won't put a dime in the kitty 'cause they drinking up all their dimes, but you take dancers, if they enjoying your music and kicking up their heels and all, well they want the good timing to continue on so they feed the kitty. Play for the dancers.

Which, of course, circle back and lead Robert mind to dwell upon Callie for a minute. He ain't never met nobody dance good as Callie, especially to his music. He would take her dancing more but when she there he don't do nothing but concentrate on her and that ain't pleasing to everybody else, even though it be most pleasing to Callie, and pleasing to Robert in a selfish sort of way, but he can't afford to be selfish. When he don't pay no attention to everybody else, the kitty starve to death. But lord, lord, lordy lord Callie sure can step.

Now see if she didn't have them three children it would be perfect, which is another reason. And just like she can dance, she sure could shake them sheets. Ike laugh at him one time, "Robert, you'se a kind of good looking young feller, how so come you go for a hen instead of a springer."

"Ike, you ever been up in church?"

"R.L., what you know about church?"

"You know every negro whatever was born up in Mississippi know something about church—church damn near all Mississippi negroes got."

"I hear you fine, but I ain't understanding you none. I ask you about going for old womens and you start to talking about Jesus."

"No, Ike, hear me good. This ain't none about Jesus, this about what you asked about."

"I'm listening, young blood."

"Well you know how them preachers says, the old sheep knows the road, it's the young lambs what got to find the way?"

"Can't say as I has heard that, but that makes sense to me."

"Well, which one you wants up in your bed: an experienced somebody what know the road or a lamb trying to find the way?"

"That depend on how good the lamb look."

"Man, looks ain't got nothing to do with how a woman feel, how she do. I takes a woman what functions over a woman what looks good any day of the week. You can't fuck no looks."

"Yeah, but I don't want to fuck nothing who top looks as ugly as her bottom."

"What you mean ugly? A woman's bottom ain't ugly."

"R.L., you know good and well pussy is ugly. All scrunched up and covered with hair. Look like a prune with moss on it."

"They told me God don't make ugly and I believes that."

"No, R.L., it go, God don't like ugly."

"Ok, but guess what, Ike?"

"What?"

"From what I understand, he ain't too particular about pretty either."

"Pretty! Boy, you trying to say pussy pretty?"

"Ike, I gots to ask you. I know you done been with womens before, but I gots to ask you, you ever look upon pussy?"

Both of the men was grinning so hard, they had difficulties saying what they had to say with a straight face. Mens likes to grin when they talking about fucking women.

"Boy, pussy ain't for looking upon, it's for fucking. You looks upon the face, you fucks the pussy. That's nature."

"So if that's the case, Ike, if you ain't been down there looking upon, how be it you come to judge that pussy is ugly?"

Ike had not answered. Ike knew a lot about playing the guitar but he ain't seem to be so up on womens.

Robert's mind was always working. He didn't know how he had come to the point where he knew so much about women, and maybe it wasn't knowing women such as much as it was that he knew peoples in general. But why was that? Why was it that one person try to understand how another person work and another person don't care how someone work? Which is when Robert realize he can't help from thinking on things, he can't never turn his mind off. It was like he was direct connect to a driving wheel of questions. He wasn't so much on answers, but he had a wagon load of questions.

"Mama, why my daddy don't like me?"

"What you mean, Robert? Dusty likes you a lot, that's why he all the time be trying to tell you right. You know he trying to steer you down…"

"Dusty, ain't none of my daddy. I means Spencer."

Robert was sixteen when he surprised Julia Dodds (now known as Julia Willis) with the intensity of his question. She was not surprised by the question itself, but the way he asked it, like as if it was life or death and he had to know right then and there.

Julia had known for a long time she would have to cross this particular stream what ain't had no bridge, which all meant that she would have to wade hip deep into some treacherous waters. The fact that she knew it was coming did nothing to make it easier to face.

Robert stood in all his angry innocence, asking what he thought was a simple question.

"Robert, sit down."

"What, mama?"

Robert sits and waits, his little hands drumming on top the table, but he fidgeting, his right leg rocking side to side like he got to go relieve himself.

Ain't no simple way to explain why the creek don't run straight, that's just the way water flow. Nature always seeks its own course and that is seldom straight up and down.

Julia kept trying to find the right words but all she could think of was, well, was nothing. No matter what she said Robert was going to take it wrong, was going to think she had intentionally lied to him, like as if she had sent him out back to collect hen's teeth.

"What, mama?"

Julia sniffle and in an instant her life flashes, lightning bolts showing her desperate glimpses of when she did what she had to do, which was things that if she had any kind of choice she wouldn't have never done, but she never had no choices. When necessity and survival mate, the baby liable to be something that will do anything, whatever it takes, and whatever it takes can be mighty ugly.

"Robert..."

"Mama, you..."

Their words collided like two bulls butting up against each other, except they weren't fighting each other, so they both stop, while each one waited for the other, and, of course, what followed was an awful long silence, well, really it was a short silence it just felt awful long.

"Robert, Spencer ain't your pa. Your pa named Noah Johnson."

"I knew it. I knew it. That's why he ain't never likeded me."

"Robert..."

"He Carrie daddy too?"

"Who, Spencer?"

"No, Noah Johnson."

"No, Robert. Spencer is Carrie pa. It's just you."

"Where he at?"

"Who? You mean your real pa? I don't know."

Both Robert's legs was shaking now. His head was exploding with questions, number one of which was: if she had been leading him on all this time, could he trust his mother now to tell him the truth? It's a powerful disturbance to wonder can you trust your mama.

"You hear me, Robert? I don't rightly know where he at?"

In his mind Robert couldn't figure... She said he was the only one. He got ten brothers and sisters and he the only one who is not a brother 'cause he got a different daddy. Did any of the others have different daddies?

"Where I was born at?"

"Hazlehurst, Robert. You was born in Hazlehurst. That's where we all come from."

We all who, Robert started to ask. But then at the same time he started to ask why me? Why I got to be the only one got a different daddy?

"So I'm a Johnson. I ain't none a Spencer."

"Robert, Noah Johnson your real pa. Spencer and me was married and him and me had your brothers and sisters. Now I'm married to Willie and he done agree to raise you as his son. I know it's kind of balled up and everything."

"So I'm a Johnson?"

"Robert you can lay claim to Johnson, or Spencer, or even much to Willis, if you of a mind to."

"But, I'm born a Johnson?"

"Yes, your pa is Noah Johnson, but Spencer took you on and give you his name, and..."

"I'm born a Johnson, I'm going to live a Johnson, and die a Johnson."

"Robert, it's up to you to make your own way, I'm just saying, you is you, don't care what name you call yourself."

"It ain't..." Robert couldn't think how to say more words. Robert lift up his head and jump up, and is surprised to see tears rolling down his mother's face. Even though it pained him a plenty, he didn't say nothing more at that time.

Days later, he went to Julia again with another question. Sometimes a whole week would pass by between questions. Julia hated that. It was like he was torturing her, but she could see it was troubling him and that he didn't quite know how to deal with it all at once, so he took it in small portions, like it was some nasty concoction for to treat worms, leave your mouth all chalky and fishy tasting.

"How come you ain't stayed with my daddy?"

"Why you left me with Spencer?"

"How come you ain't went after my daddy instead of going with Mr. Willis?"

"Who Serena is? I mean I who she is but how she got to where she, and you, was both up, kinda at the same time. I mean… Nevermind."

"I got any brothers or sisters by my daddy?"

Julia tried to answer Robert direct as she could. Straight on. No pretty words or nothing. Just plain the truth as best she could tell it. And each time he would quietly listen until she finish and then he would walk off without saying nothing more.

"Robert, I ain't too good at talking none, but sometimes they say if you talk out what's troubling you it make the load lighter."

But Robert would never answer her. He would just go off on his own, find a tree or a rock, the flowing face of a creek, sometimes a cloud would do, he would look there upon and talk to the things around him. One day when he was writing in the dirt with a twig it come to him: you got to make yourself over.

At the point when he just about had made his mind up to go off and find his real daddy, and to use that as his jumping off point to making who Robert Johnson going to be, a peculiar thing happened that helped him understand part of who he was—he started thinking on somebody else. She was young and all, but she was the one somebody he could talk with. His mama had been right, it did make his load lighter to talk to Ginny.

Talk to Ginny.

Ginny.

Sometimes the person we be loving, part of the reason we be loving them is because they be there when we really need somebody to love.

Which is when, at this particular junction in Robert's thinking while he walking, this Ford roll up on Robert and slow to a stop. Robert look over, it's a white man. Robert lift his hat and nods to the man, adjust his sack and keeps stepping.

"Where you going, boy?"

Immediately Robert is on full alert, even though he cross the state line now and he down in Louisiana, he don't forget his Mississippi understandings of how to conversate with white folks.

Telling a white man the truth is always dangerous. It's always better to tell him what he want to hear, and if you don't know what he want to hear, tell him something that make him think you don't know nothing and you just waiting for him to tell you something.

"Louisiana, sir."

"You in Louisiana. Where at in Louisiana?"

Robert should have been paying attention and had a story together long before the car come up on him. One thing for sure, Robert ain't going to say New Orleans, but Robert trapped now 'cause he don't much know Louisiana. New Orleans the first Louisiana name come to mind and he can't think of nothing else quick enough.

"Huh, sir? My mama say follow the river down through Louisiana and I gets there directly."

"Baton Rouge? You going to Baton Rouge?"

"No, sir. I'm going see my mama. She say follow the river, sir. I'm following the river."

"You a good ways from the river. But I believes you going to Baton Rouge."

"Yes, sir."

"Climb back there," the man pointed to the back seat of the car. "I'm going to take you part of the way." Robert don't move right off. He really don't want to travel none sitting up in back this white man's automobile, but Robert doesn't have any choice in the matter at this particular moment. The white man doesn't notice Robert's hesitation, instead the man is more concerned about the state of Robert's soul. "You been saved?"

"Saved, yes sir. You saving me a heap of walking."

"No, I mean do you accept Jesus?"

Robert pause just as he is about to throw his leg up into the back. "I been in church since I was a baby, sir."

"What you got in that sack."

"I plays Jesus songs, sir."

"Well, do tell. This is truly a blessing. Climb on in and sing us some songs while we motor along."

-19-

ROBERT LOOKED LEFT, ROBERT LOOKED RIGHT. HE DIDN'T EXPECT TO SEE A SIGN saying two-headed people this way, but what was he going to do? What could he do? He certainly wasn't going to stand here all night waiting for a two-headed to walk up on him. He had to do something, even if it was wrong. If he went the wrong way, maybe then somebody would set him straight, or, at the very least, maybe he would learn something he didn't already know.

One thing he did know is that he hated God. Well, at least he hated the God that the Christians said made everything. The God who had killed Ginny, killed their baby, had left his mama all alone in Hazelhurst. The God who had made Mississippi white people.

That white man probably thought he was being all good and everything, making Robert sing them church songs. Robert hated that, just flat out hated the way them Christians was always trying to make people be and do the way they wanted them to.

On more than a couple of occasions when Robert had been drinking heavy, he had took to talking against God, sometimes preaching his anti-God message between songs. One time the whole joint had cleared out when Robert challenged God to smite him dead, if you almighty and everything, well, just throw down one of your thunderbolts or whatever and strike me dead right here. Go ahead, God. Strike me down.

Of course, nothing happened and that made Robert even bolder.

"See, yall don't believe no more than I believes, but yall scared to say you don't believe, just in case, kind of, you know like, just in case it's true about hell and all, and judgment day, but if you really believed in all that you wouldn't be up in here now dancing and drinking and thinking on fornicating and what not. Yall know I ain't lying. I may be a little drunk but I ain't no ways stupid. That God you believes in, where you learn about that God from? Not from the trees. Not from the rocks. The water.

The sky or nothing. But from the same man that's kicking all our asses."

Which is when the juke owner, he come over to tell Robert the people came to hear him play and not to hear him preach. It wasn't the God talk that riled up the juke owner, it was the white man talk. The juke owner paid good money every month to the sheriff for the sheriff to let the juke be, but if the sheriff hear tell about all this talking against white folks going on, well, there would be hell to pay, and that was much, much more than the juke owner wanted to pay, was willing to pay, or, more importantly, was able to pay. Robert knew all that, so all the juke man had to say is, man, I pays you to play, not to preach.

"Well alright. I understands. Somebody give me a drink and I'll play whatsoever song you wants to hear. I guess I ain't nothing but one of them vendor machines. Instead of putting a nickel in my mouth, puts a drink in my hand, and instead of listening to the same platter over and over, I'll play your special request. Give me a drink. Tell me what you want to hear."

Then Robert he look up at the juke joint man and he wink. The man don't wink back. He just chew on his cigar, suck on it some (it ain't lit), chew on it some more, unfold his arms, and go back to tending the counter, which is when a man gives Robert a drink.

"Now that's what I'm talking about. What you wants to hear?"

The man was drunker than Robert.

"I wants to hear Amazing Grace."

Robert don't even blink as he throwing back the drink from the man's bottle. The corn liquor is strong. Robert rear back in the chair, winch, clear his throat, "Amazing Grace, huh?"

"Yeah, God damn it, Amazing Grace."

Robert set his guitar aside, stand up, pull his harp out his pocket and raises it to his lips, and proceeds to blow the prettiest Amazing Grace anybody could ever remember hearing.

He only plays one chorus, but even before he is halfway through, what few peoples was still remaining up in the place, stops doing whatever they was doing, stops thinking whatever they was thinking, and all of them just looks upon Robert in utter wonder.

The song is so pretty one man caps his bottle, gives it to his friend and say, "Man, I'm going back to church in the morning and I'm cut out all this drinking as of right now." And he walks out leaving his friend holding half a bottle of perfectly good moonshine.

Robert ain't knowed it, ain't intended to, but he pour all his heart into that Amazing Grace. What would save him? What could save him? Was there any salvation for people like him? And his mama? Sure weren't none for Ginny and their poor baby. If there weren't no salvation for Ginny and the baby, weren't nobody worth saving, nobody in the whole wide world. Damn it.

Some time stuff just come out you. Some time you don't even know it be in you. Well, you know it's in you, but you don't be thinking on it, 'cause there is a lot of stuff up inside of everybody, but we don't be all the time be thinking on all the stuff what is up inside of us. In fact, a lot of times we intentionally tries to forget some of the stuff what be bottled up in us on account of all we been through.

When the man had said "Amazing Grace" Robert thought he would just play a chorus just to please the man, after all the man had been the first one to offer Robert a drink, and, hell, Robert knowed the man was drunk and maybe was just saying that on account what Robert had said about playing anything somebody might wants to hear, and the man, he probably figure don't no juking musicianeer be knowing no spirituals and whatever, and Robert being Robert, he take pride in knowing most every song there is, church, juke, platter, or radio. He don't boast or nothing about all the songs he know, but he don't let nobody call nothing he don't know, specially not nothing like Amazing Grace, hell, they got babies' what gurgle along to Amazing Grace, so Robert he raise up his harp to play the song just to show he know the song, and when he start in to blowing the first thing pop up in his head was his mama, Julia Dodds, singing that song to him when she was a baby, and that time when she was telling him about his daddy, how Noah had helped out Julia when everybody else was scared to even much say boo to her.

"Robert, this was 'fore you was born. They run Charles out of Hazlehurst," she was speaking about Spencer. "They was trying to kill him. Had a lynch mob and everything. We was up in the house. Spencer he was already gone. Left right 'fore sundown, had my dress on and a bonnet, walking. Did it that way case one of them paid off niggas was to be spying on us, so they would think it was me and that Spencer was still up in there.

When them white mens came, it was a whole passel of them, sitting up on they horses with torches and shouting and cussing and calling for Charlie to come out before they burn the whole house down."

Robert had been almost afraid to look at his mama, the way her voice change. Got mean and ugly, he never heard her sound ugly-voiced like that before, ugly like a squished up toad frog what been run over with a wagon wheel. It was like that dead frog was croaking in his mama throat.

"Like I said, you wasn't born yet Robert. But your brothers and sisters was, all the rest of them was sitting up in the house holding on to each other like they was in a boat and was 'fraid they was going to fall in the water. So I went out there and told them white mens, ain't none of Charles here. He done run off. Ain't nobody here but me and my chillun." Sitting in the dark of the room, Willie snoring softly in the background, Robert had been listening to his mama answer his question and was now almost sorry he ask the question, 'cause now he was starting to change his opinion about everything. Spencer had never said nothing about dressing up like a woman to run off from no lynch mob. Nothing about leaving his mama behind to face off them white mens. Robert never knew none of that.

"Robert, I ain't knowed what I was gone do. I knowed I couldn't let them white mens burn down our house with all your brothers and sisters and what not in there. But I ain't knowed how I was going to stop them if they had a mind to burn us out. So I prayed on it. I mean it weren't like I had no whole heap of time to pray. I just prayed fast. Real fast and then I commence to humming, and I said Lord if you be with me, I guess I can do this. So I hums to Jesus as I walks out that front door straight on up to them white mens on they horses. Lord, it was a powerful long walk. But what else I was going to do?"

Robert cleared his throat but he couldn't figure out nothing else his mama could a done, so he just clear his throat again.

"I told 'em Charles done run off. And they said, for my sake, I best be telling the truth or they was going to burn the whole place down with him up in there if they fount him up in there. I said, I'll show you. They said, naw, nigga, you stay right here. We go see for ourself. Two or three climb down. I start to try to run back up in the house, but one of grab me and threw me down on the ground. He put his boot on my chest and shove his shotgun up in my face, he say to me, he say, bitch, you move, you dead.

After a while them other two come back from going through the house and holler out, nigga gone. Nothing up in there but a bunch of little nigga babies and children. We going to find him though. He can't get too far walking. The one what had his foot on me, he was the last one to climb back on his horse. Once he was up tall in his saddle, he look down upon me and spit, and then he say, if he come back he dead."

Part of Robert had wanted to know if his mama meant the white man had spit on her, but another part of him was afraid to ask. Suppose the white man had spit on his mama, what could he do about it? Nothing.

Robert was hurting. Powerful hurting. But he couldn't think of nothing to tell his mama. But even though he couldn't say nothing, he didn't have to say nothing. And even though his mama say she don't much like talking, she just keeps on talking now. Robert guess when you get to talking about something like this, you just keep on talking 'til you get it all talked out.

"I got up, wiped my face off, wiped the mud off my bosom, I was thinking I didn't want your brothers and sisters to see me all dirted up, and I ran back up in the house. Everything was all mashed up and throwed about, and all of them was a huddled up crying and what not. And I said it was going to be alright. The Lord was going to take care. Take care of their pa, take care of them, take care of me. I called all of 'em to me, each one by they name, and I touch each one of them. And we circle up tight together, and we prayed the Lord's prayer and sang Amazing Grace."

Robert would never forget the look on his mother's face. Never forget the sound of Willie snoring as tears streamed down his mama's face. Funny how you hear certain things at certain times. He had heard Willie snore before but he ain't never heard Mr. Willie snore like he was snoring while Julia was telling her tale. Willie's snoring was making Robert mad. Here his mama was crying and all, and this man was calling hogs.

Amazing Grace. When Robert started playing that song up in that juke, all them memories started flowing. He closed his eyes and saw his mother's tears.

"Robert, I guess you old enough now to hear the whole story."

The whole story. How could there be more? Well, yeah, there had to be more. There had to be the part about Noah Johnson, about Robert pa but... Robert didn't want to hear no more. So he had walked out the room. It took him two whole weeks to be able to take some more of the story.

When Robert come to the bridge of the song, it was like everything he heard his mama tell him about Noah, about Spencer, about Serena, even much about Willie, it was like all them things parade across Robert face and march straight up his nose every time he suck in air, and once they get inside him they mix up with the breath he blowing his harp with, and they be up in that sound.

"Robert, you see Charles had taken up with Serena on the side, but what had happened was one of them Marchetti brothers had his eye on Serena, well, she didn't like him none but what could she do, which is when she got pregnant and when the baby come that baby was dark as a black cat, so that white man knowed it weren't none of his, and, course, he got mad about that, and when he fount out who the baby daddy was he got madder. Went to saying that Charles was getting too big for Hazlehurst. Said, Charlie better look out, watch where he sleeping, even came told me, Julia, you know your nigga got a baby with another woman. I think you ought to do something about that. But what I was going to do? Huh, Robert, what could I do? That's when they told Charles to leave Serena alone. But then Serena, she say she still ain't want to have nothing more to do with that white man."

Robert had wondered why his mama was telling him all this part. This ain't had nothing to do with Robert or Noah, or nothing Robert care about.

"So Mr. Charles run off on account of the white man want Serena?"

"You could say it like that."

"But, mama, weren't Serena up there in Memphis when we come up there."

"Yeah, she was."

"I remember she was up there."

"Yeah, Robert. She was up there. She had got in a family way a second time."

"But I thought you said Mr. Charles already run off."

"No, he don't run off 'til the second baby born. He sent word back that he was going to get us out, one by one. So we start sending the oldest ones off first, but come to find out he sent for Serena before he send for the rest of yall. So Serena and her two get up there before the rest of us."

"So, that's when you went up there with me."

"No."

—204—

"Oh."

"No, Robert. You ever see a crow fly?"

Robert, he had smiled at that. His mama was always funning him. "Mama, what a crow got to do with this."

"Robert, you ever see a crow fly?"

"Yeah. Everyday."

"Well, you ever seen one fly straight."

"Naw, they zig zag all over the place."

"Yeah, well, that's the way life is, it zig zag from here to yonder. So what had happened was once Serena slip out of town, the white mens take all they meanness out on us and they get the bank to call in the feed loan Charles had made before he left. I ain't had no money. Charles ain't sent no money. I still had two of yall left with me and they made it so if I ain't come up with the money, I have to give up the property."

"So you get kicked out and Serena up in Memphis and you... wait, I was born yet."

"By then I was carrying you."

Robert get up again and walk out the room.

At this point, Robert is just about finished playing the bridge of Amazing Grace when the rest of the story come choking him up. He want to scream and cuss God, and at the same time he want to be able to do something for his mama, but he don't know what. So he play Amazing Grace even harder as he think on the last part of the story.

"Robert, your pa took me on 'til the Marchetti brothers come round again. So then I had two children and you and no where else in the world to go. Noah, he said he was going to stand and fight them like a man. I told him he would end up being a dead man and there wasn't nothing a dead man could do to help the living, so I left one day while he was out in the fields. I went and signed up on a work detail and end up in the delta working just to feed yall and all."

Robert get up to leave. Every time he feel like he don't want to hear no more, he get up and leave, but this time Julia stop him.

"Robert, sooner or later, you got to learn to face life. Things ain't always pretty."

Robert stopped but he didn't sit down.

"It took me almost a year to make it up to Memphis and to find Charles and all. And when we got there he took us in. I gots to credit him. He took us all in. And so it was Serena and her two, and me and our ten, and you. All us. Which is when he done changed his name from Dodds to Spencer, but you know, it was hard for me to swallow what all had happened. I just couldn't stay up in that house, even though I tried for all yalls' sake. I tried. I really double-d tried. I did. I tried. But I couldn't. That was my weakness. I just couldn't. Charles was taking care of us and all, but I just, I mean, Robert you understand, some things you can't cotton to, and when that happen... I had to, I couldn't... I know. I know it don't all seem to make much sense now, but I just. Maybe one day, by and by. And that's how come I ends up here in these parts and I wanted to take yall, but I couldn't take all yall and didn't want to take one or two and leave all the others, so, I..."

Robert started to walk out the room. He took one step and then he stopped, turned to face Julia, who was sitting to the table. "Mama, I guess you done answered most all my questions. Now I gots to figure out what all these answers mean."

"Robert, they mean trust in the Lord. God's grace the only thing what can see you through. The only thing what saw me through. How you think I survive all that lessing God was with me, had his angels looking over me and protecting me? Think whatever you want about peoples, but don't never doubt the Lord."

Huh, don't doubt the Lord, that ain't how Robert felt when he was looking down upon the dead face of Ginny...

And by then he was finished playing Amazing Grace.

Amazing Grace.

And that was the last song that white man in the car wanted to hear, Amazing Grace, and he had nerve enough to be messing the song all up with his singing. "That save-it, a ranch like meeee-EEEEE."

Robert had wanted to holler at the man, shut, the fuck up. But he was a white man and Robert was a colored man, and, shucks, Amazing Grace.

Robert stood at the fork in the road. Here it was April, spring time, damn near to the day, the anniversary of Ginny's death. God damn it, that was why Robert was going looking for the two headeds at this very moment. Ginny died behind him, so now he had to die too. The old Robert had to die. He was tired of being afraid to live. Tired of being a Dessie—

where the hell did that come from, that Dessie thing? White men killing us up behind colored womens, even though they says they don't want to have nothing to do with colored, they says that all day long, and ain't a colored woman nowhere safe around none of them. None of them.

And at that moment, it all come tumbling out of Robert. He let out a mighty shout. The worms in the ground beneath his feet, they paused for a second as the vibrations from Robert's hollering burrowed deep into the earth. Birds looped up and turned back rather than fly through the sound of Robert's shout almighty. It was worser than twenty negro women falling out in church. It was worser than a cow run over by a train, than a negro cut four ways twice with a straight razor. It was the sound the devil must a made when he was cast out of heaven, the sound of utter hopelessness announcing regardless of what all happens, I am. Fuck it, I am. I. Am. Ahhhhh.

After the shout, Robert felt better.

He still ain't knowed which way to go, so he waited for a sign, which is when he heard a sound that made him jump damn near in the ditch. It was one of them ah-ooohhh-GA car horns and the car was barreling down the road faster than a race horse. It pass up Robert without much even slowing down none and took the fork to the right. The white man who had let him off a ways back, said when he would come to the fork, Baton Rouge would be to the right.

Now here is where Robert's sign reading faculties was brought into play. If you was looking for a sign as to how to find the two headed peoples and you was at a fork in the road and ain't knowed nothing about where you was at, and along come a car burning up the road, and this white man is driving like he crazy, raising dust and all, and he don't slow down none, is you suppose to go right or left, what the sign telling you to do?

Robert smiled. That was as clear a sign as he ever was going to get. He had to go left. Cause he knew good and well he couldn't find no two headeds by following no white man. And before he knew it, Robert had hummed a short snatch of Amazing Grace as he made it on down the road, but just a snatch, 'cause as soon as he realize what song he was humming, he stopped.

Robert was back to his old self, which meant that he was now singing his favorite traveling song, Sitting On Top Of The World. Robert looked up at the sky and figured he had maybe another two hours or so before sundown, surely he would run up on somebody by then.

-20-

ROBERT HAD WALKED FOR A WHOLE HOUR AND A HALF OR SO, MAYBE MORE, IT was hard to know exactly. He never owned a watch, had no need for one. He came and went when he felt like it, was never in a hurry to get no particular place, never had no set time to leave. Time was not a thing he had to watch closely like it was a fish nibbling at his line and if he didn't jerk it when the fish bited he would miss it. Robert figured, whenever you doing something, take the time to do it, and at the same time don't devote no time to doing nothing you don't want to do, which is why Robert and Dusty never got along.

Dusty never could understand why folk made excuses for Robert just 'cause Robert could play a little music. The boy still ate and all, somebody had to feed him and somebody had to clean up after his shit 'cause he was worthless when it come to working. Dusty had got to the place where he was able to buy a second-hand tractor to make it easier to plow and all, and he catch Robert sitting up top the tractor playing a harp when he was supposed to be plowing. What was the use of even talking on it, when it came to working Robert was worthless, but, see, Julia, she was always making excuses for the boy, and when she weren't doing that, she would be holding out that he was going to change his trifling ways. Even though he no longer even bothered talking on it and had never so much as contradict Julia about that, Dusty had lived long enough to know a snake can change its skin, but it don't change its ways, it still be a snake.

Robert knowed Dusty didn't think much of him and Robert knowed why, Dusty had never been shy about telling Robert face to face that Robert was worthless. Out of respect for his mama, Robert ain't never openly fight with Dusty, especial not when Julia was around, but if you put the both of them in the same bottle they would separate, Dusty weighing down on the bottom and Robert floating on the top just like they live in a big house, one on the bottom floor and one on the top floor, and Robert ain't never liked going down stairs for nothing and Dusty get all huffed up every time Robert walk through the front or back door and go heading for the stairs. Guess it's hard for two different mens to live up in the same house, just like they say can't no two women run one kitchen, can't no two mens be head of one house, especially when one is young and full of fun and the other one is old and set in his ways.

Robert smile to himself on the sly, just like he used to all the time slip out the window and steal down to the jukes and such to sit up under Son House and Willie Brown. All the time, even after Ginny died and Robert done moved back in with Julia and Dusty. Just like couldn't nobody make no field hand out of Robert, nobody could stop Robert from being Robert. But even though Robert ain't liked Dusty, he respect that Dusty done right by Julia, and for that Robert had to recognize up on Dusty good side. Ain't many mens would take on a woman who done already had eleven children, would treat her just like she was a new, little schoolgirl just learning on being a woman. Dusty could of had a young girl if that had been what he wanted. Many a mama would a sent one of their daughters over to Dusty. The man had a homestead, was God fearing and church going, was not no gambler nor fornicator, worked for everything he needed, didn't want for nothing. He could of had plenty young womens, but he stuck to Julia like white on rice, he was through and through a Julia man. Robert had to respect Dusty for respecting Julia.

Thinking on which causes Robert to think some more on why old mens like young womens but ain't no mens like old womens. Robert he liked doing it as much as the next man, it just be that he come to recognize the value of older womens when it come to loving was not just in the sheet shaking business, but was also in their understanding of who and what a man was, how a man does in life.

Robert wondered what a two-headed woman was like, not just in bed—although for sure he would like to experience that 'cause fucking a two headed must be a double up. He wondered on could they make you shoot off twice at one time without having to rest between shooting off. Mens wonder them kind of things, especially mens who know women, know how a woman can gain satisfaction two, even three or four times in a row right quick, like ducks diving down in the water with their legs sticking up. Yeah, it was like that. Ducks is air breathers but they can go under bottoms up, get what they looking for, pop up for a second, and go right back under, whereas a man, he weren't nothing but a man, if he went under for a spell, when he come up he got to rest a little bit before he hard enough again to go back under. Look like mens be more crazy about doing it than womens be, but womens can get more out of it than mens can—life was funny like that.

Robert, he know that most mens don't think on these things the way he do 'cause most times all a man thinking about his satisfying hisself, whereas a woman be thinking on what it take to satisfy others. Most likely it be because women have children and in caring for their young they come to recognize how to please somebody else.

It's funny how when he walking along sometimes Robert get his mind stuck on one thing and no matter what else he try to think on, he come back to the same one thing he stuck on. Robert recognize that it be different things but most of them different things come back to womens and music, maybe that's why most of them songs be about women, and most of the songs the women sing be about men.

Like that Bessie Smith, Lord that woman could sing. All them platters she had. Robert was going to make him some platters, they most likely would not sell like Bessie Smith platters or Leroy Carr's, but they would be his platters none the less. Which bring up the issue of what it would be like to fuck Bessie Smith. Robert done heard musicianeers jawboning over that. Possum Crayton come right out and admit he would be scared to fuck Bessie Smith, said Bessie was too much woman for him.

"See I'm just a average feller when it come to fucking, I ain't got no dick like Long Dick Ned."

"Who dat you talking about?"

"You know Long Dick over to Crystal Springs?"

"Possum, don't nobody know who you talking about. Tommy, you from over Crystal Springs way, you ever hear tell of some Long Dick Ned?"

"Naw, but I can't say as I know everybody."

"I know he going to tell us anyway, but I'm going to ask Possum this question, so as he can pass this lie out the front part of his mouth: why they call him Long Dick?"

"Now you ain't even much got to ask that question. The man name advertise his specialty. In fact his specialty so special even the white folks refers to him that way. They say he can even much fuck a mare and make a mule."

The gentlemen sitting around the stove all roar with laughter. Slapping their thighs, calloused hands against work-worn denim overalls. One or two of them even pausing to feel on themselves, and most of them not so secretly wishing they had what it took to be called Long Dick.

"So, Possum, you were saying hows you was just average in the dick department."

"Yeah, I'm like most mens is. I couldn't handle no Bessie Smith. Besides they tell me she go with women."

"Ain't no such."

"Sho there is. There is women what go with women."

"Ain't such. Can't be."

"Why it can't be?"

"What a woman going to do with a woman? Stick her finger in it?"

"Well, I'm going lay it out like I plows, which is straight down the middle. Ain't going to lie. I done used my hand and I done done it with women, and the hand loose out to nookie every time. Every time."

"Yeah. Yeah. I believe Joe right about that."

Feeling like he had backup from Joe, Possum started getting loud, "Besides all that, yall knows once a woman done had some of this here good wood I got, her finger wouldn't be nothing but a toothpick compared to this tree I got down here."

"Well, I know many a man be talking," Robert looked dead up in Possum face as he drawled out a quiet rebuke, "you know, talking about they cigar and all but they don't never much even have a cigarette."

The men laugh at Robert's quiet rebuke. From time to time, they all brag, but ninety-nine out a hundred of them feel somewhat lacking when it come to measuring length and all, at least lacking when measured long side of how long they would like to be.

Just like scared men whistle through a cemetery, the average man lie, brag, and laugh when it come to talking about his thing. It's the same thing. Robert just smile because this is something he been figuring on for a long time.

Possum didn't take kindly to young Robert contradict. "Boy, what you know? You so green you still squirting water."

"I knows there is women what likes women, and they be satisfied with each other."

"Ain't such. Might be some what says that just 'cause they don't want to give you none. But just like they ain't no man I desires, I don't believe they got no women what desire a woman."

Which is when Tommy spoke up on the subject. Tommy had been around some, had made platters and all, traveled a ways, probably had more experience than most all of them put together. "Yall done all heard that song Kokomo sing 'bout if the Lord can't send him no woman, then at least send him a sissy man?"

"That ain't natural."

"But it happen, don't it? Happen all the time up to Parchman, don't it? What's the matter? Yall was all loud talking a minute ago? What you got to say now?"

"Tommy, you know good and well, when you all locked up and everything, you got to make do. I'm just saying if you had the option, some nookie or some asshole, the average man would go for the nookie every time. Every time."

"Well, Possum, ain't said nothing about every woman likes women, he said he heard Bessie likes women."

"What difference do it make what she do?"

"The difference is it ain't right."

"So, who say what right is?"

Robert peeped where this conversation was headed, "next thing some one of yall going to be quoting the bible and all." Robert looked around at each of the men, they choose not to lock horns with him and instead look off to the side or out the open doorway. Robert continues, raising his voice slightly for emphasis but not loud or shouting. "The fact that the bible say don't do it must mean that somebody was doing it, even way back then." Robert pause both to let his words sink in and to give space in case somebody want to contradict. Nobody say nothing, so Robert, he continue. "So it would seem to me if it weren't natural, it would of been died out by now, but the fact that it still going on and that it been going on since before the flood back in the bible and all, that fact alone tell me that not only is it natural but it's something God is allowing to exist 'cause if he didn't want it to exist, he wouldn't never of made it."

Tommy stare over at young Robert in amazement, the boy not only could play, he coud think. How-so-ever, Possum, for his part, remain unconvinced.

"All that sound good, but I knows womens on womens don't work."

Here it was a big old Saturday evening, they weren't even drunk yet, just sitting around jaw jacking and such, waiting for the crowd to congregate up, and already they were philosophying like they was white men up in one of them big school buildings like to over at Oxford. Normally, Robert didn't arrive until late so he would not be involved in such conversating, but he was early on that particular evening on account of he had not been home to Callie for two days, rather than walk four more miles coming and going, he had decided to head straight on over to the juke right off the road. Robert remembered it clear as clear could be and now here he was walking this Louisiana road and thinking back on that Tommy Johnson discussion.

Tommy had challenged Possum when Possum said how he knowed a woman couldn't satisfy a woman.

"Possum, how you know that. You ain't no woman."

"I ain't got to be no woman to know what a woman got and ain't got." And one thing I know for sure, a woman ain't got no dick."

Which is when Tommy quietly said, "They got women in New Orleans that got dicks."

"Ain't such."

"Yes sir, Possum. I'm telling you what I knows, not what I heard. You said you heard something about Bessie, well, I'm telling you something I know."

"How you know? If a woman had a dick that would make her a man."

"I know 'cause I was friendly up with a woman down there and she showed me."

"Tommy, you saying a woman fucked you with a dick?" Possum say laughing at the same time and making a motion like he humping the air in front of him.

Some of them snickered, but it was a nervous laughter that died down quickly, like trying to light green wood where the flame go out no sooner you pick the stick up out the fire. They was all waiting to hear Tommy's response. Tommy was generally respected and so if he said he seen it, well, it must have been so.

"No, Possum. I'm saying she told me about it and showed it to me."

"Showed it?"

"Yeah, she keep it in a box inside a drawer in this chest of drawers she had. Tell the truth, she had two boxes. One of them was white and one of them was black."

"What color she was? I know she weren't no white woman. Wouldn't no white woman show you her dick."

"Well, it's hard to say, what color she was 'cause she was mixed up colored and white. You know they got what they call that creole thing down there. They be colored but they look like they white."

The men whistle and get all big-eyed quiet like the first time they watch a stallion mount a mare. They all hanging on every word Tommy Johnson got to say.

In fact, the fact that Tommy Johnson was going to be there was a main reason for Robert to make it back to the juke. Robert liked playing with Tommy and his brother Ledell, 'cause Tommy had some ways of singing way up high, higher than most men could reach, and he could do it with such ease, so relaxed like he was talking about the weather, but hitting notes like a hawk circling up in the sky, far, far above the ground. Tommy's singing was not quite a yodel, had a quiver that get to you, make you want to try to woo-hoo like he do but it ain't so easy as he make it sound. Robert liked that and, of course, it didn't take Robert but a couple of listenings before he had caught on to Tommy and then went on further down the road and take it different places 'cause Robert put more chords up in the music, make the falsetto be more pronounced not 'cause he singing higher but because he putting it on different places, not just at the end of a phrase, and 'cause he put it on top of different notes from the simple chords that Tommy use.

Of course, another reason Tommy interest Robert is behind Tommy having the last name of Johnson, just like Robert daddy name (by now, we all knows Robert ain't got but one sure name and that's Robert, everything else depend on who telling the tale and when, and even some time Robert don't even use Robert), but anyway Tommy could a been kin to Robert through Noah, Robert asked Tommy one time he know of Noah, but

Tommy said, no, he don't know of no Noah Johnson, but still in all, it may be so, seeing as how Crystal Springs ain't so far from Hazelhurst.

Robert particularly liked to second Tommy when Tommy would take to singing "Cool Drink of Water." When Robert would play behind Tommy, Robert could shadow him with the slide, make the guitar yodel just like Tommy do, especially when Robert playing with steel strings on his box and use a driving rod (or sometimes even his pocket knife) for a slide instead of a glass bottleneck, something about that metal slide scrapping on steel strings that whine like a haint in the holler at midnight. It gets so quiet up in the juke when they do that song you could hear every note ringing clear and hear the steady flapping of Robert foot beating tme. Robert always would go out his way to hear a musicianeer he felt he could learn something from.

So anyway, Tommy he was standing up next to the stove, had his hands stretched out and was rubbing them together whilst he was relating about this woman friend he had.

"See, she likeded me by my playing and one night we was up in one of them joints they got down there and she got into a fight with this feller, said he was trying to short her or whatever and they got to cussing each other and all, and before you know it he done jumped her like she was a man. Deedee, that were her name, Deedee she roll and tumble with him and probably would a whipped him hands down but he was twice her size, well she must a bite him or something. He jumped up with blood all down the side his face, which is when he come up with a knife and said he was going to cut her so ugly not even a murderer would be able to stand to look at her. Which is when me and my friend, brother Colt intervene and suggest if he gon fight her, fight her fair. Either give her a knife or put his away. 'Course by now he so mad he don't pay me no mind and he slash at her, cut her arm good, that's when I plug him in the foot. I grabs Deedee and we high tail it out there, which all is how me and Deedee got to be friendly like. Never did lay down with her or nothing 'cause I was liking on another girl at the time, went by the name of Sandy, and it turn out Sandy and Deedee was cousins and all. I must of stayed down there a good six or seven weeks. Probably would still be there but Sandy she got killed up behind some guy she was tricking. Both of them was tricking at the time, I means Sandy and Deedee."

Just like all the others, by then, Robert was listening and sort of envious of Tommy who had done gone down to New Orleans and took up with them New Orleans womens and everybody knowed them womens traffic in all kinds of hoodoo, say they could give you a drink of sweet tea and make you change you mind. Get you in bed and make you forget everything you knowed. So they all was waiting for the part where the woman had a dick.

"So one day it was raining and I was over to Deedee, this was right when I was fixing to make my getaway. We had done buried Sandy the day before and I was saying my goodbyes and all, would have left then but it was raining. It always be raining in New Orleans, I don't know how them people can stand all that rain down there. So I was telling Deedee maybe she should pack her leaving trunk on account it weren't healthy in her profession and she say she know but she was used to it and all. So we got to drinking and talking about Sandy and I don't know how but we start into talking about tricking and stuff and Deedee she ask me if I ever see a dee-doe. I says, naw, I ain't knowed nothing about no dee-doe. Any yall ever seed a dee-doo?"

There was a general murmuring as the mens tried the new word in their mouths: dee-doe. Robert was the first one to speak up to Tommy, "is dee-doe some kind of fancy name for a dick?"

"Well, yeah and no. It's look like a full on hard on."

"So you laid your eyes on it?"

"Yes, sir. Sure as I'm looking at you, I was looking at it."

"What she do with it? I mean, she told you how she use it, how it go and all?"

"Yeah, she showed me. She had this strap she wrap round her waist and tie the dee-doe to it, and she be standing there with that thing just a sticking out and everything."

When Tommy had said that, everything got quiet, quiet, quiet. None of the five men assembled in that room could imagine themselves being fucked by a woman with a dick strapped on her. Hell, it made them uncomfortable just to think on such a thing. Again, it was Robert what was the first and only one to speak up.

"Tommy, I don't rightly know how to put this, so I don't mean no offense or nothing, but she show you or, I mean, she told you how that thing go? I mean, she say they be some mens who wants her to put that dee-doe, or what-so-ever you call it, to put that thing up in 'em, I mean stick it in they butt or what-so-ever? Huh?"

"Man, I don't know all that. When she strapped it on and I looked upon that, I couldn't think to say nothing. That shit was scary, and yall knows I ain't no scary man, but brother, let me tell you, when you see a woman with a hard on dick strapped to her, it'll scare the shit out of you."

"What it made of?" Robert had asked, still curious as all get out.

"She told me I could touch it if I wanted to but I ain't wanted to. From what I could see, it looked like bullwhip leather, at least the black one did. I don't know what the white one was, 'cause by then I was fully sobered up and was anxious to get out there. I ain't cut out for all that crazy stuff they do down there."

All the fellers were thinking the exact same thing: get out of there. Get far away as you can.

Far away as you can, Robert repeated the phrase in his mind. Louisiana was another world compared to Mississippi. And now here Robert was walking through Louisiana where the womens got dicks.

-21-

ROBERT NOTICED IT WAS CLOSE TO SUN DOWN AND HE STILL AIN'T RUN UP ON
nobody.

"Brother."

Robert jumped a little, surprised by how close the voice sounded. He
looked around but he don't see nothing, so, of course, Robert go in his
pocket and put his hand on his knife—he know you can't cut no ghost, but
he sure can cut some flesh and blood. You know how it be spooky to be
thinking on something and for it to happen.

"Best get off the road. Sundowners coming through. They catch you,
you be in beaucoup trouble."

Robert was steady looking to see where the voice was coming from.
The trees was growed almost right on top the road. The Louisiana landscape
was spooky. It remind him of the backwaters round the Yazoo swamps,
ain't no telling what all was up in there and, for sure, you didn't want to
be stumbling through there at night without no torch light or nothing. But
the voice ain't sound menacing or nothing. In fact the voice sound more
afeared for him than Robert felt afeared of the voice.

"Come on this way. Hurry on. They be coming through soon."

Robert saw a bush shaking, but that was all he could see. The voice
sounded fully growed. This was one of those moments when Robert had
to totally rely on his instincts, his ability to get a quick understanding of a
crossed-up situation, like when somebody about to pitch a rock at you and
you trying to real quick figure which way to jump to keep from getting hit.

Robert wasn't the strongest and with his bad eye, he wasn't the best
at seeing stuff, but he was real good at reading a situation and figuring out
how to get out of tight spots, and as a result Robert trusted his instincts,
except at this minute he was getting mixed signals, something was telling
him it was ok, but something else was telling him there was more going
on than it seemed like, which is when he heard the dogs in the distance—

now if you a colored feller in Mississippi (for sure, he was in Louisiana now, but he wasn't too far away from Mississippi and Louisiana weren't no picnic), so if you Mississippi colored and you hear hounds baying in the distance, and they sound like they getting closer, both your first and your second inclination is to not let them hounds get no closer. The bushes shook again.

"We got to go. Come on."

Robert ain't had to think on it no more, he hurried over to where the voice was. But there was nobody by the bush that had been shaking a couple of seconds ago. Robert was mixed up and sort of worried, which he had a right to be. Robert had some of the best hearing of anybody he knowed. He had heard that voice clear and it was real close, coming from this very bush he was now standing next to, this same bush what had been shaking when he first looked over this way—the hounds was getting closer—and Robert had not heard no commotion, and couldn't nobody move through this thicket without making no sound. All the while he trying to figure up what was happening, Robert was looking around, trying to catch any movement he could—damn, them hounds was closing in fast.

Robert weren't no scary man, being a walking musicianeer, Robert, he done been in all kinds of situations, a bunch of scrapes with some mighty unsavory folk, even much some plain stomp-down evil peoples, he done had his instrument smashed all up, a couple of hickies from bottles and what not throwed at his head, even was kicked once when he tripped and fell (the foot's owner was a jealous somebody who didn't like that a woman he liked had decided she liked Robert), but in all those cases there was usually somebody also helping Robert out, even if it weren't no more than that girl jumping up on the back of the man with the boots who was trying to stomp the living daylights out of Robert, but this time was different, not only was he not in Mississippi, there wasn't nobody around Robert knowed. So here he was, standing in he-don't-know-where Louisiana, a voice he can't see somewhere close by, evil-ass sounding hounds getting closer and closer by the minute, the sun almost completely gone down, and Robert could hear his own breathing and feel his heart starting to pound louder than if he had been dancing all night, he was holding his sack cross his back with his left hand, and had done already pulled his knife out his pocket and slapped it open on the side of his leg, everything Robert knowed was telling him he was in a sticky situation.

"Man, don't just stand there. Come on." One of the bushes moved, which is when this hand reach out from nowhere, it seems. Really, the man had been kneeling by the tree near to the bush. His grip was like one of them traps for four-legged beasts, hard, quick hitting, you felt the force of the grip in your bones. The man had grabbed low on Robert's wrist so as Robert couldn't twist his hand or nothing, so even though he held a knife there was nothing he could do 'cause at the same time the man grabbed Robert's wrist, the man also jerked Robert with a force that almost made Robert fall. One thing Robert was clear about, this man was way stronger than Robert and there weren't no sense in even much trying to resist. Before Robert could realize what all was happening they were trotting off away from the road.

The ground was soft and mushy. Robert kept stumbling, bumping into bushes, scrapping up against tree branches and such while the man pulling Robert just seem to blend into the woods without making a sound or even much disturbing a leaf. After about ten yards or so, the ground start to turning to damp mud and was sucking on Robert's shoes with each step.

Robert was trying to get a clear view of the man but there was always some kind of leaves and branches and such between him and the man, even though the man was pulling him along. The man stopped suddenly and Robert bumped into him. Although it weren't all the way dark, it might as well been 'cause even though Robert done damn near fell on top the man, Robert can't hardly see him.

"Get in."

Get in what? Robert started to ask.

"I got your sack, you get in."

If those damn dogs weren't getting so close, Robert might have hesitated. The man stepped to the side, Robert looked down and saw a really small, flat-bottomed boat. Now Robert, he liked to look at water but he was not no swimmer or nothing. He ain't knowed nothing about boats, didn't have a clue as to how he was supposed to get in a boat, especially a boat this small.

"Step in the middle and sit down at the same time."

Robert was scared he was going to turn the boat over and fall in the water and drown or get bit up by a cotton mouth or one of them big fishes with teeth Robert heard tell they had down here in Louisiana. Robert ain't been up in this strange land one whole day yet and already he done rode in a automobile with a white man, got bloodhounds chasing him, and done met up with some stange somebody taking him in a boat that was barely wider that Robert, hell, if he sat his guitar sideways it would be sticking over the sides.

When Robert step in, the boat moved while Robert was trying to sit down and he kind of tipped to the side like he was going to fall in the water, but the man had grabbed the back of Robert's shirt and pulled him upright.

"Scoot up some."

Robert's feet were already at the front of the boat. The man place Robert's sack behind Robert, jumped in the boat like he was jumping in the saddle of his favorite filly and before Robert knew it they were gliding along into the darkness, into shadows, trees, all of which seemed to grow up out of the water. And then the boat slowed and swung around. Robert felt the boat rock a little. Robert looked over his shoulder and saw what Robert thought might of been the man's back except he was covered with leaves and twigs or some such. Robert could only clearly make out the man's hands. He was using some kind of long stick in the water, it was not no paddle. Robert had seen a paddle before. This was just a long stick.

"Bend down, watch your head." The man instructed Robert, some kind of something crawled all over Robert's head and shoulders.

"Ok. We clear."

Less than a minute later, Robert hear the hounds just a barking and barking. They must of got to the water's edge. Robert was so…, well, so concerned about what all was going on that he didn't realize he was still holding his knife, which was why he had almost fallen over when he got in the boat. He had not wanted to let go of his knife and he tried to steady hisself with his knuckles on the side of the boat but he had not been able to. He had slipped, but he wasn't going to let his knife go, even though Robert knew, knife or no knife, he didn't stand a chance against the man.

The man laughed softly to himself. "They never catch me."

They went on for a long time more, neither of the men saying anything to the other. Actually, it was only eleven minutes more, but it seemed to Robert like he was journeying to a far corner of some nameless swamp or something. By now it was fully dark, and there was no fire light nowhere. And no way in hell to tell one tree from another. The only thing Robert knew for sure was which way was up, and the only way he knew that was because they were floating in a boat and Robert figure the sky was above him 'cause the water was below him, and that's about all Robert was sure of. This was worst than the first time he jump a train and was sitting up in an empty boxcar in the dark. At least then he had somebody with him that he knew.

While they were floating through the swamp, Robert saw a big old white bird standing stark still on one long, slender leg, his (or was it a her?) other leg folded up. As they drew near to the bird, it casually turned its head, seemed like all the way around, watched them and then, in no particular hurry, slowly spread its big wings, and took off, flying slow and low over the water. After a short while, even though it was the whitest of whites, it disappeared into the dark shadows. It was like the swamp was a gigantic mouth and just swallowed the bird up, feathers and all. For some reason that made Robert sad, real sad.

At first, naturally, Robert had kind of wished he had wings and could fly away whenever he needed to. Like most Southern negroes, Robert had often dreamed of flying. He didn't know that dreams of flying was a common sleeptime image among the descendants of black people who had been slaved up and brought here in big ships, and kept here with whips and chains, guns and dogs, and shit. Robert had never much thought about asking nobody he knew about flying, I mean how you run up on somebody with some stuff like, hey, man, you ever dream of flying? Robert had not even much asked Ginny and you know if he ain't asked Ginny, then he weren't going to ask nobody else. But he should have asked. If he had asked he would of found out there was a lot of people flying around in their dreams at night. Negroes like to dream of flying. Partly because we got an eleven dozen thousand hundred million reasons to fly away. And Robert just got sad all of sudden caught up in this swamp and wanting to fly away and not having nothing but feet—and don't care what the bible said, can't nobody walk on swamp water. Or run away from hounds.

For a minute, Robert kind of resigned himself to maybe not surviving this time. Who knows? Robert watched the bird until it disappeared, and then Robert himself felt like he was just disappearing, kind of fading into this swamp, and nobody would never see him no more. And then Robert wondered what it would be like to be dead. Could it be any worse than what his life was now? Like, yeah, there was some good times and all, but after awhile it don't seem like it all lead to nothing but dying, so if all you was going to do was die eventually, why keep on living when shit keep turning out fucked up? Like Ginny?

Them church folks be sometimes talking that Ham shit, drawers of water and hewers of wood. So how come white folks born to be race horses and we born to be mules? It weren't right. Some people was saying Chicago was heaven compared to Mississippi, but at this point Robert was yet to visit Chicago, so he ain't knowed nothing about all of that. All he knowed was hard times Mississippi and now this swampy Louisiana. Dogs on his trail before he even much even met up with anybody except this leaf-covered man pushing this little boat cross the waters. Besides, who would miss Robert if he was never to come back? Callie might miss him for a minute, but she would get over it, just like she got over them other men she had done been with. Who else? His mama, but there weren't nothing special about that, your mama supposed to miss you. Maybe his sister, Carrie. Yeah, Carrie, would miss him. But that was about it, and even them, they would go on living, just like most people go on living after a beloved done died.

Robert even thought about jumping into the water.

Robert look down. It was dark now, so there was nothing much he could really see. Inside his head Robert saw himself stepping off into the swamp water and going under and just kind of floating under water for a while and then he would be dead.

The boat bump to a stop.

"We here."

Robert came back to his good senses and started to thinking on surviving and catching up with the two-headeds, learning some more hoodoo stuff about making music. Robert force himself to think about a good future, about how good he would be able to play, about making platters, about people throwing money at him, but, of course, first he had to escape this particular predicament.

The man had said, we here, Robert tried to turn to see where the hell "here" was but Robert couldn't see nothing that he would recognize as a particular place, everything up in here look the same to Robert. The man had already got out and seem like he was gone off somewhere. Robert just sat there. What else could he do? He almost fell in the water getting in the boat, he wasn't about to drown now that they were wherever in the hell they was at, so he sat and waited. It was a powerful long wait, and again, just like the journey here, the wait was actually a lot shorter than it seemed.

While he was sitting there a lot of things run through Robert's head, his thoughts was bumping around like tadpoles running all up into each other and such. One thought was how was he going to get out of wherever the hell he was at. Whenever he go up in some place for the first time, the first thing Robert do is try to make sure he know the way back out, make sure he can see the door, or a window, or some such way to escape should he have to de-ass the place in haste. Robert don't like being no where when he don't have no knowledge to where he at or how-so-ever to get out of there, so you know Robert was quite uneasy sitting up in that small boat in the middle of some Louisiana swamp. Hell, that leaf man could hand him one of them telephone things and let him call who-so-ever Robert might want to call, what was Robert going to say? Where he was going to say he at? How somebody going to come save you if you can't tell them where at to come?

Robert still had the knife in his hand. He look down at it. It was useless. Even if he was to cut the man down, how in the hell would Robert get back to the road where at he had been lost in the first place. Shit. He didn't know where he was when he was on the road. He double lost now that he up in this swamp. Double lost! That's a whole lot of lost. And on top of that, he got to pee. He ain't peed since round noon. It's after sundown. Which, of course, put Robert in mind of that time up in that white man upper room when he had to pee. Being a walking musicianeer Robert used to relieving himself whensoever he feel a need. Holding his bladder is not in his habit.

At that moment something bites on Robert left arm, feel something like an ant bite. Robert realize he still holding the knife so he don't swing at whatever it is biting him until after he close the knife, careful to push the knife's metal loop over so that the blade don't close all the way, that way if he need to utilize the knife fast, he can open it up as he pull it out his pocket—Robert had practice that move til he could do it so easy, it seem like he had a straight knife in his pocket. Of course, by the time Robert slap at the first bite, he done been bit seven or eight more times.

"Come on."

The man startled Robert. The man was spooky, the way he could move without making no noise.

How in the hell do you get out of a boat?

Robert start to try and reach one leg out at a time as he bend over holding on to the side of the boat, but that don't work. The man laugh at Robert.

"Stand up first. Hop out."

Hop out? Robert wondered how in the hell do you hop out a boat. What was the man talking about. And before Robert could say any thing them buzzing bugs took to biting him on the side his neck and all up on his face. So here he is standing up in a boat, buzzing bugs biting all on him, and some strong-ass man he don't know is laughing at him, plus Robert got to pee. How in the world he suppose to hop behind all that?

The man bent down and grabbed the side of the boat holding it to dry land, "jump!"

Robert jumped and landed on sort of solid land. Look like all this ground give way some when you step on it. The man is steady laughing low like he enjoying himself.

"Come on. I got your sack."

"Mister, I got to pee."

"Well, go head. Ain't nobody stopping you."

The man just stand there and look upon Robert, who is steady slapping at the buzzing bugs—them damn bugs buzzed louder than a horse fly but they weren't big at all, instead they was so small you could barely see them.

Bad as Robert had to go, he hesitated a little, how would he stand it if one of them buzzing-bugs was to light on his dick and start in to biting on it while Robert was peeing? In fact, Robert's fear of being bited all up was stronger than his embarrassment about taking it out and peeing with somebody looking upon him, but what else he going to do? When you got to go, you got to… hell, your body always win out.

As he empties himself against the tree he standing next to Robert throws his head back and gives out a long exhale—it feels so good to let it go when you got to let it go. And when he finish, just before he shake himself off, Robert look over to the man standing next to him and the man is looking back at Robert, which make Robert really uncomfortable to have a man looking upon you while you standing there with your thing in your hand.

This the first time Robert get to see the man's face. He dark and got a big bushy black beard and some kind of hat or crown made of leaves and got leaves and twigs all over his shoulders, if he close his eyes and his mouth and don't move, you could be standing right up on top of him and not see him. That was how come Robert ain't seen him back on the road.

"OK, follow me." Robert thinks on what the man just said. What else was Robert going to do but follow along? The man sling Robert sack over his shoulder and starts troding off somewhere, and Robert, buttoning up his britches as they walk, is right behind the man. Out of nowhere, there is a small clearing and a slight rise in the land, like a little hump on a bull's back or something, and next to a big tree with roots sticking up every which-a-ways there is a little hut or something with a small fire beside it.

"You sleep here tonight. We'll push off just 'fore day."

And what will we do in the meantime Robert wondered but didn't say nothing. The man put Robert sack down by the opening to the hut, you couldn't hardly call it no doorway. There weren't no door, just an opening and the hut was low, too low to stand up in fully.

Robert stood there, steady slapping at the buzzing bugs. The man laugh somemore at Robert and then brushes past Robert, goes into the hut and comes back out with some stalks or something in his hand. He crush them up and squeeze on them and then rub them on Robert arms and neck and face.

"It smell strong but this keep the mosquitos off you."

Robert don't know what to make of this moment. He ain't never had no moment like this when a man was feeling on his face and what have you. It don't seem to bother the man none, but it kind of spook Robert some, you know, Robert used to a woman's touch but a man's touch is troubling.

"I am Brother Bras. You're safe here."

But where was here and what is here? Robert looked around. How could you live out here? There didn't seem to be nobody else living out here except birds and four leggeds, fish and turtles, and them, what he call them, mosiquitos. Caught up in thinking on the nature of where he was at, Robert forgot his manners. He didn't even introduce himself back, nor did he say anything to Brother Bras. Bras, for his part, only smile and slap Robert on the shoulder real friendly like.

"I know this is a lot to tussel with, especially since this your first time up in here. In the morning I'll take you some place where you can be more comfortable."

Robert still don't say nothing.

-22-

"Isn't it true…" the white man questioning Robert leaned back in his chair, perfectly relaxed, his legs crossed, his thumbs hitched into his dull red suspenders, decorating his face was a slight sneer causing his heavily mustached top lip to quiver in the kind of delight a cat takes with a cornered mouse.

"Isn't it true…" Robert listened, irritated like when a meddling relative, say a younger brother or sister, is intent on pestering Robert with questions delaying and shortening the time Robert would get to spend with the then object of Robert's interest.

"Isn't it true that you fucked that girl Dessie that night she so graciously took you in when you had no place to stay during your, ahem, visit to Natchez?"

A hushed murmur snaked through both the upper and the lower gallery like the commotion that sounded in service two Sundays back when freckle-faced, innocent-looking little Josie, the county sheriff's incorrigible youngest daughter of five, with her strawberry-blond self, had showed up to the Mighty Rose of Our Savior Jesus Christ (segregated Southern) Baptist church in a dress a little too tight and a little too red.

It was not that the man had said "fuck," because, really, there was nothing unusual about a white man saying fuck, especially when referring to colored people and particularly with respect to colored women, so, no, neither a white man saying fuck, nor a white man fucking women, none of that was unusual, what set the gallery's tongues to wagging was that the gentleman from Natchez was putting that expletive on the permanent record when even all the white people there abouts (or should we more accurately say, particularly all the white men) knew that don't nobody colored mess with Dessie, yet, for all times to come, when anal retentive investigators turn to the record, they going to pull out this court transcript and say, see, that proves my point, Robert did fuck Dessie.

In the upper balcony, Reverend Samson, no admirer of Robert Johnson, but still since he was a Reverend and since the boy's mother was a stalwart deaconess, the Reverend felt it his duty to attend to the hearing even though he knew there was no hope in hell that Robert would be admitted to heaven. Rev knew that Robert was no angel, in fact was rumored to be a devoted follower of Satan, playing the devil's music and all, but all of that notwithstanding, Rev knew what the deal was: although Robert might be a follower of the devil, Robert weren't the only devil, and these men who were supposed to be the pillars of society, it was these very men who were most responsible for a great deal of sin and wrong doing, which is when Rev, a militant in his own quiet way, leaned over and whispered into Deacon Jones' ear: they make the law and then use the law to say we breaking the law. Was no need to say who "they" was.

In his mind, Robert answered the question about Dessie with a quiet, no sir, but out loud, Robert said nothing 'cause he recognized that this was not a trial but a judgment, a summing up of how his investigators and interrogators felt about Robert, not about what Robert felt or did.

Had it been a fair trial, Robert would have spoke up and let them know, yeah, I thought about it but I never touched her.

And, of course, through it all, Dessie sat with that characteristic vacant look on her face, the look of cattle watching one of their own get slaughtered, the look exhibited by negroes forced to watch a whipping. She was just the alleged fuckee, so nobody—at least not none of the white men—was the least bit interested in what she had to say, and hence nobody even much bothered to ask her what happened, and even if they had, who would believe such a luscious-piece-of-colored ass had any intellectual information to offer.

Robert recognized the inherent unfairness of what all was going down, and also recognized how depressingly normal all this bullshit was, since day one up in Mississippi—and in most of the rest of the good old USA for that matter—from the jump the deal been foul.

"Isn't it true that you, Robert Leroy Spencer, took advantage of the hospitality offered by your host and assaulted her in the middle of the night while she soundly slept in her own bed? You woke her and engaged in your own sadistic pleasures and then left at first light in the morning. And after promising her the world, you slipped off when her back was turned without even offering any explanation or apology on your part?"

Robert clutched his upright guitar case close to him like he were hugging and trying to console an injured child. The whispered asides in the lower gallery were even sharper now that it was clear that Robert offered no answers to the direct questions. The upper gallery fell into stony silence.

"Isn't it true that you are, through and through, a professional philanderer? That you use your musical talents to seduce your victims, and once you have had your way with them you, heartlessly and without any concern for their subsequent well being, walk away and generally do not return to them?"

Robert held his tongue but in his heart he cursed these cruel men, most of whom routinely used their power and privilege to do far, far more harm to colored women than anything Robert had ever done, and besides, Robert never raped nobody, never engaged in any unwanted or forced act with anyone. Never.

Which is when another white man rose. He was dressed in an immaculately pressed seersucker suit with a dark blue string tie, his jacket was unbuttoned, so that when he pushed back the sides of his jacket and placed his hands on his waist for emphasis, the back of his jacket flared outward almost as if he had a fleshy behind, which, of course, he didn't, but the gesture made it look like he did. This scion of southern aristocracy was both more delicate in his language but also more cruel in his accusations.

The white man's eyes narrowed like he were squinting beneath the spotlight of high noon sun. He puckered his lips. He brushed his mustache—what was it with all these rich white mens and mustaches? Some even had little whispy goatees, and when they lowered their chins and peered across their spectacles they resembled billy goats, especially those of the men who were well past their thirties and had heads partially covered by limp crowns of wavy white hair.

"Isn't it true that you were not even present when your unfortunate wife died in childbirth? Isn't it true that you were off somewhere cavalierly engaged in frolicking while she died trying to bear your child? Isn't it true that she had returned to her mother's home to give birth mainly because you were not a reliable companion and…"

Robert knew it was dangerous to publicly contradict a white man, especially when other white men were judging you, but what could Robert do, what could any colored man facing a jury of Mississippi white men, all of whom were presented as experts, what could anyone do? They said they had all the facts. They knew what Robert was thinking. How many teeth he had in his mouth. What hand he used to wipe his ass. What the circumference of his dick was. They claimed they knowed everything, had talked to everybody who had ever seen or heard of Robert.

Robert knew the score, it was a tune played over and over again. They took the facts that suited them and twisted them up until they accused a bull of acting like a cow and then condemned the bull for not giving milk. What Robert hated most was not that they were liars and tormentors, not even that they had power over him, but that even now that he was dead they would be the ones who established who he had been and what he had done while he was alive, and there was nothing he could do about it.

Dead? When had Robert died? Robert looked around. He didn't know where he was and he surely didn't know that he was dead, but that's what the sign said hanging from the ceiling: Judgment of the Dead.

So, is this what happens when you die—white men decide what your very living had been about? If this was what colored people had to go through, then for sure there was no life after death.

"…and further, I submit that this same Robert Leroy Spencer did marry and abandon a second wife, a woman named…" and the man paused in his accusations, poked around at papers on the podium where he stood and shortly came up with Callie's name.

Robert just shook his head from side to side, no, this weren't right. He liked Callie a whole lot but he was not married to her, indeed, he had even been thinking on leaving her. Meanwhile the white man droned on.

"…you moved her to Clarksdale, away from her family and friends, so that she would be totally dependent on you, and then, like so many of your kind, you abandoned her. Isn't that the case?"

Robert surveyed the scene and thought that the Robert who was sitting in the dock looked tired and weary and sort of discouraged or something. And then it occurred to Robert that the old Robert might not have married Callie but who knows what the future held, except he was dead, so how could a dead man marry a woman?

"And further more, your second wife died of a venereal disease she contracted from you, and which same social disease eventually caught up with and killed you, isn't that the case? Look on the back of the death certificate" the man waved the document above his head, "here it is in plain English, sealed and notarized. Syphillis, I believe it was. Isn't that the truth?" and with an unsteady arm, ending in a trembling fingertip, the man crouched over slightly and pointed in Robert's face, then stood to his full height while his finger was still pointed at Robert's nose, and the man sort of turned his back on Robert, still with that finger all up in the middle of Robert's face, and the man commence to raising his voice like he was urging on a game cock, "he is not just a philanderer, an abuser of women, not just a shirker of his responsibilities, not just a hard-hearted killer and carrier of filthy social diseases, but, worst of all, he is a plagiarist!"

Although the Robert who was watching the scene understood, few among the upper (or, for that matter, even among the lower) gallery knew what a plagiarist was.

"Isn't it true that you stole all your music from others, changed one or two words here and there, altered a note or two, and then proclaimed far and wide that you had composed those songs when the horrible truth is that you are nothing more than a two-bit, musical copy cat. You are no artist, no professional musician. Isn't it true that you are a cold-blooded, two-bit thief, a hack who has never had an original idea in your life?"

"No, sir," Robert mumbled.

"What did you say, boy?"

"No, sir."

"No, sir?" The white man was befuddled as he repeated Robert's two words. "No, sir? Are you saying our experts are wrong? What about Mr. Son House's Preaching Blues, which you stole? What about…" the man sputtered in rage, reached down into his well-worn, dark brown leather, over-sized brief case and pulled out about twenty platters and threw them at Robert's feet, naming each in turn and indicating what song Robert claimed was his that he had actually stolen from some other recording artist. "…and then there's Kokomo Arnold did Milk Cow Blues, you stole it and called it Milkcow's Calf. LeRoy Carr had a hit with When The Sun Goes Down, you copied it as Love In Vain. And look, here's another Kokomo Arnold. Let's see, yes, it's Arnold's Old Original Kokomo Blues, which you called Sweet Home Chicago. And another Leroy Carr. This time it's I Believe I'll Dust My Broom, which is actually Carr's "I Believe I'll Make A Change. Boy, you are a complete and utter, through and through fraud. Isn't that the truth?"

Robert looked at the man both in bewilderment and in veiled anger. Nobody had ever, ever before accused Robert of not being a musicianeer, even when Mr. Son House was admonishing Robert not to play the guitar, even then Mr. House had acknowledged that Robert could play the harp real good, that Robert was indeed a musicianeer even if, at that time, he wasn't even half the guitarist he became. Besides, everybody knowed that a lot of the songsters all sang the same song, just sang them in their own way—didn't no one body own the music. The music was for everybody to use, each according to their own way. Couldn't be that no one body could own all the music. But Robert remained silent. He knew that white men liked to claim property and would have no understanding of a song belonging to everybody.

Not satisfied with Robert's silence, the man piled on more accusations.

"Are you saying all the evidence and information we have gathered on your, your rambling about, your philandering, your cruel and callous behavior toward the women of your own race—and we have not yet brought up your considerable drinking problem—are you saying that all of this is a lie? Are you calling us white men a lie?"

"No, sir."

"Speak up, boy. This is your chance to defend yourself, to tell the truth for once in your miserable life."

"Sir, all I can say is, no, sir. I ain't got nothing: no papers, no books, no experts, no witnesses. All I got is me and my music, and all I can say is no, sir. Make of me what you will. In life or in death. All I got to say is: no, sir. No, sir. I'm already dead. Yall done done everything you could to make sure I never lived. You got the power. You got me sitting up here listening to you run me down like I was a dog and you was in a buckboard. You got most everybody afeared of you. Afeared you going to kill them and all they family too. Even some of yall what tries to helps us, yall still wants us to sing your song, yall still wants us to accept you into our circle of loved ones. I can't say nothing more but I sure can say this little bit, and what I'm saying is: no, sir. No, sir. What-so-ever you got to say, I says no, sir. No, sir. No, sir. I'm dead now, you can't do me no more worse than you already done me. Well, I guess you could try to scrape away my name from people's ears like them teachers used to ask us to erase they blackboards, but even so, even if you erase me, I can still say, no. And when you finish figuring up on me and come up with whatever sum you come to, I still say, no, sir. No, sir. No, sir. That's what my music says. That's what my life says. That's what my death says. That's what I wants people to remember me by. Whatever yall was trying to do to me, I said, no, sir. When I couldn't say it with my mouth, I said it with my feet. When I couldn't write it in a book, I fixed it into a song: no, sir. No, sir. NO. Sir.

By then all the negroes was dancing. They ain't had no reason to be dancing. They ain't had nothing but hard times and barely getting by. It was 1931. Depression had camped out all across the country and was especial bad news deep down south. There the black and poor had been overworked and so severely underpaid, it might as well been never paid. They had worms in their stomach and mouths invested with rotted teeth. They had undisclosed illnesses and a heap of miscellaneous mutilations. They had scattered and shattered dreams and near-useless hope buckets what the bottoms done dropped out of. Where was their joy, their evidence of having lived? It was in the "No" of their music, their dance, their singing.

Some of them sang on Saturday night. Most of them sang on Sunday morning. A few of them sang at both services. And one or two of them sang at neither. But, in general, it was this singing, this no that said yes, it was this that was the substance of Robert Johnson. It was this "no" that even in death Robert stood for. And no matter how much they tried to understand the music he made, tried to figure up on the power of it, the force of it, the essence of it, at the center of the music was a refusal to not exist, a refusal to be insignificant, a no that was a yes, an affirmation of life.

The white men pounded their canes hard against the floorboards of the courthouse. One of them banged and banged with his little wooden hammer, shouting out: order, order. Order in the court.

But the assembled negroes paid them no mind. That was how the colored survived—whenever they could, they paid the white folks no mind. And in those moments of unmindedness, when the only authority was the spirit, at precisely those moments Robert smiled and felt satisfied that all his music making had not been in vain. There was something too beautiful about dancing negroes. It was almost like they were electric generators or batteries jumping off sparks. And even Ginny was there, doing her little side-to-side two step, she never could dance worth spit, but even she had her own way of getting down.

It made you feel like singing extra hard. You take six days of hard labor and stomp it down.

"Isn't it true you don't believe in God."

"No, sir."

"Isn't it true you have blasphemed and denied our Lord and Savior, Jesus Christ?"

"No, sir. I believes in life. I just don't believes in you."

"Isn't it true?"

"No, sir."

"Isn't it?

"No, sir."

"Say, 'yes, sir,' boy!"

"No, sir."

Finally, Robert got tired and just stood up and took in to walking. Just plum walked on away. Robert knew they was going to come after him, knew there wasn't going to be no hiding place, but Robert figured if he kept moving, they would have a devil of a time catching him. And more than that, Robert also took a vow: he would never own nothing more than he could carry. There would be absolutely nothing to tie him down.

It was a hell of a hard way to live, but when Robert compared the tough life on the road to the deadly softness of a cotton boll, when Robert thought about the whichever-way-the-wind-blows of hiway traveling compared to the certainties of field work, the fleeting pleasures of occasional love compared to the stable joys of family life, in Robert's mind the choice was easy to make even if it the choice was hard to handle. For Robert was determined not to be up under no white man's command and because the white folks wanted to own everything they could lay their hands on, Robert ain't had no choice but to be like his brother the wind.

Now you might think such a choice meant scurrying around like a rat trying to dodge two cats, but Robert knew that the secret of running off was to run slow, in fact, to slow walk—make friends everywhere you go, but not to stay so long in one place that your feets grow roots.

Robert walked like a gypsy. Showing up when you least expected him, gone when you tried to find him.

And that's when the white men cut the dogs loose. The dogs. They said they sicced the dogs on him because he was evil. The dogs sniffed everywhere trying to catch his scent. The dogs sniffed at trees and rocks, mules and tractors, women's underwear, and the seats of juke chairs where it was rumoured Robert had sat down to play. Everytime they heard a radio playing amongst colored people, the dogs would circle around the edges of the gathering, in search of Robert's spoor. And don't let two or three negro males be drinking, the dogs would trot up and stick their noses to the tops of open liquor bottles trying to determine had Robert's lips been there. Whenever a train pulled into a station, the dogs hopped up and went from freight car to freight car. A couple of times they even sensed a faint trail gone almost cold.

Even though it looked more like it was going to be later rather than sooner, in fact it had become increasingly apparent that it was going to be much, much later, yet and still the dogs were not discouraged, they kept on the trail of Robert Johnson.

Robert got so he could hear the barking even when it was four or five days away and, unless he got drunk or something, Robert was able to keep them at least three or four days off, not letting them get no closer, but it called for Robert being vigilant and not letting down his guard, plus, Robert knew a lot of the others walking along beside him weren't able to sense the dogs like Robert could, so sometimes when the dogs was starting to get close, like a couple of days off, the other guys wouldn't hear nothing, nothing at all. So those guys not knowing nothing about the hounds, well, those guys would be a liability to Robert and a liability to themselves, so Robert he took to traveling alone a lot of times, and even when he was with somebody, sometimes, for their own good, he would leave them and take off.

Robert knew how to dodge the hounds, how to throw them off his trail, but some of the musicianeers who wanted to follow him, well they didn't know about the hounds, and since Robert knew the hounds would pounce on anybody who was close to Robert and since Robert ain't wanted nobody to get hurted up behind him, well, whenever the hounds was getting close, Robert, he would take off by himself.

"Mister."

It was Brother Bras. This was the first somebody Robert met that could sense the hounds, in fact, seem like he was better at it than even Robert was.

"Robert, you is guided by ways you don't rightly remember. Your mind done forgot, but your spirit catch the feeling, and when you catch the feeling—you call it the 'no, sir,' and when you get into that 'no sir' manner of being, that is when you are at your best. Our power is not the power of flesh. Our memory is not of this world."

Brother Bras talked all night that first night, chanting incantations. He used words that Robert had never before heard, words that Robert did not understand, but what was more important than meaning was spirit and the existence of another world. Bras said even if you never reach it, always remember there is another world. There is another world. You can't walk there. You got to go there in spirit and in truth.

When Robert woke up he was delirious like as if he had been running a fever, which, once he felt his forehead, Robert decided it was definitely the case that he was running a fever. Being a walking musicianeer, Robert was in pretty good physical shape and was even used to doctoring and dentisting on himself whenever he was feeling poorly. He even knew a little bit about teas and herbs, not much, but enough to get by. So, as his whole body ached like somebody had been beating him with a licking stick all night long, even as he retched and vomited up emptiness because he had not eaten since early yesterday, even amidst all that sickness, Robert was aware that he had had a strange dream, but he couldn't remember much of it, partly because after the first night in the swamp, instead of thinking on his dream, he spent the day upchucking, belching and retching in horrible spasms that led him to moan and roll from side to side like a calf what done ate poison weed. And when the runs hit him later in the morning, Robert's miserableness was so complete he started in to praying that he would die so it would all be over.

Brother Bras gave Robert some flat bread to chew on, but even Robert's teeth was hurting him, every time he bit down it was like chewing on barbed wire. And shortly after noon is when his bowels first loosed up, and there was no where to go but just off to the side of the hut by the tree, in the bushes. As he tried to squat and keep his balance and keep from splashing loose shit all on his clothes—the shit had come shooting out him so fast, he barely had time to pull his britches down. How could he have so much shit in him when he had not eaten in over twenty-four hours? And it stunk to high heavens, all runny and smelly, and look like it smell even more worse than skunk juice, which all just made him even sicker, and having to wipe his ass with handfuls of small leaves ain't helped none neither—seemed like there weren't no plant up in the swamps that was flat and big-leafed. Robert was more miserable than he ever remembered feeling in all his life, physically that is, not like heartache or the pain he felt when Ginny died, but just a general body misery, like as if he done been poisoned by somebody.

Brother Bras had said they would wait until tomorrow to travel, wait until Robert was feeling better. But he ain't never felt no better, not at high noon, not on in to what was usually supper time, and not even at dusk when he started to cool down some, and the night noises was even worse. Robert was sick, so sick, he felt like one foot in the grave.

Robert couldn't sleep but for short snatches. Some times he had to crawl over to the tree to shit. Some time he just lay there and moaned, and moaned, and moaned some more. And one time, when he thought he was just passing gas, he was actually shitting on himself, and he was so sick he lay their in his soiled trousers and cried. He was feeling so miserable, he cried. Not sobbing but silently, tears streamed and he kept blinking his eyes, his hands with bits of shitty leaves stuck to them, seemed like even dipping his hands in the swamp water was not enough to remove the smell and whatnot, so by that night, both hands were too filthy to wipe his eyes, so he kept brushing his face against his shirt sleeve. Oh, it was awful. Awful.

The next morning he was all shitted out and he was mighty thankful that the runs was over. When he opened his eyes and looked around, there was some clean field-hand overalls near by and, best of all, a bucket of clean water and a rag and some hard soap. Brother Bras was nowhere to be seen or heard, which, of course, did not mean he weren't not around 'cause Bras had a way of being there and you wouldn't even know he was there even if you was looking for him and listening out for him.

Brother Bras must have been somewhere nearby though, for as soon as Robert finished washing up—and it had taken him more than forty minutes, shucks he spent almost twenty minutes washing his sore butt what was all raw and tender from shitting all day and all night, and even though it hurt, Robert had wanted to make sure he was clean. He hated being dirty, and being this filthy was embarrassing. Anyway, no sooner was Robert finished, Brother Bras appeared and took away the bucket of now slimy water and also took Robert's soiled trousers. Bras left behind a gourd with some liquid what had leaves in it. It didn't smell too bad but when Robert took a taste of it on the tip of his tongue, it was so bitter it make Robert screw up his face. Brother Bras smiled and motioned for Robert to drink it up. The potion made Robert drowsy and before he knew it, Robert lay down and slept some more. He felt so weak. He wasn't as feverish as yesterday, but now he was feeling empty, and he was actually feeling more thirsty than hungry. He wished for more of the flatbread. It was sort of tasteless but it had settled in his stomach and seemed to help absorb his gas so that he wasn't passing as much gas and fouling up the air so much. Finally Robert fell asleep and did not awake until the middle of the next morning.

By now he had almost forgotten about the dream. Almost. How could he forget being dead and being judged? But no matter how hard he thought on it, Robert could not remember the specifics. He just remembered being judged and people dancing. The white men was judging him and the colored was dancing, at least those that came to the courthouse, at first he had thought there was a lot of people at the courthouse but the one thing he remembered in detail is that he had counted the colored people who were present, there was a grand total of thirteen people dancing around him. He weren't playing his guitar. He was just standing up clapping his hands and singing out and people was circling around him. Or was he sitting on a log? Robert couldn't remember. He tried, but he couldn't remember.

Brother Bras had cooked up some brownish-looking soup in a pot. The soup had leaves in it too. Look like everything Brother Bras ate or drank had leaves in it. The soup was tasty but hot, like somebody had put too much pepper in it. All day Robert ate soup and flatbread. And then he fell asleep early and slept so soundly that when he woke up he was looking up at trees and sky, flat on his back in the little boat floating through the swamps. By now he was totally dependent on Brother Bras and he judged that Bras was doing all he could to help poor Robert get back on his feet. So Robert surrendered himself and before long, as they drifted across the swamp, Robert fell off to sleep again.

When Robert came to the second time he was still on his back, so the first thing he saw was a beautiful blueness. Open sky. But he was on dry land now, not in the little boat. He sat up and felt himself, literally felt his face and rubbed his legs. He was in his own clothes now. Brother Bras must have dressed him—his sack? Where was his sack? No sooner Robert look down, he see the sack beside him. Everything was ok.

As he slowly gained his feet, Robert tried to remember everything he been through, especially that dream, but the harder he tried to remember, the less he could rightly say what had really happened and what he dreamed had happened, it was all so jumbled up. He had been in a boat in the swamp and there had been someone else there, but that is all he could remember. That and the strange taste in his mouth. That's all. A small boat. A big swamp. An invisible black man. And a strange taste in his mouth.

Yet, somehow, it did not frighten Robert that he could not remember anything much. In fact he felt at peace, somehow he felt like someone or something had told him that what he was doing was right, was good. Robert stood to his feet. He felt strong.

Even though he had no idea where he was, he felt no fear. So he picked up his sack and started walking again. What would he tell Callie? He didn't know. How could he explain any of this? He couldn't.

It was almost like he had had a night vision, maybe Brother Bras was a two-headed, but he had not told Robert anything about playing the guitar. Nothing. But still and all Robert had that feeling he get when a song want to come out of him, except this time it was a deep feeling, like it was ten or twenty songs what wanted to come out of him all at one time.

One thing Robert knew for sure, he wasn't dead yet, so Robert set out to walking.

Robert must of walk for about two hours or so and the sun was steady coming up but it was still low, so it weren't too hot, and there was a breeze that kind of cooled Robert as he walked.

Birds was just a warbling and chirping. And then Robert heard a singing. Sounded like a woman, way off in the distance. And since Robert had no particular destination, finding that pretty voice seemed like a good thing to do. Robert knowed the distant woman couldn't be too far off and so, even though he had to get off the road and cut into the woods, he followed after the singing, after all, this singing woman was a combination of Robert's two driving interests in life.

He had to go find the woman who was singing all pretty like that, more pretty than any woman singing he had ever heard before. In that moment of quick decision, Robert pushed aside the bits and pieces of memory that he had been puzzling over. Those hard days and nights in the swamp was gone. This was a new day. A new adventure. Robert figured he had plenty of time to catch up to the two-headeds, but he might never again have a chance to run up on an angel-voiced woman like what he was hearing now.

-23-

When the woman's singing sounded like he was drawing nearer to it, Robert started stepping slower and more careful like, trying not to make no noise, and pausing every few steps to make sure that he was not disturbing nothing and also that he was headed directly toward the source, sound can get tricky in the woods.

Soon he saw a little creek. The singing was clear now and even more beautiful. There was two big trees growing side by side and the voice seemed to be emanating from the other side of the trees. And he could hear splashing water and the gurgle of the creek flowing over rocks.

Robert sat his sack down real careful like and eased up close to the two trees. She was still singing, and if he had been thinking about it, he would have wondered how come her singing sounded so quiet now when just a few minutes back when he was on the road he had heard her singing clear like she was just a few yards away even though back then she must of been a good three hundred feet or so from the road, a good ways off, but now she sounded soft and low, like she was singing to herself. But he wasn't thinking about any of that now.

Robert had stuck his head up in the small opening between the two trees to see if he could see his angel. She was still singing so sweet and all.

What he saw stunned him.

A black woman, real tall, naked in the water, washing herself. And singing.

This was not just any naked woman. Robert done seen many a naked woman so he had a basis for comparing. This woman was, well, was… damn. Just god damn.

Dark skinned everywhere. A shining, licorice dark. Even the insides of her hands was tan. Firm breasts, round like medium-sized cantaloupes with nipples dark as raisins. Tight waisted with hips like cracker barrel hoops. A butt sitting up high, like what them rich white women's bustle be modeled on, except her flanks was muscular. And thighs thick as huge hams. Her arms were long and lean, well formed. She had big hands with strong-looking fingers. Her hair, cast iron black, was all over her head, wet and crinkly like she had just let it growed and had never hot combed it, or greased it, or even tied it down or nothing, or combed it out, or even plaited it. Her eyes were almond shaped, but large like prunes. A big nose. Real big, not unattractive, but bigger than average. And a mouth bigger than her nose. As she sang her teeth flashed. Her ears were kind of long but they fit in right nice with her oval face and high cheek bones. Now her neck, that was long, real long, made her head sit up proud, and she had pronounced collar bones, that flared across the top of her chest. And breasts, those breasts again. And down there, her sex was lightly covered with curly hair, but she was so dark that even with her being less than twelve feet away it was hard to distinguish her pubic hair from the insides of her thighs.

This weren't no any ordinary kind of woman, not no Indian, and certainly not no white woman, and neither was she Mexican or gypsy or nothing like that. From the singing Robert had already assumed she was black, even though, this being Louisiana, she could a been a mix up of a lot of things, but, looking upon her, there didn't seem to be nothing much mixed up about her, from hair, to butt, to the size of her thighs, the full body profile of her was straight breed black.

When she paused in her movements and stood stark still, she even took to looking like a statue or something. Her angular face neither smiling nor frowning, but fascinating all the same. Time and again, whenever Robert look upon another part of her, he get drawn back to her face and how it look like she was wearing a mask on top of her real face, well not that she didn't look real. She looked real real, more real than any woman Robert ever dream of seeing—which momentarily confused Robert, how could a dream be real? How could this be a real woman, and yet, looking upon her, you could not deny that this was a real woman.

Nor could you avoid how fascinating beautiful she was, except if you did not like powerful looking women, 'cause she sure was powerful and Robert knew there was men who was scared of powerful women. It was a combination of power and beauty, or was her power the source of her beauty?

Now Robert didn't know he was an appreciator of African art. Far as he knew, he had never even much ever seen any African art, but the irony was that whatsoever it was that Robert thought of as beautiful or good when he look upon people or things, well a lot of Robert's judgments was real close to the beliefs and preferences that African carvers and musicians had. Lots of Mississippi born and bred black people had that kind of preference deep up inside of them, so deep inbred that it didn't seem like no choice or nothing, it just seem natural, so natural that no amount of exposure to other ways or other instructions could bleach that blackness out of them.

Now if you're wondering was Robert thinking this, the answer is no. Robert was just real caught up in enjoying the sight of this woman he was looking upon and sort of imagining he was getting with her, you know his hand moving up and down the sturdiness of her hefty back, the bulge of her butt, up between the twin pillars of her thighs, thick as oak trees. Man, a woman like this.

And that's one way womens teaches men—a man be attracted to her and wants to learn how to do whatsoever it take to get and stay close to her, which was one of the many thoughts racing up and down Robert's spine: one second he thinking with his hands and imagining touching her, another second he thinking with his head and wondering what he got to do to get her to like him, another second his dick take over and he just want to get to know her in a real close up way (which include wondering do he have what it take to satisfy something like that, and if he don't have it, what was the chances of him getting it or learning it?), and every now and again, even his music sense take a turn reflecting on the woman 'cause hot damn it sure would be a sack full to be able to play like she singing, indeed, what would it sound like for them to play together, and then what about… he must of stood there for two or three whole minutes just a looking at her and listening to her.

Robert was used to hearing all kinds of womens singing on the radio and all. He had an ear for catching the different ways they inflected notes, how some sung up high in their head with a kind of voice full of air, wispy and soft but still sharp, and this woman had some of that sharpness to her sound but she also had a power, like how an owl sound fuller than a wren or a sparrow, or a jaybird for that matter, but not sharp like a hawk. So she had some of that owl strength up in her voice, but she also had this fullness to her sound, a real pleasant turtle dove cooing that was warm and inviting. But to tell the truth, the sight of her was so entrancing that even though her sound is what had initially made him want to see her, now that he done seen her, he was so wrapped up in what he saw, he almost stopped hearing her.

Suddenly Robert became aware that he was holding his breath 'cause he had to exhale so he could take in more air. Upon first spotting her gleaming wet in that water, he was so shocked he must had sucked up about three square feet of air. Maybe it was because it was early in the morning and nobody ever expects to walk up on a naked woman like this. Maybe it was because it was out in the middle of lost-found. Maybe it was because he didn't expect an angel to be a black woman shocking you with her beauty—not that he thought it would be a white woman or nothing, shit, he didn't know what an angel looked like, which is why he had left the road to come up in these woods and see. Maybe it was because she was so big and black and beautiful, a big, black, beautiful woman, Lord it made his nature stand up straight. Maybe it was because he hadn't had no nookie in going on over a week now. Or maybe it was because of all of that, kind of mixed up together, or none of that. Maybe it was just because she was looking at him.

Damn, she was looking at him.

Or, at least, it look like she was looking at him.

It be an embarrassing thing to be caught peeping on somebody. When you get founded out doing something you know is wrong, most people turn all shame-faced and looks away, but Robert couldn't stop looking even though it look like she was looking right at him, except she was still singing and now was stepping upon the bank like as if he wasn't looking at her. She wasn't in no hurry or nothing, or wasn't trying to cover up her nakedness. So maybe she didn't see him. But even if she did see him, Robert couldn't stop looking at her.

She reach down and pick up a cloth from on the ground and when she stand up, she stop singing and look at him again. Then she extend her arms out unfolding the cloth, it was a pretty-pretty, deep dark blue, almost black, with little, white-kind of, seed-shaped designs arranged all along the border of it. She shook the cloth and then flips it over her head and extends her arms again, this time with the cloth stretched out behind her, and she spreads her legs some and stands straight and tall.

"You don't have to try and hide. You can come out. I'm not going to hurt you."

Well, right then, Robert should of knowed he was dealing with a higher power, 'cause most naked women would have been afraid of a strange man spying upon them, but here she was telling him he didn't have no reason to be afeared as though he was the one in danger, which should, right off, established who had the upper hand.

And then she smiled right at Robert. Hummed a little snatch of the wordless song she had been singing—or, it seem like to Robert the song was wordless 'cause if what she had been singing was words, they was words in a language Robert ain't never heard tell of, a language that didn't sound like no language Robert knew anything about. And then she proceed to wrap the cloth around her body. It go around her one time and a half, and then she roll the top of the cloth down a couple of times, fitting under her arms and right across her breasts. When she finish with her wrap, she slide her feet into some slipper looking shoes with little white stones on them. And then she clasp her hands in front of her, her hands resting on her thighs, right below her privates, and she patiently wait on Robert to show himself.

Robert was transfixed by the way the thin cloth cling to her wet nakedness, like do a sweat-drenched shirt after a long day in the fields. Seem as though that fabric was searching out every curve and crevice of her body to settle up close in, which all was disturbing Robert, and though he heard her talk to him, he was still so much up into looking and thinking on her, he couldn't function, didn't respond.

For maybe the first time in his young life, Robert hesitate to approach a woman he interested in. Why? He don't know why. For a second he felt unworthy. She look so queenly and he ain't had no present to bring to her, like they say in the bible, you brings presents to kings and queens. She look so good. She look like something you supposed to give gifts to, but he ain't got nothing. Except his guitar and his playing shoes and his good hat. She would look funny in his hat and she don't look like she would wear none of his shoes. Robert had seen womens in men shoes before, lots of womens wore them in the field. He could not imagine this woman in the fields with brogans on. While he was hesitating, she smiled some more and then spoke up.

"I'm Zooley," which is when she reached out her hand to him, offering to shake, which, of course, was an invitation he could not refuse.

Yes, this was one of those, what they call, turning points in Robert's life. In fact, it is always a turning point when a man who's used to having his way with women run up on a woman he desire but a woman who is clearly superior to him. As Robert float closer to Zooley—it ain't felt like he was walking, it was like her open hand was reeling him in, not that he was trying to fight the feeling or nothing, but even if he had been of a mind to resist, he knew it wouldn't made not one bit of difference.

As he draw neigh, Robert realize she so tall, he got to raise up his head some and look upwards at her in order to peer up into her eyes. The woman was easy well over six feet tall, almost a whole head higher up than him, plus, she had hypnotizing snake eyes all up in her pretty face.

Robert was speechless.

Zooley laugh some more at his mouth hanging wide open. "Ain't you never seed a woman before?"

"I done seen lots of women, but, but you, you something else."

"Well, thank you."

By now he was touching her hand and what he thought was going to be some feather-soft, dainty, high class, limp-wrist handshake was instead a firm encasing of his long-fingered hand. Zooley briefly pressed her palms together around his right hand, and instead of just letting go, her left hand patted the back of his right hand and then traveled up to his shoulder and gently guided him into a welcoming but very brief shoulder to shoulder hug, almost like a dragonfly buzzing against your skin.

"Come on, we don't have a whole lot of time."

Robert hated to seem contrary, but time was not hardly no issue as far as he was concerned. In his mixed-up mind he sought the right words to convey to her that he was available to her for how-so-ever long she might want him around.

Robert hated to say anything that sounded corny or hick-like. A big part of him wanted to be hip, wanted to avail himself of all the swift language the radio musicaneers used, but whenever he tried them words in his mouth around all the people he was usually around in Mississippi it didn't ring true. He just always came off as odd and fake when he tried to talk like that and so he usually didn't talk like he was as up on the latest trends, leastwise not with his mouth even though he was constantly thinking about talking the latest talk, and though she—"Sue-Lee" he needed to remember to call her by her name: Sue-Lee. Robert wondered if she liked being called Sue, you know, by just the first part of her name. Sue-Lee had not said anything to indicate that she talked that hi-dee-ho talk but somebody as fabulous as Sue-Lee, well she just had to be up on whatever was the latest whatever.

Meanwhile, Robert still ain't found the right words to say, so he just kind of blurts out, "Lady Sue, I got as much time as you need."

"It's Zooley, not Sue Lee."

"Zoo." Robert repeated hearing now that she was meaning her name start with a zee and not an "s". He knew what a Sue was but he ain't knowed what a zoo was, well, he had read about a zoo, some place where they had lions and tigers and such, sort of like a circus, but instead of traveling around it was stayed up in one particular place, but though Robert imagine Zoo-Lee was a wild somebody and probably had a lot of tiger up in her when she was in bed, still he don't believe that's what all her name meant or nothing. "That's a new one on me, but I believe I got it now. Zoo-Lee."

"Yeah, you got the first part right, Zoo. The second part is more like lay than like lee. You know in most of our peoples tongues you pronounce the a, e, i, o and u as ah, a, eee, ooo, ooh and the y sound be a kind of short e."

And all Robert could do was marvel at how intelligent this woman was, and like wet follow water, Robert found himself wishing to be a special student up under Zooley's instruction, in what he imagined was her especial one room school house with one teacher—her, and one student—him, and school in session year round, which was an odd way to be thinking upon Zooley seeing as how Robert didn't much care for school even though he do like to learn new things, but all of sudden school seem real appealing to him—a teacher you likes can make you want to learn anything.

"Zooley. Alright, I got it."

"Yeah, that's it. You got it." Damn, this woman was still holding his hand, and her palm was still damp from the creek water, but, shit, Zooley could of poured a whole bucket of water on Robert's head and it would not have made him no never mind. "Come on," Zooley tugged softly on Robert's hand, "let's go."

Robert start to step off with her when he remember he done left his sack up by the two trees. He hold back. Zooley feel him hesitate and drop his hand, turns away and just starts in to stepping off back up creek.

"Zooley, ah I got to get my traveling sack."

Zooley don't seem to pay no mind. Robert scrambled up the slight embankment, scurried behind the trees, snatched up his sack and scampered right back, but even though it didn't take Robert even one whole minute to secure his sack, Zooley still was a good twenty or thirty feet on down the way. For sure, this weren't no woman that was going to wait on you.

Robert was fashioning a mental profile on Zooley, looking for every little piece to help him unpuzzle what kind of woman this woman was.

Robert trot to catch up behind Zooley like a milk calf following its mama, and while he trotting, a warning come upon him sort of like the sound of a rattler shaking its tail. Robert pull up abruptly. He was supposed to be down here looking for them two headeds and now here he was chasing after some fine-ass woman—for sure she was fine, finer than anything he ever seen in Mississippi but still, this ain't what he come down here for. If he ain't be careful, it was going to turn out like Ike had warned him: what-so-ever it is that you crazy about is the thing what can kill you, so you got to mind yourself when you going after something you wants that you really likes. But shit, this woman weren't just fine, she was smart, he could learn from her as well as enjoy her, surely that weren't the same thing as just going after a woman on account of wanting her.

Somebody looking upon this little dance might not have seen what was really going down. To the outside it probably just look like Robert stumble a little bit and pause to catch his balance, and it might also have seem like Zooley was unaware of what was going on behind her back, but that was not the case. Robert had not stumbled he had hesitated, he had second-guessed himself, he had felt a warning that he was about to jump into some still waters what was way deeper than he could imagine. And, as for Zooley, well there was nothing shallow about her, she knew she had an ocean of knowledge compared to the pond Robert was coming from, but she also knew that Robert needed a long drink of what she was willing to offer if Robert was ever going to grow to his fullest potential.

How did she know this? Well, black women, like all women, are born with a maternal instinct, but added up on top of that instinct is the instruction that living black in white America imparts to a woman, an instruction what makes clear to the black woman that she be the main sustenance for a strong black man who got the mighty task of withstanding the trials and tribulations of America in general, but most especial, the never-ending trials and tribulations of living up in the face of Mississippi, and that don't be no job for the weak 'cause you see Mississippi, well Mississippi will take and whittle down the average black giant into a rather ordinary nigger midget, turn a throne into a footstool, a wise man into a babbling fool.

So Zooley was testing Robert. If he took too long to catch up or hollered for her to hold up, she would know he was not ready. Zooley kept watching and hoped that Brother Bras was right about this one.

Fuck it, Robert thought, if you don't play you ain't going to never win, so he run and catch up with Zooley, and when he do, Zooley look over at him and smile.

Zooley stop, and place a hand atop his shoulder. "If you come with me, there are two things you must accept. One, I will change you. Two, I will not be your woman."

Now, this was a crossroads: go where-so-ever with her or return to that hiway yonder and keep on stepping searching for the two-headeds. Like he do in the jukes when he looking upon a woman and trying to decide whether he can pull her, Robert do some mental arithmetic. She had sounded some serious when she said she weren't going to lay down with him, so what would be the reason to go with her if he couldn't fuck her? Sometimes with a man it get down to that basic a calculation.

Robert look deep into Zooley's eyes but he can't fully figure her out, so he decide to play for time, see if he can get more information to help him decide what all to do. "Zooley, I could be somebody out to do you some harm. How come you trust me? You don't even much know my name. You don't know who I am?"

Like a checkers champeen what sucker you into a jump so they can get a triple decker and end up with a king, Zooley responded to Robert without hesitation, "Do you know who you are?"

"What?"

"Do *you* know who you are?"

Robert start to answer, I'm Robert Johnson, a Mississippi musicianeer, but he didn't. At this moment, his mouth hanging open for a second time,

all the implications of Zooley's question rush over him like getting caught up in a stampede.

Who was he? Robert didn't even know where to start.

What was his name? He went by some many different names. Which one was him? Were any of them really him?

Do you know who you are, she had asked him, and that was a damn good question: who was he? Zooley started singing again. And walking.

If Zooley could help him answer that question this would surely be worth whatever the cost.

Although he felt some real anxiety, Robert gave the most honest respond he could give to Zooley's profound question: nothing.

Though Robert did not say a mumbling word, he did make a decision: he decided to join her, to follow her lead, and hopefully to find out the answer to a question what had been a botheration to him ever since he learn how to think on things.

Silently, Robert fell in step, stride for stride with Zooley, and though she obviously was not rushing, he still had to extend himself some to keep up with her long-legged gait. Plus the terrain was uneven and sometimes they had to wind through trees and bushes as they followed along side the creek.

All the while Zooley was humming like as if she was a jaybird messing with a cat, flying just out of reach, dipping and what not, and steady singing knowing good and well the cat want to catch her but can't 'cause she stay out of reach even as she be almost close enough to touch. So Robert, he do like the cat, and try to forget about catching her at the same time that he delight in listening to her.

Robert's conscious mind was trying to catch the drift of her song so he could hum along with her, and hopefully impress her, meanwhile his subconscious mind was deeply wrestling with the one seemingly simple yet truly powerful question that he had never before been able to answer.

Who? Who? Who am I?

-24-

THEY HAD NOT BEEN WALKING EVEN TEN MINUTES, THE CREEK ABOUT THREE minutes behind them, when they come to a clearing and what look like a little hut or something. It seemed sturdy enough but it was built in a circle shape, like the way people forms up when they watching somebody dance. Most houses Robert seen be build like boxes.

"We are here."

"Yeah," was all that Robert said, but what he really wanted to ask was, where the hell was here? Was he still in Louisiana or back in Mississippi or someplace else? Was there a town nearby? Was this on a map somewhere? What? But as was his way when traveling, Robert ain't asked no questions out loud. He just kept his eyes and ears open, wide open. What now?

"Come on."

Robert had a habit of surrendering to his fate rather than trying to challenge or change the outcome of situations. Hell, if he did not like what was happening, he could always walk away, except now he was in so deep that just walking away would have been another kind of adventure, even though, to be truthful, he wasn't in no way desirous of walking away. Zooley was too fine to walk away from.

Like most men who be standing next to a woman they like looking upon and with whom they hope to do more than just look at, Robert was ready to put up with a lot of uncertainty just for the chance to stay up close to this woman. Now some might say Robert was being obsessive, but the truth is deeper than obsession.

We all have dreams, fantasies, peoples, and situations we would like to be all deep up in, and when a dream be standing next to you, living and breathing, and warm, and you can hear them, look over and see the texture of their hair around their ears and down the back of their neck, like in this case with Zooley and that mass of black hair sticking every which a ways all over her head, making Robert wonder about how she manage her hair, what she do with it and all, and while he looking at her hair and thinking on what it must feel like to have his hands all up in that hair, not to mention have his hands on other parts of her, damn, anyway, while he standing there transfixed, a butterfly come along and alight on the top of Zooley head, which is when Robert make up his mind, this woman is what he been waiting his whole life to be with, don't care what it take to make it come true.

The butterfly flap a few times and jump off, flit around her head, and Zooley act like this butterfly anointing is something that happen all the time. She don't even look like she paying it no mind. The butterfly fly off and then loop back around and land on her leg. Zooley look down upon it and smile at the butterfly. The butterfly flap its wings in slow motion.

Now Robert ain't superstitious or nothing, but he do believe in signs, and he don't need no book to tell him that he standing next to a special woman. Meanwhile, the butterfly done flew off.

Instead of going up in the hut, Zooley go over to a patch of flowers and what not, she stoop down and when Robert come up behind her, he see that these are strawberry plants. Zooley picks a couple of big fat red ones. She stands up. The butterfly come circling nearby. Zooley slowly raise one of the strawberries to her big lips and bites a piece of it. She closes her eyes as she tastes it.

"Hmmm."

By now Robert's mouth is moist, like somebody was holding out a hambone to a hungry dog. Zooley turn the strawberry toward Robert. He can see her teeth marks, the deep red on the outside of the berry and the pinkish-white center of it. Robert sit his sack down and go to reach for the strawberry, but Zooley done already put the berry up close to his lips. Robert open his mouth. Zooley places the strawberry about halfway in. Robert bite down on it. The berry so sweet he like to pee on himself when he suck on the juice and the taste of it goes shooting all through his mouth and down his throat. Then while all that wonderfulness was happening, Zooley wipe his lips with her fingertips cause he had a piece of the strawberry stuck on his lips—he would of got it but she just quick like reach up her hand to her mouth and lick the little piece of strawberry off her finger.

Now, as far as Robert was concerned, that one little motion sealed her fate. The casualness of the way she wiped his lips with her fingertips, not to mention the feel of her fingertips, it was like she was already familiar with him, real familiar, and comfortable doing something some womens would do for their children in a minute, but would never think of approaching they man that way, but she ain't even much hesitate or nothing, just reach out like she birthed him and wanted to make sure he was presentable, even though there wasn't no public around to see him drooling. She wasn't afeared to touch his spittle, so that told him she was probably a real outrageous type of lover who would not hesitate to handle up on him any kind of which ways might pop into her or his head, and, of course, Robert he like a woman who like that.

He don't say nothing as he watch her watching him watch her lick the little piece of strawberry she done wiped off his lips onto her fingertips. Robert is fascinated by the length of her tongue, the Mississippi mud red of it—he suspect she a Louisiana woman, although he done seen she ain't got no dick, well, maybe she got one in a box somewhere or something, but ain't no dick part of her anatomy, he seen that she was woman built when he look upon her back down at the creek—the color of her tongue remind him of Mississippi earth. He thinking of how her tongue would taste all up in his mouth, how it would feel as he gently suck on that long-ass tongue, and the way it curled around her finger, damn, bet she could touch her nose with her tongue tip.

And it wasn't that she was teasing him or nothing, 'cause it look like she just did it without even thinking about it, it was so quick. She didn't linger like to say look at me or nothing. But just that one casual gesture informed Robert about how sensuous this woman was and, not being nobody's fool, especial when it come to women, Robert, he pick up on how Zooley comfortable with natural things, including some of the stuff that uppity people think is nasty, which all lead Robert to speculate whether Zooley had children, 'cause lots of women that got children understand how to deal with tears and piss, snot and shit, and all them liquids a body be giving off, which kind of prepare a woman to deal with all the liquids and such a body be giving off when you really be getting down.

Ginny used to deal with it but she would wash off afterwards, and wash him off. And Dessie, just judging from how she was dealing with him in that upper room and judging from her being with that white man—

and everybody knowed some of them rich white folks was downright nasty, well anyway, Dessie she was probably good at dealing with the liquids of lovemaking too. But this Zooley, she seem like she in a whole other league. Like she would taste anything. Without hesitation and smile like she smiling at Robert now, and Robert would enjoy her smile like he enjoying her smile now. Would she lick him like that?

Then she offer him the other strawberry she holding. This time he don't reach out his hand for it, he just close his eyes and open his mouth and wait until he feel her gently put the sweet fruit up against the eagerness of his teeth and he slowly bite down upon it, and move the little nip of strawberry to the back side of his mouth and then mashes down with his big teeth like he one of them wringer contraptions on one of them new fangled washing machines and he squeezing out every last sweet drop of juice, and then he swallow, and, ahhhhhh.

When Robert open his eyes, he see Zooley done moved off a few feet bending over some bushes. When she stand up and turn around she got a hand full of blackberries and the juice of them has stained her fingers. She got one finger in her mouth sucking on it. She must of stuck herself. Robert know a blackberry bush is terrible thorny and you can't hardly harvest no blackberries without getting all stuck up. These berries are huge, just like the strawberries was jumbo size.

Robert is not too particular about blackberries, but then again, he don't generally care no whole lot about strawberries but since tasting that strawberry Zooley gave him, Robert is kind of sure he could learn to really love strawberries, and if he could learn to love Zooley's strawberries, well then her blackberries couldn't be too far behind.

It never occurs to Robert that he hungry. By now, the only thing Robert thinking on is that he must be the luckiest man in the whole wide world.

Zooley still don't say nothing, but just walks up to him and puts a blackberry up in his mouth. It's a strong, strong taste with little seeds that troubles Robert's tongue but it is not unpleasant. In fact, it is sort of good but not pleasing like the texture of the strawberry. The strawberry was smooth, this was gritty. Still, he liking it. And Zooley know he liking it. With all this up round her front door, Robert could hardly imagine what delights might be up inside her cabin.

Just then a rabbit dart across the clearing, moving so fast Robert could not hardly tell whether it was brown, or tan, or off white, or what, which is when Robert hear a hawk shriek. Robert look up and there the bird is way up, circling. For a second he stand there, shade his eyes with his hand, and look up.

Robert start wondering what it would be like to live out here with Zooley. When he finish spying upon the hawk, Robert take his time and look around more closely. Now he notice that where he standing is part of a long garden patch that stretch on to the back. And further on he even notice what look like it could be a road.

At first it did not register with Robert, but then he realized this is one real quiet homestead. Weren't no dog barking, he ain't heard no cattle or no horses or not even no chickens, or nothing. And, likewise, there wasn't no fields. All around the little clearing, which was maybe two hundred feet wide and about twice that deep, was trees growed up tight and close. She didn't seem to be the hunting type, but then again, from the way she move so easy through the woods, she could of stole up on a deer and stroke it with her bare hand. Maybe she ate fish. Maybe there was a lake nearby. She couldn't just live off of berries and what-so-ever greens and such she had growing up in this little narrow garden. Robert stomach was talking to him but his mind was on Zooley, so Robert stomach had to speak to Robert through questioning what Zooley eat to gradually get Robert to understand his stomach need for Robert to eat. Meanwhile, Robert was checking out how healthy Zooley look, not just fine, but glowing healthy, which meant she was eating regular, or at least eating right.

As they get nearer the hut, Robert notice now there was flower bushes and, as he draw closer to the door, he see that the bushes is roses. Pink ones in full bloom and some other flowers he didn't rightly know the name of. The pink blossoms look all beautiful contrasting to the deep dark blue of the cloth Zooley got wrapped around her body, showing off every curve, and her curves are soft like a rose petal's curves. Robert wonder did she have thorns, was there a dangerous side to her that he had not seen yet? Probably was. Couldn't nothing this pretty be without some kind of defenses.

The fragrance of the roses and the jasmines intertwined in a delightful bouquet that makes Robert's nose dance. The flowers smell so powerful pretty, they almost momentarily call his attention away from looking at

Zooley's butt—fortunately for Robert he can smell one thing while looking at another without the one disturbing his appreciation of the other.

Zooley reach up and unlatch her door, which was held in place by a long nail with a wire tied to its head, so when she pull the nail up out the ring and swing the latch back, she leave the nail go and it just hang their up by the doorway. Guess it was to keep raccoons and what not from roaming up in there when she was away, 'cause it sure would never keep no mens or whatever from going up in there, but then too, way out here—wherever here was—Zooley probably don't hardly get no whole bunch of visitors, friendly or otherwise.

At this moment, the taste of strawberry and blackberry all a gentle blazing in his mouth, and a taste for Zooley firing up his imagination, Robert is figuring all is right with his world. He ain't hardly thinking on finding the two-headeds. He could do that later, right now he wanted to enjoy this moment and even see if he could stretch it out some, you know, like slow eating a particularly satisfying piece of yellow cake, maybe with pecans in it, but definitely with Karo dark poured atop, and you eating it with your hands and sucking the syrup and the crumbs of your fingers, sort of like Zooley had just sucked that small piece of strawberry off her finger from after rubbing it off Robert's lips. He could not stop thinking about her tongue. Cat tongue, that's what it was. Yeah.

Robert ain't knowed what to expect up inside Zooley's place but he didn't expect this. First thing he saw was a big old brass bed off to the left—when Zooley had led the way in, she stepped to her right and gesture with a graceful sweep of her arm, almost look like she was throwing corn feed in extra slow motion, so when Robert step forward most of the light coming up in the room from the open door was shining to his left, so he look that way, which is when he see the brass bed.

He done seen gleaming brass beds before but none with a quilt like the quilt she had on it, full of all kinds of crashing colors and signs and symbols and such that Robert had no idea what they mean. And above the head of the bed was a big old drawing of a black woman, naked from the waist up, holding a spear across her body and she is fiercely smiling.

While he looking at the woman with the spear, Zooley has gone to a window and throwed back the curtains, hanging them up in a little bunch on a hook set off side the window, look like just for the purpose of holding the curtains. Light immediately spills into the room behind Robert, sort of like somebody switch on electric.

To the left of the bed is a small bookcase with four rows of books and a little night table in front, just about the same height the bed be, with a lamp on it. There is a window above the bookcase. Zooley brush pass Robert and go over to that window and throws the curtain back, which is when Robert notice she got glass on the windows.

When she hike up the curtain on its hook and then swing the window open a breeze blow through the cabin. Robert turn around and see the window that Zooley first throwed open. By that window is a small table with some kind of checkerboard game on it, well, at least the board look like checkers, but the pieces are shaped like little figures and they ebony and ivory colored. In the corner, behind the door is a rack with all kinds of colorful cloths draped all over it. And more items of clothing are hanging on hooks upside the curved wall. On the far side of the room is a fireplace, next to which is another little table with a wash basin on it, only this table is taller than the one by the bed.

Robert turn back to looking upon the bed, mainly 'cause Zooley had done sat down on it. Robert peep that she is watching him look upon her living space. Robert start to take note of what he don't see: ain't no chairs and no sitting-down table. No chest-of-drawers or chiffoniers. He don't see no pots or nothing for cooking, and only the one lamp on the table by the bed.

Zooley flips her slippers off, sort of hikes up her covering a little bit, scoots over and some kind of way folds one of her legs up under her, almost like she sitting Indian style, but the other leg is sitting out straight upon the bed. She leans forward some and pats the empty space on the bed beside her.

"Sit."

It sounded more like a command than an invitation, so Robert being Robert he hesitates, where upon Zooley just laughs and rolls over on her stomach, reaching to the other side of the bed. When her long arm raises up, she holding what look like it could be a footstool or something, but the top of it curved instead of straight flat, like when you make a swing bottom out of a strip of leather.

Zooley rises up out the bed, walks to the wall next to where Robert standing, sits the stool down and then squats upon it, leaning her back against the wall and stretching them long legs out before her, but she don't say nothing. It's up to Robert to make the next move.

For some reason it remind Robert of the time his mama, Julia, caught him trying to come tipping up in the house after he done snuck off and hung out in the juke. When he had opened the door and was going to tip toe on into the back, even much had his shoes in his hands, she just light the lamp on the table and sit there waiting on him to say something, and he didn't know what to say. He remember he could hear Dusty off in their bedroom snoring, and the fire was most out in the fireplace, so it wasn't crackling or nothing, and it was real, real quiet. For some reason Zooley sitting all still and all remind Robert of that time with his mama and how she ain't said nothing but just stare upon him as he stood there froze up in his tracks. She was waiting for him to move.

How do you tell somebody you want to be with, that you don't want to sit on their bed next to them, not 'cause you scared of them or nothing but because you don't want to mess nothing up? You don't want to let your lusting overcome your judgment and fuck everything up. You want to act like you know better, even though you know you really want to act out.

Every time Robert look upon her, Zooley hair be beckoning to his hands, like the strands of it is singing: come tangle with this. Still Robert don't say nothing, neither do he move, not even to sit his sack down. He just stand there.

Zooley still looking him dead in the eye. Finally, she smile, sort of, folds her arms across that ample chest of hers, and closes her eyes like she's going to sleep or something. Her long legs is still stretched out in front of her.

What was Robert supposed to do with this situation?

"You going to tell me your name or should I call you Standing-Man-Who-Does-Not-Talk?"

Robert look down at Zooley. She is not looking at him. Her eyes are still closed. He get the strange feeling that she is doing more than joking with him. It sound like she know him, referring to his Indian blood and all, just out the clear blue. Clearly, this was much more than Robert could handle, and yet, this was exactly the kind of situation he loved to be in: something new, something unexpected, with somebody he deeply attracted to, and all kinds of signs and wonders up around him.

"I talks when I got something to say."

Once again he try to shift the conversation to her. He know if he don't say nothing, he won't reveal nothing and besides, this way, he can learn what she about. When you ain't got the upper hand, keep your cards hid.

There is a long pause of quietness. Zooley does not look up, she just sits there, leaning back on the wall, those long legs outstretched almost to touching up against the bed. Robert stands all silent and still like he hunting deer, waiting by a stream for one to come along.

A big old fat bumblebee buzz through the window. Zooley don't seem to take no notice. Robert play like he don't notice neither.

When Robert realize Zooley ain't going to say nothing if he don't say nothing, he decides to tell her his name.

"My name Robert. Robert Leroy Johnson. You ain't told me your name."

"Zooley."

"No, I mean your whole name."

"Zooley is my whole name."

Robert smile.

"So you ain't got no last name?"

"You ain't neither. None of us know our last names. They took our names. Until we in a position to name ourselves, I'll stick with a first name of my own choosing."

"Your mama ain't named you?"

"You know a slave does not even own their name?"

"But we ain't slaves now."

"And we ain't free neither, is we?"

Robert just look at Zooley and don't give her no reply. After a few seconds, Zooley closes her eyes again.

Robert starting to get tired standing up.

There is more silence.

Before he can decide what more to say or do, Zooley slowly pulls her legs back and sort of floats upward. Robert looks after her.

She don't say nothing, just walks out the door and closes it softly behind her. Robert don't know what to think. Maybe she stepping outside to relieve herself.

After ten minutes she is not back. Now Robert really don't know what to think. Finally, he decide to go to the window and peer out. Maybe she sitting outside, sulking or maybe she just trying to play with his mind. But when he stick his head out the window, he don't see her.

Robert go to the door, open it and step out. He still don't see her. He walk back of the hut, he don't see her but he do see a automobile sitting a ways off. So what he had thought was a road is actually a road.

The sight of the car really confuse Robert. Just when he had started to judge that Zooley was some kind of hermit or something, living way off by herself in some kind of secret fashion, here it is he find out she got a vehicle. But it's confusing that she would seem so comfortable in the woods and down by that stream like that was her natural self and here she got a automobile and it look new too.

This Zooley is a strange woman. What else she got?

After a few minutes of thinking up, one by one, all sorts of foolishness, and one by one throwing them foolish thoughts out of his mind, Robert turn around, to trod back around the hut and go back inside, but this time he go on the other side of the hut, which is when he see a little outhouse, sitting up close to the tree line.

Soon as Robert step back inside he freeze up. His sack is not where he left it. His guitar is leaning up against the bookcase. His shoes are sitting by the wall, his good hat is hanging on a hook. Next to his hat, hanging in a neat little row are his playing clothes.

Robert spins around, she must be watching him, but he don't see nobody. He couldn't of been gone that long. He was just out back. He would have heard her.

He run to the door and step outside but he don't see nothing. No Zooley.

He step back inside and think to go check on his guitar to make sure… really his guitar was his anchor, the only thing he could hold on that he was fully knowledgeable about. As he reach for the guitar he see a plate of yellow cake and a cup of coffee sitting on the night table. The coffee got little wisps of steam rising up out of it. He touch the top of the cake. It's warm.

Robert spin around again. Looking for he don't know what. Something. Anything that could help explain what all is going on. He go over to the fireplace—it's cold. He go back over to the cake. It's still warm. Which is when he heard the automobile start up out back.

Robert run outside, round back the hut but by the time he get round there, all he see is the car driving off raising dust in the distance.

Back inside he suddenly feel really tired, so he sit upon the edge of the bed, close to the table and commences to eating the yellow cake and sipping on the coffee. The cake is sweet and soft, like he like it, except there ain't no pecans in it and no Karo on top it. The coffee is sweet too, and strong, and sort of strange tasting, sort of a little bitter at the same time it warm and sweet. When he finish, he kick his shoes off and lay back atop the pretty quilt. Before he know it, Robert done fell off fast asleep, a deep and dreamless sleep, or at least he would not remember dreaming when he wakes up.

It was a strange waking up. At first he thought he was dreaming he was playing in a juke what was on a little island up in the middle of the river. He was playing that nonsense song, Hot Tamales. He guess he was thinking on Zooley, when he realize that he was laying down, but he swear he was playing, which was when he open his eyes.

In his sleep, he had turned to facing toward the back wall. Was that Zooley playing his guitar?

When Robert turn over, he ain't seen Zooley. He saw a black man sitting upon the stool strumming, just a playing like as if that was his guitar instead of Robert guitar, which who guitar it was Robert could see right off without even having to so much as look over and see if his guitar was still by the bookcase. Sure enough, Robert's guitar case lay open on the floor.

Robert freeze up and just look. The man is looking down, playing with his eyes closed. The man was playing real good. In fact, he was playing some chords Robert ain't never before heard used up in that song like that but even so all the chords seem to fit into Hot Tamales without throwing it off or nothing.

After a short while the man look up and sees that Robert is looking at him. Robert sits up. It ain't right to be laying down in the presence of a strange man. This time the man just hit the passing chords and Robert can hear the progression real clear. Robert don't have to watch his fingering 'cause he already know all the chords, he just got to listen to how they fitted up into the song. That's what was different.

One more again the man play the chords, and when he finish, he get up, walk over to the bed and give the guitar to Robert. Then without saying nothing else the man walk out the hut. Now that's the second time somebody walk out on Robert without saying nothing.

Robert sit without moving and look at the door for a whole minute. After trying to figure up on what to do, Robert decide to try playing Tamales with them chords up in it. He find it easy to do once he put his mind to it, which lead him to wondering if he could do them kind of things with other songs he know. Before he know it Robert done spent two hours fitting new chords up into old songs. Two hours without stopping or nothing. Finally he sit the guitar down beside the bed and lie back.

First off he feeling good about learning something new, well not really new, 'cause he already knew the chords, but learning a new way to hook those chords up into a song where he usually don't use no chords like that, and all that make Robert feel powerful good. In fact as he laying back staring up at the ceiling, he's smiling and in his mind going over another song he could quilt up some chords in. Yeah, that's what it was, it was like quilting where he took bits and pieces of what he already know and hook them up in interesting ways. While he feeling good and thinking and such, before he realize it, he done feel asleep again.

When he wake up the room is dark except the lamp is burning real low on the bedside table. Robert swing his legs off the bed and as he stand up, he realize he got to relieve himself, so he stumble off to the outhouse.

When he get back inside the hut, Zooley is sitting on the little stool, leaning forward.

"Are you ready to talk now?"

Odd as it may seem, what with thinking on the new chords and old songs, and wondering who the guitar playing man was, Robert had done clean forgot about Zooley, and her confronting him like this sort of shamed him. How could he forget her? It didn't seem like she was offended or nothing, but still, it was embarrassing. He had been sleeping up in her bed and some kind of way his mind got to working over the music and he clean forgets her.

Robert just stands at the foot of the bed, speechless. Zooley pushes over and makes room for Robert to sit down but Robert don't move none.

"What you want to know?"

"I know what I want to know. You the one seeking something. You keep thinking you want to get to know me but you will never know me if you don't know yourself and how can you know yourself if you're always running from place to place. There's a big difference between going somewhere and running from something."

What she said hit Robert like a mule kick. It was like she had a way of looking up inside him. It made him feel like he was slipping down a bluff or something, falling off into a deep hole. Robert reach out to one of the bedposts and steady himself.

Mentally he tries to get his bearings by looking around for something he might recognize as real rather than all this mash up what been happening since, well since he took off for Louisiana and climb up in that car with that white man.

In a flash he feel a little dizzy and he close his eyes trying to hold on. When he open his eyes and look upon Zooley she is patiently sitting and looking back at him.

Robert look around Zooley's hut. All of sudden none of this seemed real. It was like he was in some dream world where things happen all kinds of different ways, all crazy mixed up and not making sense when lined up one behind the other.

Robert look at the brass bedpost he holding to and then he look down at the quilt and the bed he was just sleeping upon. Would there ever be a time when he could sleep without waking up all funny kinds of ways, all kinds of stuff happening around him? Wake up and not be in some strange place? Not sleeping up next to somebody he ain't seen before? Not in no place where he feel obligated to leave as soon as he can?

It all just rush over him, this desire for a resting spot, some place where he wouldn't need a traveling sack, a sun hat, some sturdy shoes. Somewhere where at he could just drop down and be at ease. And still yet not be…, not be alone.

Was all this really happening or was this one of his crazy dreams?

Zooley swing her legs round and stands up. Robert sort of notice that she is wearing trousers like a man and a shirt tucked in all around and she got her head covered with a scarf—sort of, because he really don't pay it no mind, like he see it but he don't see it 'cause he don't make nothing of it. He don't figure what she wearing mean nothing in particular. He don't even think on it. He just think on what he wearing he been wearing for going on a whole week now, or maybe longer, the same clothes. By now he should be used to wearing the same clothes for eight or nine days at a stretch, you would think so, much as he do it. But, now, all of a sudden, he feel worn out like these traveling trousers he wearing. They started off dark brown but now they almost khaki. They dust colored. Dust covered. Dust dyed. Sun bleached. Rain washed. Now they most the same color as dirt.

"You look tired. You should rest."

Robert started to protest that he weren't tired, but he was. He was tired trying to figure all this stuff out. It was like Zooley had reached into him and pulled out a plug or something and all kinds of stuff started flooding up into his consciousness. Overwhelming him. And for no good earthly reason that he could think of, Robert suddenly felt like crying, and he didn't know why he felt like crying. He felt all sad and all, but he didn't know why he felt sad. He had some new music, but it was the old him. More than some new music what he really wanted was a new him. He was only twenty-one years old but he felt like an old man, a used up old man.

Zooley reach down to the bed and pull the quilt back some, and fluff up one of the big pillows.

"Get some sleep. We'll talk in the morning."

And then she gently put her hands on him and guided him down onto the bed. Robert was trying hard to keep from crying. This was all so confusing. Nobody had ever told Robert that everybody cry at some time or another, or if they don't cry they wall off their tears behind a dam of making like they don't feel. They cut off their feelings. But if you feel, you cry. Sometime sooner or later, if you feel, you got to cry.

There was something about Zooley that made Robert feel all kinds of things. And Robert realize he ain't really feel this deep down since the last time, since he was holding Ginny. And yes, that was the last time he had cried. How could he ever forget crying like that? But there was no Ginny he was holding now, not unless his life was his Ginny and he was holding his dead life in his hands and looking down upon it and seeing it all stillborn and everything, 'cause he really weren't fully alive, wandering around from place to place, taking whatever he could get, whatever scraps of leftover love people offer him, sometimes more than scraps, sometimes everything and he ain't had nothing he could give back. And it's a horrible feeling to take love and not be able to give love, it's horrible when you think on it even if most times you don't think on it. That didn't make no sense.

No. What didn't make no sense was his life up to this point.

But who was to blame for that?

Robert sank down to the bed. Zooley was holding him, easing him down slow. She was strong. He felt all weak. The urge to cry was coming and going—and he was mad about that. Mad about feeling like he wanted to cry. Mad about feeling that he weren't going to allow himself to cry. Suddenly there was all this mad at something, everything kind of stuff riled up in him. But mainly mad at himself.

Zooley stretch him out and pull his shoes off. Then she reach over and cover him with the quilt and turn him over face to the wall, and then go into humming and rubbing the back of his shoulders.

By then Robert losing the ability to control his mind. He can't even think straight. Can't even much think one thought after another. And all she had said was: you the one seeking something.

After five minutes or so of massaging him, Zooley gets up and turns the lamp all the way down. She looks upon him for a few seconds and then turns and walks out the room. Soon thereafter Robert roll over and look at the door.

It briefly cross his mind to get up, grab his sack and split, just to walk away from this situation, but he don't. What stopped him? Was he thinking on what the conversation with Zooley would be like in the morning? Or was he wondering whether the man would come back and show him some more ways to fit chords he knew up in songs he knew? Or maybe even it was the hope that Zooley would come back and climb up in the bed with him? Or, was he thinking that he would wake up and this would all be some real messed up dream and he would be back up in Martinsville with Callie and the kids? Or he would not wake up at all and he was dead. Or, who know who going to come through that door next.

At one point Robert try to get up but he can't move. He can't make none of his limbs move or nothing. While he can't move, Ginny walk up in the door and reach out to him. He start to get up and she turn into Julia who turn into Sweetwater who turn into Dessie who turn into Eula Jean who turn into… and Robert want to get up and go stop people from walking up in the door. But he don't get up. And just like all them womens come up in that door, they stand before him for a little while and then they just disappear. Just plum disappear right off into the air.

Robert suck on his saliva. It's bitter. He don't fully remember the bitter but the bitter is faintly familiar. It's the same bitter that was up in that tea he had up in the swamps. The same bitter as in the coffee Zooley left for him, but he don't really place it. It's a faint bitter. Too far off in the fog of his confusion for him to make out what it is.

Maybe she done poison him. Or maybe it was that leaf man what poison him. Maybe he weren't poisoned at all. Maybe he just feel poisoned. But he don't feel sick no more or like he going to die or nothing. He just feel strange. And he can't move. Like invisible ropes got him tied down.

And he know any minute, Zooley could come walking back up in that door with a handful of strawberries. He could see her all black and tall and naked with her hand outstretched, both hands cupped together, carrying a bunch of strawberries. Or her nipples blackberry colored. Blackberry nipples. But she didn't come through the door. No Zooley. Even after watching the door for a whole half hour. No Zooley.

The lamp light was down all the way low and the room was real dim, and the door was up in the shadows, so she could of snuck up in there and he might not see her come in. She move around so quiet and all. Just once he would like to see her coming. Robert never did see none of that parade of women he saw come marching through the door, never did see even a one of them go back out the door. He never did see Zooley come back through the door neither. And when he did see her, he wasn't sure he was seeing her or if he still asleep, but eventually, he do wake up, or at least he come to consciousness and is able to move: first he wiggle his toes and then he move his fingers and then he reach his hand from under the covers.

There was sunlight in the room and it feel like morning. Zooley was sitting on her little stool reading a book and there was a plate of strawberries on the table, and when he stirred, kind of reached up and rubbed his eyes, and feel his face to see if he really awake—how do you tell when you really awake if the only people around you is the same people what be in your dream? Which is when he hear Zooley call to him.

"Good morning."

Zooley mark her spot with a little piece of blue ribbon, close her book, set it aside and stand up. She wrapped like she wrapped herself down by the creek, except this time the dark blue cloth got a different design on the top part of it.

She lean back to the wall, clasp her hands in her lap, and patiently wait to see what Robert going to say.

"Zooley, how do you know when you alive and not just dreaming you alive? You understand what I'm saying?"

Zooley smile at him and repeat herself, "good morning."

Yeah, that was Zooley always trying to play mind games. Robert threw the covers back and swung his legs around, which is when he realize two things. One thing he knew for sure was that he had a morning hard on and the other thing was that he suddenly realize he naked.

Zooley looks upon him and laughs quietly to herself, shaking her head no, but meaning yes, this is some funny.

"Go out back and relieve yourself."

As she speaks, Zooley stands up, goes over and reaches down a big piece of cloth what was hanging on one of the hooks. She throws it to him, and giggles as she watches him fumble with trying to wrap himself at the same time he reaching around looking for his trousers.

"Hurry on, I don't want you wetting up my bed."

When Robert runs back up in the hut, Zooley is gone. There is a cup of coffee and a piece of yellow cake sitting up by the plate of strawberries. So this is how it was going to be.

As soon as Robert about finish with the coffee, he look up and Zooley standing outside looking at him through the window.

"When you finish your personals, come outside and we can talk."

Robert take his time with the coffee. It don't taste so bitter no more. He take his time pulling his clothes on and even stop to pick a few notes on his guitar. He's in no hurry. No hurry.

When he was relieving himself this morning he realized, there was no sense in trying to swim upstream. He would just roll over and float on his back and see where the river took him.

When he finally got around to going outside to talk to Zooley she was working in the garden. For about seven or eight minutes, neither one of them said anything.

Finally, Robert, stoop down beside Zooley and say, "good morning."

"Good morning, Robert. Are you ready to talk now?"

"Yeah. Yeah, I reckon so."

And then they smiled at each other.

-25-

ROBERT IS A SMALL-BONED MAN, NOT NO MIDGET OR STOMPED-DOWN SHORTY OR nothing, but definitely smaller than the average feller. Zooley, she a healthy woman, over six foot tall and not lacking for neither flesh nor bone. Which meant that Robert was aware of her strength, her advantage over him, so he felt like he had to watch what he say to her. Besides, look like she was quicker of tongue than he was. Seem like she could think up words much, much faster than his brain work at guiding his own mouth to speak. Plus, there was the other thing, the wanting her thing, even though she had clearly said "no way" when they were back at that creek, still, you know, when a man want a woman, the fact that he got no chance of getting her don't necessarily damper down his wanting her none. In fact, sometimes covering a pot make it come to a boil quicker.

Which all is what was kind of happening at this moment as Robert stood there looking down upon Zooley, who was sitting on a little, three-legged, down-low-to-the-ground stool as she tended her garden, and Zooley, for her part, was looking up at Robert as he was standing there trying to act like they were having a casual conversation, even though he really wasn't fooling nobody, not himself, and certainly not Zooley. There was nothing casual about this mid-morning meeting in the sun.

"What you want to talk about?" Robert asked Zooley.

"It's not a matter of what I want. It's a matter of what you need. You know?" Zooley wasn't even looking at him. She had turned her attention back to pulling up weeds. Didn't as much as pause to see what his response would be. Even started humming something to herself.

Robert looked around, not really expecting to see anyone else, but hoping for some kind of diversion or something, a way out of having to talk with this woman who was faster than a preacher reaching for his bible, or for a piece of chicken.

"Robert, what you 'fraid of?"

Robert started to fake it and say, I ain't 'fraid of nothing, but he didn't, not because he was afraid to lie to her, but rather because, well, maybe he didn't have to pretend with her. Maybe he could be like he was with Ginny and just be, you know, just breath and be and let whatever come out, well, just let it all come out howsoever it had a mind to come out. After all, Robert weren't the one what put all what was inside of him deep into him. Robert didn't ask not to have no daddy. Robert didn't beg white people to treat him the way they treated him. And so forth. But still whether you had a hand in making yourself be who yourself is, whether you lie and cheat or you try to be honest and upright, no matter, you got some stuff in you that you don't normally let nobody see, and though she had not said so, Robert was getting the feeling that Zooley was asking him to show himself, to show her the real Robert, what all Robert had deep down all up inside hisself. Ginny were the onliest person Robert had ever showed all of himself to. Of course, it was also true that back then Robert had less of himself to show than he does now, but still, it was the same principle: it's dangerous to let somebody see all up inside you, or at least Robert thought it was dangerous without ever examining why he thought it was dangerous. On account of all of that, Robert didn't quite know what to say.

"I don't know." Robert spoke out before he could catch himself, and no sooner he spoke, he thought to try and grab the words and pull them back, but of course it was too late, 'cause words once they are spoken, once they are in the air, they take on a life of their own, no matter if you glad you said them or if you wish you could call them back, words was like grown-ass children—they issue from you but once they out your house, out your mouth, it be awfully hard, neigh on to impossible to tell them words what to do. So Robert's "I don't know" had to stand for now, but still, Robert wanted to clarify what he meant about not knowing. He didn't mean that he didn't know what he need—not that he did know, but not knowing what he needed was not what he was meaning to say, nor was he saying that he wasn't afraid of nothing, 'cause that too would be a lie if he was to tell it. Robert was afraid he was going to die without making a platter, without accomplishing nothing. Die and be like Dusty said, be worthless, or like Dusty put it, not even worth spitting on if somebody set him alight. Not worth saving. Yeah, that was it. Robert was afraid he would die before he had accomplished something to make his life worth living. So, yeah he kind of knew what he was afraid of, so his "I don't know" was really meant to mean "I don't know how to say all this 'cause I ain't never even much talk upon this before."

And suddenly like a friend what sneak up behind you and cover your eyes with their hands and force you to guess who it is 'cause you ain't heard them coming up on you, you don't know, you just know it probably somebody who close to you, well, like that this feel come up on Robert and the next thing he know, Robert recalling being all up inside Ginny one time and he had been going at it hard, like he was digging a well or something, just a grunting and groaning, a sucking up air real loud on the upstroke and sounding a steady moan on the downstroke, and some kind of way, a strange feeling come over him, like a spasm or something, and he felt it in his feet first, and it was rolling up his legs and by the time it got to his hips try as he might he couldn't control hisself, and he was a thrashing and a lunging all at the same time, and usually no matter how good it got, usually he stayed aware enough to make sure that he didn't hurt Ginny or nothing, but this time he couldn't catch hisself. He was gone and all the back his thighs got tight, tight, tight, and his butt-hole draw up tight and he could feel himself about to come real hard. Real, real hard. And he holler out to Ginny: "Ginny. I wanna. I wanna. I wanna come in you. I wanna come." And Ginny she had threw her little legs open wider, wider than it seem she could. Wider than any woman could. And she had grabbed his behind and pulled him deeper into her and, and, and Robert was still babbling, I wanna come, and by now Ginny was answering, come on, come on, Robert, come on. And it was funny. Most times Robert he remember that great good feeling when he come, but he ain't remember this time when he was saying he wanted to come 'cause just at the moment he exploded, he screamed and he lost awareness and next thing he knowed, he was crying and Ginny was holding him and caressing his head and shushing him like he was a whining baby or something, and telling him it was alright, it was alright, and he was crying, he couldn't help it, he was crying and she was holding him, it's alright Robert, it's alright, and then it scared him that he was crying, that Ginny had made him cry, scared him that he was so into Ginny that she touch him that away. And their bodies was all sweaty and everything. And eventually he stop jerking and slowly he stop crying, and Ginny had just pressed herself all close all over him, had pulled his face down into the hollow of her neck and stayed holding on to him with her arms and her legs and her shushing and all, and it's alright, Robert. It's alright, baby. And at first he couldn't hardly stop himself from crying so he kept his face buried down by her bosom like as if he was trying to strain to reach down and suck on her breasts but he weren't, he had just been crying, his tears flowing like a fountain, just a rain falling down upon the sweet dark earth of Ginny's deep brown skin. Coming like that had scared him. He felt so helpless and at the same time felt so comforted by her, by the way she was holding him, cooing in his ear, rubbing his head, her legs hitched up either side of his hips, and he was soft but he was still in her, and still crying, and she was rocking him, gently, not like no storm or nothing, but like a soft breeze rippling the face of a deep still pond, and when he finished crying, he ain't said nothing to Ginny and Ginny ain't said nothing to him about it. She just lay there close to him, kissing him, and snuggling slick skin to slick skin, and some of her hair damp sticking to the side of her face, and so quiet, you could count the crickets chirping and all, even what sound like some dog way off somewhere barking, but way off, way, way off like you ain't had to worry none about him, and at that moment in Ginny's arms feeling too safe to be scared, but afterwards the next morning feeling too scared to say nothing about what had happened that night before when they were making love. And Robert ain't never said nothing more about it and Ginny ain't never brought it up but they both knowed, they knowed that Robert had cried and Ginny had held him, Robert had come so hard he cried, and Ginny had just opened up wide and wider and took him into her, took all of him into her. And what could he say behind that? What could anyone say? And now standing here before Zooley he was afraid of telling her about that, afraid of telling her he had been afraid when he was crying, but he ain't knowed what he was afraid of when he was crying. He knowed Ginny weren't going to hurt him or nothing, that she ain't meant him no harm, that she was loving him, that she would die for him—that she did die for him. Ginny died. Birthing his baby. Sure as sun is hot and white men is mean, Ginny did die for him. And he was afraid of that little woman what made him cry and who died for him. He was afraid. Afraid he would never be worthy Ginny's death.

But, or so he felt, he could not tell Zooley this.

So all he said was, I don't know—meaning I don't know how to say to you any of the stuff I'm really thinking about in response to your question about what I'm 'fraid of.

Zooley understood.

Zooley smiled at Robert.

Her smile both delighted and confused him—he expected her to be a little put out with him, but here she was reacting to him like as if he done something to make her proud.

"And how did your guitar lesson go?"

"What?"

Robert blanked out, couldn't figure what she was talking about. His guitar? Where? It was back in her house, inside. Secure. Safe. Then he suddenly remembered the man who had been playing his guitar. Robert wasn't for sure he had not been dreaming of the man playing. Was it real? Was that what Zooley was talking about?

"You mean..."

"Yes," Zooley cut him off with an even bigger smile.

"Well, ah. I don't rightly know, I mean it weren't hardly no lesson like Ike would do. He just played some and ain't said nothing."

"Did you understand what he played?"

"Yeah. I mean it was just some chords with extra notes in 'em."

"Extra notes? What you mean?"

"I means he kind of stack up his chords, playing four and five notes at a time, most times we use two or three. Open tuning. You understand? I mean, you play? You know what I'm saying?"

"Could you play what he played?"

"Yes mam, afterwards I mean, after he done it. I mean after I hear him play like that, I could play it too, but, you know, I always could do that. I always could play whatever I hear."

"Had you heard music like that before."

"Well yeah, and no. I mean it wasn't no one note or one chord in particular I had never heard it was the way he kind of hook them all up together, how he put one behind the other, what lick he hit in passing while moving from one to the next. That's kind of what was different about what he done."

"An huhhh. So what you learned was how to use your imagination?"

"I don't rightly know that I learned nothing in particular."

"It's not a matter of what you know but rather of what you can imagine."

"What you mean?"

Robert was neigh 'bout to the bottom of this particular sack. He ain't had nothing more to draw on in this discussion. Zooley smiled again, leaned forward, pulled at a particularly stubborn weed, and jerked it out the ground. The loose top of her dress gapped open exposing her breasts, those same eggplant-colored, cantaloupe-sized breasts that he had stared at when he first saw her naked and all, standing in that stream. The fleeting sight of a dark, dark nipple on her right breast aroused him. He couldn't help it.

Zooley looked up and caught Robert staring down at her breasts.

"Why you think it is you men folk get all excited looking upon a woman's breast?"

Robert turned away shame-faced.

"Well? Don't turn away now." Zooley started laughing out loud and stood up. "You ain't ready to talk, you got other things on your mind." Zooley walked off toward the cabin. Robert remained rooted where he was standing, embarrassed, dumb-founded, like when the teacher had lined up four of the boys and made them hold their hands out to received a slap with the ruler and Robert was number four in line and was standing there waiting for his turn, and he could hear the loud slap, really a hard popping sound, WAP!, as Miss Anderson hit the first boy's hand. It was Johnny. He whimpered and jiggled up and down, obviously in pain. Ronnie was next, old slick Ronnie. He tried pulling his hand back just before the lick landed so it wouldn't come down as hard, but Miss Anderson was a veteran executioner, she knew the flinching trick, the way you moved your hand down and away at just the right time so that the contact was only glancing. Miss Anderson stayed the expected blow and patiently waited for Ronnie to raise his hand again. Slowly she lifted the ruler above her shoulder. Ronnie was going to get it now. She looked Ronnie in the eye and without saying a word and without moving a facial muscle she waited until he was looking back at her instead of looking at the ruler. She waited. And Robert stood there looking. And Johnny was still whimpering. "Johnny Charles shut up your puppy-dog ways before I truly give you something to cry about. Shut up this instant." And it was when she had said "this instant," in that less than a split second when both Robert and Ronnie had momentarily glanced at Johnny, in that brief milli-moment Miss Anderson had unloaded on Ronnie, catching him full on with a hell of a lick. Ronnie had hollered out, not too loudly, but in pain none-the-less, and was shaking his little hand fast-fast like he was trying to spin some hand made ice cream or something. Charles was third. He said nothing. Offered up his hand. Took his lick. Said nothing. No flinching. No hollering. No hand shaking. Nothing. He just took his lick. His face remaining a motionless mask. None of them had even so much as thought of running off or trying somehow to get out of the punishment. Robert had wanted, of course, to be like Charles—impassive in the face of a whipping, but that was not Robert's constitution. His feelings ran in two streams. One stream close to the surface that everybody could easily see, and another stream so deep running that nobody really knew about it. WAP! When Robert's lick came he gave off a brief yelp, like a stray dog run off by a pitched rock. But inside he found out he was not afeared. This licking was not enough to stop him.

Robert felt like he had been slapped. Zooley had caught him doing wrong, but her admonishment was not enough to make him stop. As she walked away, though he was a little embarrassed about being called out on account of looking at her beautiful breasts, he didn't stop thinking about sucking on Zooley, wondering how sweet was her nipple.

Then it come to him that she must of knew who that man was.

"Zooley, wait up. I do wants to talk."

Zooley stopped just before stepping inside her doorway. She turned and waited as Robert walked toward her. She was not smiling.

"You right, that's what I was thinking about."

"What?"

"What you said?"

"What I said?"

"You said I was thinking on, you know, I was looking on you and ah…"

"And what?"

"I was thinking on laying with you."

"How is it, you can use your imagination when it come to getting with a woman, but you stifle your imagination when it comes to picking out your notes?"

"What?"

"I'm going up by Bogaloosa. Maybe you ought to go down there to the juke and I come back and get you in the morning."

Robert was confused. He had never heard of Bogaloosa. Where was it? What was it? How far was it.

Zooley said nothing else. Turned and walked into her cabin.

Robert was still standing there when she come out. A big hat on her head and she had trousers on and a man's shirt except she ain't looked like she was dressed like no man. She had his guitar case in her hand.

Robert ain't knowed what to say, so just like he had quietly walked back to the little chair that was his spot in the classroom, in a similar fashion he found himself quietly following Zooley around the back of the cabin over toward the dark blue automobile sitting to the side of the road.

Zooley paused as they neared the vehicle.

"You want to drive?" Zooley asked without looking over at Robert.

"I can't drive."

"That's alright. Driving is my specialty. I take great delight in traveling. Come on."

Zooley placed the guitar case in the rumble seat, climbed into the front, waited patiently while Robert gently closed his door and then she started up the vehicle, smoothed-out her trousers, took off her hat and handed it to Robert, smiled as she did so, paused, looked him up and down, then turned her attention to the road ahead and without any warning floored the accelerator and laughed out loud as the automobile shot down the dirt road.

-26-

It was Sunday. Sunday morning. Early. Robert was sitting on the side of the road. Somebody had abandoned a leaving trunk. It was all broke up. Wasn't nothing in it or nothing. Rain damaged, the handles done come apart. The latch all twisted up and ruined. Maybe it fell off a wagon. Maybe it was throwed off. Whatever. It was a good enough seat for Robert.

Robert smiled he had eight dollars and sixty-seven cents in his pocket. Last night's chicken and potato salad was still resting easy in his stomach. Last night. Man, it was a good night. Good money. Good music. A good, fun-loving crowd. Man, there must a been at least 28 or 29 peoples crowded up in that lil funky, one-room, hole-in-the-wall that some fool had nerve enough to name "The Outhouse."

Should of called it the "Who Dat?"

Robert actually laughed out loud. Good golly them people was some friendly to him. When Robert had started into "Shake 'Em On Down," instead of singing along on the chorus, some drunk had shouted out "Who Dat, Nah!" and quicker than a rattler can spit, the whole crowd was saying "Who Dat, Nah!"

It was Petey, leastwise that's what he said his name was. Petey. Big hunk of a laughing man, hands all scarred up. He must of like to fight. But he was in high spirits last night. Had plunked a whole jar of shine down on the table next to Robert. "Boy, long as you keeps playing like that, I'm going to see to it you don't lack for no liquor."

Yes, it was a good night.

Robert played and played. Hell, he would of played all night without worrying so much as about collecting even one lousy nickel. It seem like it had been months since he played for a room full of folk, even though it had only been maybe a week and a half, going on two weeks, still it felt like a real long, long time. And it felt really, really good to be back to playing like that. Especially how the peoples danced and shouted and sang along and kept on dancing and clowning and what not. By midnight, maybe one or two had left, but four or five had taken their place and then some.

When he had been walking around town, earlier during the day, getting the feel for the place, playing for a bit by the main general store and nearby the road where the lumber trucks rolled through, and people was obliging him with nickels and dimes, well, right then and there, Robert had knowed it was going to be a good town to play in, even though it weren't no bigger than a sparrow's egg.

And you know they had some frisky women up in there, and you know they all was spoken for, and you know that didn't matter none to Robert, or at least wouldn't have mattered if he had been of a mind to talk to one of them dimpled mamas. But he had not been of a mind to, and not 'cause he was scared or nothing. No, don't care where he was, first time or been down the road and back, Robert weren't never unprepared to conversate with a woman about whatsoever she wanted to conversate about. Hell, one time he had held a thirty-six minute conversation about sewing jeans and shirts and whatnot.

She had said—funny, he couldn't rightly recall her name at the moment, but anyway, she had said: You the first man I ever knowed, ah, what takes some kind of interest in sewing.

In his mind, Robert had noted every word what came slow rolling out her mouth, her inflections, the way she had been looking down, but looked up directly at him when she said "I ever knowed" and caught herself and kind of half-covered her mouth with her tiny hands. And Robert had reared back in his chair instead of pulling forward like most mens would have thereby betraying their intentions to capture the game. Instead, Robert had allowed his lids to droop, sleepy-eyed as though he weren't but half-interested and had looked down when she looked up at him full on, and did not look back up at her until she had kind of looked off sideways, and then slow like you catch a mosquito hawk he had uncrossed his legs, and scooted up some, rested his elbows on his knees, slow sucked his teeth and exhaled loud enough for her to hear, and then caught her completely by surprise when he responded in a way that was appropriate for the situation but, in a way the average fellow wouldn't have never thought to do.

"You know, you got some pretty hands," and Robert had reached over and gently held one of her upraised hands, "but they ain't no where near as pretty as your smile. Why don't you drop your hands on down so as I can look upon your comely face. You looks like that woman that David in the bible was talking about." And then he had paused to allow his words to sink in and hook her good. "Well, you knows I'm a musicianeer, just like David was, and you probably knows I done had the opportunity to look upon many a woman, so when I tells you, you got a pretty smile, I ain't just funning you. I knows what I'm talking about 'cause I done seed many a smiling woman in my time."

And of course she turned away. And of course Robert reached over and gently touched her trembling jaw, nudging her face back around towards him.

Which all, of course, had made her smile even that much harder, wider, even kind of blushed a bit, her copper-colored light-skinned cheeks noticeably turning both a bit brighter and darker at the same time, her hands fidgeting and fussing with one another about whether they should be still, clasped there in her lap, or dare she reach up and hold his hand.

Robert backed off, again, and sucked his teeth, again—damn, that chicken had been some good. He absent-mindedly used the fingernail of his right index finger like a little pick to try and dislodge the piece of chicken stuck between the upper teeth on the left side of his jaw. When he finally loosened the sliver of dark meat—Robert really liked the leg and thigh part of fried chicken—well, he pulled his finger out, briefly examined the morsel on his fingertip and then quickly sucked it off, sucked his teeth once more to make sure he had got it all out, and then leaned forward toward this young woman who was still fussing with her hands, reached and briefly covered her hands with the warmth of his own, just long enough to still her nervousness, and, as he pulled back from her—he didn't want her to get the idea he was try to feel on her on the sly—Robert smiled and then asked her, so, what you likes.

She said: Huh?

He said: I mean what you likes to do? Me, I loves music and all, I guess you can tell from my playing 'cause I'm a walking musicianeer, I travels all over making music, but you know what I really likes. I likes pine cones and tree leaves. Likes to look at them. Examine them up close. Did you know ain't no two pine cones exactly the same. And it's the same way with tree leaves. I don't much know the names of trees or nothing, but I just like to look at the leaves. Look at they shape and all. I got to hold them close to my face, 'cause my left eye kind of slightly kind of damaged. My sister had bought me some glasses when I was in school but since I been left school, I don't need no glasses to play music. I can play music with my eyes closed. But anyway I likes to look at pine cones. What you likes?

She said: (Nothing.) Just kind of blushed a little bit more, and finally scratched the side of her nose. Yeah, she was still a bit nervous. Robert could see that.

He said: Your hands are soft. Your smile is pretty. But right now, what I really wants to know is what you likes?

She said: Well, I like to sew and stuff.

He said: Yeah?

She said: Um hum. And looked down and then away. And took to playing with her fingers again.

He said: You mean like quilts?

She said: Naw. Yeah. Sometimes. But any kind. All kinds of sewing. I just likes to sew.

He said: What you sew?

She said: Whatever needs sewing. Whatever I feels like sewing.

He said: Any which thing. Jeans and shirts and things?

She said: Any thing. If it be made out of material, I can sew it.

He said: Oh, you like me then. No wonder I likes you. I plays any kind of music there is, 'cause I likes music. And you sews any which thing needs sewing, 'cause you likes sewing. That's good.

And then they went on and on, like that. At one point, Robert look up and out the corner of his eye, Robert saw two men looking upon him and this woman. Shucks, try as he might, he couldn't remember her name. Couldn't even remember what town he had been in when he talked about cross-stitching and button-sewing, hemming and letting out. But he had done it, not out of boredom or even 'cause he was trying to get some pussy, no, he had done it because once she had started talking he saw that it was giving her a great joy to talk about needles and thread and all, and Robert knew that almost any woman was grateful for the attention of a man willing to laugh, smile and conversate with her when she was talking, especially when she was talking about something she wanted to talk about and not talking some shit to make the man feel good.

Them two men who had been looking upon Robert sweet talking that woman didn't know what to do when Robert stood up and said he had to be shoving on, but if he was to ever come back, he definitely would return on round hear abouts and would love for another chance to conversate. And then Robert had reached out to shake the woman's hand and as he slow-walked away, he had nodded and paused a moment, even winked, if he remembers correctly, and said to the fellers, "Gentlemens, yall have yall a good night. You got some lovely women up in here."

So, no, if Robert had been of a mind to, he could certainly have talked-at at least one of the nine women who was up in The Outhouse last night, but he really weren't paying them no mind.

Robert had been minding his music, had been working on making the changes, finding different stepping stones to cross the creek, whereas before he might of left a gaping hole, now he slide a passing chord in there, and he found it not only filled up the music and gave it a fuller sound, he also found out that it was his sound that he was putting into music that everybody already knowed, so what happened was, even though he was playing old songs, them same-old, same-old songs sounded new to everybody.

One guy, who had a little, slight speech impediment, he kind of kind of repeated his self a little bit, well he said, uh, he said he played, played a little and wanted to know did Robert make up them songs he was singing 'cause they sounded familiar but not quite like what he was used to hearing.

Robert smiled.

"So, so, man, tell, tell me how you be, be doing that?"

"I plays just like everybody else plays. Same songs. Same old guitar. Ain't nothing different about me."

Later on Robert had looked up and peeped that the man was trying to look upon Robert's finger work, so Robert turned away. He could listen all he wanted to, but Robert wasn't going to let him look upon how he fingered his passing chords. Shucks, Robert himself was just learning on this, and, that's when it had hit Robert, he didn't know nothing about the nameless silent man who had come up in Zooley house and showed Robert about using passing chords. Nothing. In fact, Robert wasn't even for sure there had even much been a man. Robert could of dreamed it up. The man had not mumbled or otherwise uttered one word. Just played. Didn't sing or hum or nothing. Just played. And when he finished playing, had handed the guitar to Robert. Or at least that's what Robert had remembered. So the guy from last night asking for Robert to show him how to make music reminded Robert of the man he didn't know what showed Robert another way to make music.

Man, that guy from last night had stayed up under Robert even though he ain't said no more to Robert. When they finally weren't nothing but the two of them left up in The Outhouse, Robert start to put his Stella away and the guy come over to him and reach out to shake. Robert didn't act out or nothing, Robert had just looked up and without no hesitation reached out friendly sort of and accepted the handshake of fellowship. The man's hands were much rougher than Robert's, he probably worked in somebody's fields.

When their hands had joined together, the man he not only shake, he took his free hand and covered up their shaking hands and he had patted on their shake and squeezed as if to say this is real special, and he had looked Robert dead in the eye and just give Robert a real quick and vigorous head nod, sort of as if to say, we is going to be friends for life, or at least that's the way it seem to Robert.

That man, he weren't skinning back his teeth or laughing or nothing. He was serious. Serious about the handshake, serious about the head nod, serious as he gave Robert's hand one more pat before he spun around abruptly, shoved his hat down deep onto his head and stretched his lanky legs on out The Outhouse.

So now, sitting upon an abandoned trunk, Robert got to feeling so good he reached down, opened up the case, took out his guitar and commenced to playing just 'cause he felt like playing.

Weren't nobody around to hear him. Nobody except some birds flying by and one of them alight nearby and just look upon Robert with that lil jerky-jerky head motion like flying birds on the ground do when they look around, swiveling their tiny heads this way and that. Seem like the bird was fascinated by Robert's playing because the bird, he stayed there on the ground a good little while, look like close to two or three minutes, which is a long time for a mockingbird to be stationary without flying off.

It had been a long time since Robert felt this good. He ain't run up on none of them two-headed, not unless Brother Bras was a two-headed but if Brother Bras was a two-headed, he sure didn't show Robert nothing about playing a guitar. Now come to think of it, maybe that man what come to Robert while Robert was dreaming in Zooley bed, maybe that man was a two-headed except he ain't said nothing. He didn't talk and everybody knowed that two-headed peoples had a lot to talk about. And Zooley she couldn't be no two-headed 'cause even though she had the talk, she didn't show him nothing about no guitar. Maybe there weren't no such a thing as two-headeds. Or maybe all the two-headeds was now deceased and they was just something that used to be, if they ever was.

Didn't matter. Robert was feeling good. Ike had taught him a bunch of technique. And that man had showed him how to fashion passing chords. Now all there was left to do was wait for Zooley to come pick him up and for Robert to see if he could pick Zooley up.

Deep down Robert knew he couldn't get nowhere with Zooley unless she wanted him to, so all he had to figure out was how to get her to want him to get closer to her. Hell, that's all you had to figure out with any woman. Figure out how to get them to want you to be closer to them. It was sort of like catching a filly in a corral. If you run at her hard, she going to dodge you, but you just be calm and slow walk up to her and talk real low and loving like, well, she'll respond in a calm way just like you be calm, or at least that was Robert's experience.

Plus, you know, if Robert had wanted some any old kind of companionship, he could of founded it last night. After all he did have money now. Over eight dollars. That was enough to buy more than a week or two worth of attention. But hell, Robert knew there weren't enough money in the world to buy Zooley attention, particularly if she didn't want to be bothered. There was just something about her that let you know she didn't give a care about what you thought about her. But she must of cared somewhat about Robert. She let him sleep in her bed. She let him look upon her beautiful nakedness.

She could have been playing hard to get or holding back like women's do, especially pretty women who used to men chasing after them all the time. But naw, this pretty woman took Robert all up in her home. But then on the other hand she did say she weren't going to be none of his woman. But maybe that was a test to see how serious Robert was about her. Maybe she was saying she weren't going to be no fun-girl for him to have and move on. Well, hell, Bogaloosa was alright. He could live here abouts. At least for a short spell.

But what about Callie? Now see that was a problem. When that girl was dancing last night trying to attract Robert's attention, she ain't knowed that there was no way she could of made him want her by dancing because her dancing was a limp and a crawl compared to Callie, and she weren't doing nothing but making Robert long to be dancing up against Callie's plumpness.

God, Callie sure could move to say she was as big as she was but, come to think on it, that's what made Callie's loving seem so strong to Robert: Callie was a big woman working it and you ain't never been worked until you had a big woman moving naked meat and muscle, twisting and gripping your flesh, turning you every which way but loose, her softness was so strong, a strong softness. Man. Made Robert close his eyes and look inward and remember-up on all them loving-up times with Callie, especially that time she had took to looking at him over her shoulder when they was in the kitchen and how the first time she told him come on in my kitchen and he ain't knowed what she meant.

The children was gone somewhere. It was daytime and it was raining. That's right. That's when it had been. Callie had done come home on account of the rain.

"My kids going to be with Ida Mae, so we ought not let this here rain go to waste." And she had push the little table up close to the back door which was propped part of the way open with a chair in it to keep the door from closing and the kitchen window was throwed open too and the rain was a falling and blowing in part ways and it seem like she didn't even much care. And she danced as she shoved the table up by the door, just like she had danced when she throwed the window open, and danced as she opened up her dress front and had put her left breast up against his lips and rubbed up on the back of his head at the same time. He was just sitting there in the chair by the wall.

"Take my dress off, Robert."

But she weren't helping him none. Had both her arms wrapped around his neck and shoulders, pulling him into her bosom. He couldn't pull the dress top down from off her shoulders, so he reach down to the tail of her dress to try to raise up the white cotton, red polka-dotted, rough textured fabric, which is when he discover weren't nothing under her dress but trembling flesh and it aroused him in the worst way, in a good way, that is, 'cause when he reach around to the back of her thighs, she clamped her legs tight with his hand stuck up betwixt her big-old, big-boneded legs. She squeezed on his hand with her legs like as if her thighs was bulldog jaws, that's how she had hold to his hand.

"Take my dress off, Robert."

It was like she was pleading but also like she was teasing, 'cause try as he might it was not easy to pull his hand from twixt her thighs, especially since she was hugging him to her so tight he could hardly breath, seem like he couldn't get no air, all he could breath in was just some of Callie skin.

And then she done something he would never forget, first she reach down and grabbed him hard, right through his pants and all, she grabbed him, almost to the point of hurting him, almost, if she had just squeezed even an ounce more harder it would of hurt him, but she squeeze him just hard enough to make him hard and hard enough that he dare not move out of fear he would hurt himself.

"Shit, Robert. Take my dress off."

And by now the wind was blowing rain on them, but it was day-time rain so it was sort of warm, cool but warm at the same time. And she pulled him up by tugging on him. He had to stand up, she might of pulled it clean off, if he didn't stand up. And some kind of way with one hand still holding him, she used her other hand and undid his belt and then stuck her hand down his waistband and grabbed him for truth then. He had never been grabbed like that before, like over to the mill, when one of them grappling hooks catch a log and be shoving it towards the saw.

He had to get up, stand up. And when he stood up, she push his pants down, and some kind of way she did one of her dancing moves or something, some kind of way, throwed her leg up and over without leaving go of him and next thing he knowed she was holding him with her right hand what was now between her legs and she was reached back, down and up under her crotch, how she did it, he didn't know, she did it so fast he couldn't rightly tell, except one minute she was facing him and the next her back was to him and she had never let go of him, and with her free hand she had reach down and flung her dress tail up as she bent over and exposed her naked ass to him, and before he could figure out what all she was doing she was pressing him all up against her wetness, and of course now he was all excited and moaning, and she still wasn't turning him loose, and she was leaning over the table, her face in the wind and rain coming through the back door, and he felt like he was going to bust if he didn't hurry up and get inside of her, but she was still holding hard on him, still controlling him and pressing the length of his dick up against her, until finally she moved a little and pushed him back and up against her—he remembered thinking, no she wasn't, and, yes she did, she reached back with her free hand and grabbed him and guided him into her butt, all at the same time looking back at him and saying, "Come on into my kitchen, Robert."

And once he was up in there, she baked his bread good.

Robert looked up to see if anybody was looking at him remembering up on coming into Callie's kitchen. Of course, wasn't nobody nowheres around. Even the mockingbird had done gone on about it's business, leaving Robert sitting there, his guitar in his lap, his fingers still on the strings, his mind tricking his body, him getting aroused again, thinking on Callie. Hell, couldn't none of them girls last night do like Callie. They didn't move like Callie and Zooley—who was the only somebody what could take Robert mind of Callie at this moment, well, Zooley had said, naw, wasn't going to happen. But Robert couldn't help wondering what Zooley's kitchen was like.

You wonder about what it would be like to be with a woman you don't know but at the same time you wants to get to know. You can't help wondering about that. Just like you wonder about some things you done already experienced but couldn't figure how the thing went down. Like he was right there. Hell not only was he there, Callie had had holt to him, like one of them faith healers grabbing a rattle snake, she had him like that, right in the palm of her hand, and they was face to face and then some kind of way she had swung her leg up and over and next thing he knowed they was stallion to mare but she had never let go, not even for the briefest of seconds. Never. He had seen it—or at least seen some of it and he didn't know how it had happened, but it had happened. He was there. She was there. Had him in hand and all. She done it. Womens is amazing. They can do all kinds of things a man can't explain.

And then he made himself stop.

Robert took off his hat and fanned himself for a minute.

Zooley had said she would come back and pick him up on the road just outside of town. He was sitting near where she had dropped him off. He had been here over an hour. He couldn't have missed her.

Then he put his hat back on his head. Oh, well. If Zooley didn't come, he'd just walk back into town and maybe this time he would talk upon somebody. But he wanted Zooley. He really wanted Zooley. Even though he was thinking on Callie just a minute ago, he was thinking on Callie in a carnal way, but this Zooley, there was something else about her besides her beauty, something else he was curious about. Maybe that was it. Yeah, that was it.

Yes, Robert was attracted to her body, but Callie's body was plenty enough body when it come to body, but see Zooley had this mind thing, the way she speak up and speak directly at you and make you draw up inside and it fascinate Robert how a woman could make him draw up inside, and yes, he was certainly attracted to her nakedness, especially since he seen her nakedness and he know what she look like naked, and he like what she look like naked, but it was, hell, it was the way she drive that car. Was it her car? Or how she pluck them fruit and feed it to him. Or how he could not find no way to out talk her, and Robert knew he could talk. But. Damn. Zooley.

After about forty-some seconds of confoundment, Robert replace his hat on his head, turn back to his guitar and start into a song about kitchens and rain. Sooner or later it would come to him how to turn all this into a song, and maybe that was the key to his music: figure out how to turn everything into a song. Put it all in there. Put everything. Even the most secret stuff. Everything.

Before he even realized it, Robert had played for another seventeen minutes when he hear what sound like a distant train, only coming up close, and softer than a train, no, not a train.

Robert look up and sure enough here come Zooley barreling down the road. There was a big old bend in the road a little ways off and so when Robert look up, he get to spy the side of the car as it top-out the bend and start directly on toward him although it still got about a quarter of mile to go before it reach him.

Robert bend over his guitar and play. He play the guitar but he also play like he weren't worried about whether Zooley would come for him. He knew it was best if he didn't look all eager and anxious because then for sure he would never get to her. But he was going to get to her, especially since he had set his mind to the task. Just like he was going to figure out this kitchen song, he was going to figure Zooley out. No doubt. Just might take a minute, but he was going to do it. When the car stopped in front of him, he didn't even much look up. Everything was alright.

-27-

WHAT IS A CROSSROADS? A CROSSROADS IS WHEN THE WAY YOU GO, YOU CAN'T go back again. It's not just further down the road, 'cause sometimes it's not so far, but once you step off that way, there ain't no other way. You either keep going or you die, but you don't go back.

But, see, the funny thing about a crossroads is that you don't always recognize it when you there. Sometimes you don't know that you was there until after you been there and gone on further up the road, and then you turn around one day and look back and you see it. You see just how you have really changed into something, maybe, you never intended to be, not like talking about it, not like you made up in your mind to be it, but like it's really you. You have become some other you. What you are is not what you were, not nothing you ever wanted to be, but you is what you have become and in the becoming have established...

Robert was trying to make his mind think on something else because he didn't want to think on Zooley, but, you know, thinking on other than the one who he is obsessed with is a hard thing for a man to do, especially when the object of his avoidance is about to be standing right in front of him.

Robert heard the car stop.

Didn't hear the horn blow, or nothing.

Heard the engine cut off.

Didn't hear her call to him for him to brought himself on over to sit beside her on the front seat.

Heard the hard crunch of footfalls on the roadside (she must of been wearing boots or something).

Didn't hear that whiskey voice she had—husky and low with a lot of air in it, like she was breathing into his ear.

Neither what he heard nor what he didn't hear, neither one of them forced him to look up.

Robert didn't look up because he was intent on controlling the situation with nothing but the power of his will.

He would not be denied.

She would speak up first.

He would not be suckered.

Instead of just saying something to mess with his head, he would get her to express her heart.

He would remain calm.

She would end up wondering about him.

He was Robert Johnson, the future king of musicianeers.

She was a woman—a special woman for sure—but still, a woman.

Robert kept playing his guitar and silently humming inside his head, not making no sound even though he was hearing the sound of his singing as he fingered the licks while pretending to ignore Zooley.

Robert knew: if you be anxious or nervous, you liable to blow it. You don't catch a butterfly by trying to snatch it.

When they had been riding over the day before, Zooley had not said much and Robert had said even less.

"Robert, we like you." (Robert had been so moved by the verb, he forgot to dwell on the noun. He heard that "we" and kind of a little bit wondered who else made up the "we" but the "like" part of what Zooley had said got to him so such a much that he forgot to figure up on the "we" part.)

When Zooley had said "like you", Robert had smiled (but not too much, he caught himself, so instead of grinning like a fool in love, he kind of half smiled, slouched down some in the vehicle's seat, was almost tempted to kick back and hang his foot out the window or something 'cause he was feeling real good to know that he done made Zooley like him, which is when he did that winking thing he like to do when he know he done got his point across, except he wasn't winking at Zooley, he was winking at himself, saying to himself, yeah, I'm getting to her).

Robert had made up his mind to go ahead and fully head on, jump the fence, cross the field, and with his sack cross his back and his guitar on his shoulder head on down the can't turn back road, don't have to think on it no more, ain't gonna never turn back. This particular jurisdiction done seen the last of Mr. Robert Johnson.

After a short while and Robert ain't heard nothing from Zooley, he decided to cut off singing and look up. He, of course, was expecting to see Zooley standing there, and he would smile, and wink at her, and take his time finishing off this little Zooley song he had thought up sitting here waiting for that car to come round the bend.

At some point a man had to be a man. This was his time and he kind of knowed—well, not really all the way knowed for true but he felt it like something you reach for in the dark expecting it to be where you left it when the lamp was lit. Now was the time. And at that moment, when he was as certain as Sunday morning following Saturday night. At that very hour like when you hear the cock crow for day and know it is time for you to get up, well, RL was for certain—this was his life, it was teetotally his. Not his Momma, not Dusty, not Mr. Son House, and especial not Zooley, not nobody but his own self and he would live his life the way he want to, which is what a real man do. He lives his life the way he want to, accepting that there be things he don't control, like the sun, the moon and all the stars in God's great heavens, but down here on the ground, come the hell of hot Mississippi highways or the high waters like the flood of twenty-seven, at this very moment Robert was of one mind: don't care what-so-ever life reveals, Robert was going to be his own natural born self. Yes sir. I'm going to be me.

But when Robert look up, there wasn't nobody or nothing standing there. No Zooley. No man who don't say nothing. No car—but he had heard the car, or thought he had as much heard the car, but there wasn't no car. Neither was there no boots. There was nothing.

Robert stood up, momentarily throwed off.

And suddenly it was clear. He had tricked himself. The sun was shining. The air was crisp. Now was not the time for singing. Now was the time for moving on further down the road.

Life was what it was. Not what you expect or what you hopes for, but what it was and either you moved on or you stayed where you was at, but either which way, life was going to be life.

Robert shake his head, look down for second, then looks up and around, not really expecting nothing more.

Zooley disappearing was a wonderous rainbow sign.

After you see what is there in front your eyes, well, the next move was up to you. The day had revealed itself. The only question was: not what did this day mean but rather what were you going to do?

And for the first time, Robert seed as how his whole life he had been moving on but not fully realizing that he was moving on. He had been drifting from place to place, person to person, but now drifting days was over. Now he was moving on, on his own steam, fully conscious of who he was even if it was impossible to know what the future would be. Didn't matter. Come whatever, regardless of what tomorrow drug in, didn't no never mind what the future was, Robert was ready to be Robert.

So he rear up to his full height, adjusts his hat on his head, puts his guitar in his crocus sack, and heads on down the road. Confident. Happy. Whistling.

ABOUT THE AUTHOR

KALAMU YA SALAAM is a writer, editor, photographer, and retired educator. He was born Vallery Ferdinand III in the Lower 9th Ward of New Orleans. Inspired by the poetry of Langston Hughes and the civil rights movement, Salaam became interested in writing and organizing for social change. He was a founder of BLACKARTSOUTH and changed his name to Kalamu ya Salaam, which is Kishwahili for "pen of peace." Salaam was also a founder of NOMMO Literary Society and Runagate press. Among many things, he has been Executive Director of the New Orleans Jazz & Heritage Festival, a DJ on WWOZ, administrator of the Lower 9th Ward Neighborhood Health Center, and the editor of The Black Collegian magazine. He blogs at kalamu.com/neogriot

Made in the USA
Columbia, SC
30 January 2025

52974981R00178